Understanding and Teaching English Spelling

Concise and engaging, this text provides pre-service and practicing English language teachers with the knowledge they need to successfully teach the spelling of English. Offering context and explanation for the English spelling system as well as uniquely addressing specific problems in learning the spelling of English words, this book empowers readers with strategies for coping with these problems. Divided into six accessible sections, Brown covers the history of English spelling, the influence of technology on spelling, the role of punctuation, the features of present-day English spelling, teaching strategies for coping with difficult spelling, and the future of spelling and literacy. The short, digestible chapters include practical learning objectives and end-of-chapter exercises to help teachers understand and explain English spelling concepts.

Adam Brown is Director of Research at Auckland Institute of Studies, New Zealand.

ESL & Applied Linguistics Professional Series
Eli Hinkel, Series Editor

Reflective Practice in English Language Teaching
Research-Based Principles and Practices
Steve Mann, Steve Walsh

Teacher Training and Professional Development of Chinese English Language Teachers
Changing From Fish to Dragon
Faridah Pawan, Wenfang Fan, Pei Miao

Research on Reflective Practice in TESOL
Thomas S.C. Farrell

Teaching English to Second Language Learners in Academic Contexts
Reading, Writing, Listening, Speaking
Jonathan M. Newton, Dana R. Ferris, Christine C.M. Goh, William Grabe, Fredricka L. Stoller, Larry Vandergrift

The Politics of English Second Language Writing Assessment in Global Contexts
Edited by Todd Ruecker, Deborah Crusan

Transnational Writing Education
Theory, History, and Practice
Edited by Xiaoye You

Understanding and Teaching English Spelling
A Strategic Guide
Adam Brown

For more information about this series, please visit: www.routledge.com/ ESL--Applied-Linguistics-Professional-Series/book-series/LEAESLALP? page=2&page=1

Understanding and Teaching English Spelling

A Strategic Guide

Adam Brown

NEW YORK AND LONDON

First published 2019
by Routledge
711 Third Avenue, New York, NY 10017

and by Routledge
2 Park Square, Milton Park, Abingdon, Oxon, OX14 4RN

Routledge is an imprint of the Taylor & Francis Group, an informa business

© 2019 Taylor & Francis

Library of Congress Cataloging-in-Publication Data
A catalog record has been requested for this book

ISBN: 978-1-138-08266-3 (hbk)
ISBN: 978-1-138-08267-0 (pbk)
ISBN: 978-1-315-11238-1 (ebk)

Typeset in Bembo
by Swales & Willis Ltd, Exeter, Devon, UK

Contents

Preface

Background

This book is a sister volume to my *Pronunciation and Phonetics: A Practical Guide for English Language Teachers* (Routledge, 2014). However, there are similarities and differences between this book and the previous one.

For both books, the intended readership is trainee English language teachers, and in-service teachers. As a result, the emphasis is on what teachers need to know in order to teach spelling effectively.

Both books contain about 30 short chapters. This breaks the subject up into digestible parts, which is desirable for English spelling, which has many influences and therefore many strategies for teaching. If you read one chapter per day, you will finish the book in about a month.

However, one difference in this book is that it is perhaps less practical than the previous book. The reason for this is that there exists a huge number of books, websites, etc. with good materials to teach, practice and test English spelling, whereas materials for pronunciation teaching are variable. This book is therefore not entitled *Spelling: A Practical Guide for English Language Teachers*. Instead, the thrust is for teachers to understand the nature of English spelling, why it is a complex system, and why it is difficult to teach in its present-day form. Nevertheless, every chapter contains exercises, either in the body or at the end, that may be easily adapted for classroom use.

Teachers of English may be native speakers or non-native speakers. In terms of pronunciation, this may create a distinction. Native speakers have native pronunciation, without any interference features from the pronunciation of other languages. They may be speakers of a nonstandard variety of English pronunciation that may be questionable in terms of its validity as a model for foreign learners. Nevertheless, learners will seldom question the pronunciation proficiency of native speaker teachers. Non-native speaker teachers, on the other hand, may have an English pronunciation with clear interference features from their native language. These may be a handicap, especially if the class is multinational.

In terms of spelling, however, native speakers are at little advantage over non-native, apart from usually having larger vocabularies. The variation that exists in pronunciation does not exist in spelling, apart from the difference between American and British spelling which, as is argued in Chapter 15, does not amount to a large variation.

Nor are native-speaker teachers at an advantage in terms of spelling proficiency. There are native-speaker teachers who are good and bad at spelling, just as there are non-native-speaker teachers who are good and bad at spelling.

The focus of this book is therefore on making teachers aware of the nature of English spelling. Most teachers, for instance, know little about the history of English; however, this history is still clearly manifested in the present-day spelling of many words. This knowledge is necessary in order to teach spelling effectively.

Structure

The book is divided into six sections.

The first section (Chapters 1 – 5) sets the scene by explaining the nature of spelling systems in languages of the world and describing the history of English spelling.

Given that most writing nowadays is carried out on a computer, the internet, or a device (smartphone, tablet, etc.), rather than with pen and paper, Section 2 (Chapters 6 – 8) looks at the influence of this technology on spelling, and the attitude of users to correct spelling, much of which is taken to be whatever the technology states is correct.

Section 3 (Chapters 9 – 11) deals with aspects of punctuation. While readers may question whether punctuation belongs in a book on spelling, there are aspects such as hyphens and capital letters that straddle punctuation and spelling.

The fourth section (Chapters 12 – 21) represents an investigation into various features of present-day English spelling. Many of these features are vestiges of the long history of English spelling, do not occur in other languages, and may represent barriers to easy learning of the system.

Chapters 22 – 26 in Section 5 explain the strategic approach promoted in this book for coping with teaching the difficulties of English spelling. The strategies avoid the common practice of giving learners a list of English words whose spellings are to be learned and tested, without giving any instruction in how to learn the spellings. Pointers as to how to teach and how to test spelling are given in Chapters 27 and 28.

The final section (Chapters 29 – 32) looks towards the future. English spelling has never been systematically managed, but an improvement in literacy rates seems unlikely without some kind of change. The example of Malay, as a language whose spelling has been managed, such that it is easy to learn and literacy rates are high, is given as a comparison in Chapter 30.

Conventions

In this book, standard linguistic conventions are followed:

- Letters of the alphabet and example words in spelling are printed in italics, e.g. the letter *a*, *salmon*.
- Sounds are printed in slant brackets (but see the next section), e.g. /sæmən/.
- The meanings of words and expressions are printed in quote marks, e.g. "a type of fish."

Phonemic Symbols

The following symbols are used in describing the pronunciation of English in this book. Since the book is about spelling rather than pronunciation, some flexibility and simplicity has been employed in representing the two main worldwide accents of English: American English (AmE) and British English (BrE). Slant brackets // have been used to represent sounds (phonemes), although the phonemic status of some sounds, especially in historical forms, is debatable. For more accurate, detailed discussion of these issues, see Brown (2014).

Consonants

Symbol	Sample word	Symbol	Sample word
/p/	*pan*	/s/	*sit*
/b/	*bit*	/z/	*zone*
/t/	*ten*	/ʃ/	*ship*
/d/	*dame*	/ʒ/	*vision*
/k/	*car*	/h/	*home*
/g/	*go*	/m/	*money*
/tʃ/	*church*	/n/	*need*
/dʒ/	*judge*	/ŋ/	*sing*
/f/	*fat*	/l/	*lamp*
/v/	*very*	/r/	*reach*
/θ/	*thin*	/w/	*well*
/ð/	*this*	/j/	*yet*

Vowels

Symbol	Sample word	Symbol	Sample word
/ɪ/	bit	/u:/	moon
/e/	ten	/ɜ:/	herb
/æ/	bad	/eɪ/	mate
/ʌ/	mud	/aɪ/	like
/ɒ/	not (BrE)	/ɔɪ/	boil
/ʊ/	good	/oʊ/	go
/ə/	agree	/aʊ/	cloud
/i:/	agree	/ɪə/	dear (BrE)
/ɑ:/	park, not (AmE)	/eə/	care (BrE)
/ɔ:/	author	/ʊə/	tour (BrE)

The symbols /i, u/ are used for unstressed vowels of the /i:, ɪ, u:, ʊ/ type as in *pretty, glorious, situation, arduous*.

Copyright Acknowledgement

Thanks are due to the following people for their kind permission to reproduce copyright material:

- Prof. Jerrold H. Zar and *The Journal of Irreproducible Results*, the science humor magazine, for the "Candidate for a Pullet Surprise" poem (p. 58). It was inspired by lines by Mark Eckman, and the title was suggested by Pamela Brown.
- Simon Jenkins, editor of Ship of Fools, for the SMS text version of the Lord's Prayer (p. 65), written by Matthew Campbell.
- Johanna Stirling, author of *Teaching spelling to English language learners*, for the summarized list of historical morphemes (pp. 199).
- Doug Hendry of the Puzzle Company, for word puzzles (pp. 231).
- The English Spelling Society, for the poem illustrating the effects of Lindgren's SR1 (p. 251).

Dedication

I would like to acknowledge my lecturers at the University of Edinburgh who elucidated the nature of English spelling; and Christopher Upward (Wikipedia, n.d.), a former colleague at Aston University, Birmingham, UK, who later rekindled my interest in the topic.

References

Brown, A. (2014). *Pronunciation and phonetics: A practical guide for English language teachers*. New York, NY: Routledge.

Wikipedia (n.d.). *Christopher Upward*. Retrieved from en.wikipedia.org/wiki/ Christopher_Upward

Section 1

Background

1 Introduction

The palest ink is stronger than the clearest memory.

Chinese proverb

Learning Objectives

At the end of this chapter, readers will be able to:

- explain the primacy of spoken language
- make a case for the importance of accurate spelling
- show how spelling relates to punctuation and typography.

Introduction

The subject matter of this book is the spelling system of English, its features and patterns, and how teachers should go about teaching it in class. In various places in the book, we will be reminding readers that the spelling system being discussed is that of English, and that the features and problems found in English spelling do not necessarily exist in the spelling systems of other languages. It is really surprising that many books that cover the English spelling system and how to teach it do not even contain the word *English* in their titles. This gives the impression that English spelling is somehow representative of all spelling systems, and that is certainly not the case. In many respects, English spelling is an outlier in terms of the spelling systems of languages worldwide, as will become apparent in later chapters.

As this is a book aimed at teachers of English, rather than applied linguists and academics, the word *spelling* is used mostly throughout, as it is a common, everyday word which teachers understand. A more technical-sounding word – *orthography* – is often used in more academic works, but is generally avoided here. Spelling is what ordinary people do every day when writing, and what learners do in class. Orthography, on the other hand, is a more abstract term for the writing system of a language, and encompasses not only spelling, but also other aspects of written language such as the use of hyphens, capital letters, word divisions, punctuation marks, and typographical devices available on computer including the choice of font, font size, italics, bold, and color. These features are touched on in this book, partly because they are often overlooked by teachers. However, other aspects of the writing process, such as handwriting, are not covered.

The term *orthography* may also carry connotations of correctness. In fact, this is the historical origin (etymology) of the word. It comes from the Greek *orthos*, "correct," and *graphein* "to write."

To avoid all these implications, the term *spelling* is used in this book. One can, for instance, talk about *misspellings* and *spelling mistakes*, as often made by learners and other users, but the terms *misorthography* and *orthography mistake* are never found.

The term *traditional orthography* (TO) is commonly encountered and is used in this book to refer to standard modern spelling, especially when in contrast to reformed spelling (see Chapter 29).

The remainder of this chapter introduces a number of basic points that need to be made before delving into the English spelling system.

The Primacy of Spoken Language

In discussing any language, we can use two dichotomies. Firstly, are we talking about producing the language, or receiving and interpreting it? Secondly, in what form is the language being transmitted? The two main media through which a language can be conveyed are the spoken and the written, although others exist, such as Braille, a tactile medium.

These two dichotomies thus give us what (in language teaching circles) are known as the four skills: reading, writing, speaking, and listening (Table 1.1).

Which of these two media is the more important? Many people will answer "the written medium," because it has, for some centuries, been considered the only form worthy of scholarly study. Writing, being marks on paper, is more tangible than the ephemeral sounds of spoken language. Dictionaries have until recently tended to concentrate on written (spelled) forms, and meanings, often saying little if anything about pronunciation.

However, modern descriptive linguistics, pioneered by figures such as Ferdinand de Saussure (1957–1913), Edward Sapir (1884–1939) and Leonard Bloomfield (1887–1949), pointed out that there were many reasons why the spoken form of the language should be considered to have primacy.

Table 1.1 The four language skills

	Written medium	Spoken medium
Production	Writing	Speaking
Perception	Reading	Listening

- *Historical*: All human languages have a spoken form, but not all human languages have a written form.
- *Biological*: All humans without physical or psychological defects learn to speak their native language, but not all humans learn to write it.
- *Instructional*: Children acquire the spoken form of their native language by exposure to it, while the process of learning to write the language is one of conscious instruction. The age at which children master the medium differs too, spoken language being acquired in the home much earlier than written language, which is typically learned once they start school.
- *Structural*: There is no restriction on the combination of letters in writing, but there are awkward combinations of sounds in pronunciation.
- *Functional*: The spoken medium is used more often, and for more purposes, than the written.

In light of all the above, the spoken form of a language is considered by linguists to have primacy. In short, writing, including the spelling system, is not "the language." If anything, speech is the language, and writing is simply another method of manifesting the language. Bloomfield (1933, p. 21) wrote, "Writing is not language, but merely a way of recording language by means of visible marks." During the 20th century, various approaches and methods for teaching English (and potentially other languages) were proposed, emphasizing the importance of initial teaching of the spoken form: the reform movement and the International Phonetic Association, the natural/direct method, audiolingualism, total physical response, the silent way, humanistic methods, communicative language teaching, etc. (see Brown, 2014; Larsen-Freeman & Anderson, 2011; Richards & Rogers, 2001). Eventually, dictionaries included comprehensive information about the pronunciation of words, and grammars, previously seen as relevant only to written language, were published examining the grammar of speech, e.g. Biber, Johansson, Leech, Conrad & Finegan, 1999; Carter & McCarthy, 2006; Palmer, Blandford & Kingdon, 1976.

However, before it is assumed that writing is unimportant, two caveats must be presented. Firstly, there are counterarguments against a strong view that writing is merely a medium for representing speech, and emphasizing the importance and nature of writing.

- Some uses of writing could not be spoken, e.g. timetables.
- The differences between speech and writing are much greater than most non-linguists realize.
- The social prestige of writing is often higher than that of speech, e.g. their legal status.
- Loanwords (Chapter 16) may enter the language first through written language.
- The speech of many literate speakers is heavily influenced by written language.

Also, is it correct to claim nowadays that "The spoken medium is used more often, and for more purposes, than the written"? With technological advances over the last couple of decades, of texting, social media, etc., and in the light of commentators' common criticism that younger people nowadays are spending a lot of their lives reading and writing on devices, and conversely lacking face-to-face spoken interactional skills, it may be the case that written language is more commonly used than spoken for some people.

Secondly, even if we accept that spoken language is primary because, among other reasons, children acquire speech at an earlier age than writing, this does not necessarily imply that people should learn second languages the same way. This assumption has underlain several of the approaches and methods introduced above. However, second language learners have already learned what language is in general and what it is used for; the features of their native language; and what written language is, including the Roman alphabet, if appropriate. They do not come to second language learning as a clean slate, the way native children do. While many learners require good speaking skills, many do not put great emphasis on speaking because of job requirements. Throughout this book, we will be talking about "learners," but that description covers both native-speaking children and non-native L2 learners, and the two groups differ in certain crucial respects.

The Purpose of Spelling

At the outset of this book, it is appropriate to ask a very fundamental question that underlies much of what will appear in subsequent chapters: "What is the purpose of a spelling system for a language?"

Exercise

Consider the following suggested answers and state whether you agree or disagree with them. Note that we are not asking whether these are the *effects* of having a spelling system (if you have a spelling system for a language, then this is true), but whether they are the *purpose* of having one (that is why a spelling system was devised at some time for the language).

- To allow foreigners to learn the language more easily.
- To allow users of the language to record what would otherwise be oral traditions.
- To allow people not to get lost when traveling.
- To allow children to achieve 100% literacy in an acceptable timeframe.
- To be able to test children's mastery of spelling.
- To bring knowledge and education to all users of the language.
- To allow dictionaries to be produced for the language.
- To be able to distinguish between literate and illiterate users of the language.

- To allow users of the language to read and write.
- To allow users of the language to take part in spelling bees.
- To show the relationship between words in this language, and words in sister languages.
- To allow tourists to get by in the language.
- To show the relationship between modern words and their historical origins.
- To allow users of the language to record accounts of historical events.
- To give speakers a written form that can be learned by heart.
- To allow users of the language to play with words in writing as well as in speech.

If you, as a teacher, had to choose just one or two from the above list as the main purposes of a spelling system, they would probably be to allow users to read and write, and achieve literacy and facilitate education. The others may or may not be true, or may simply be by-products of having a spelling system – not the purpose for its creation in the first place.

Basic Skills

Literacy, including the ability to spell accurately, is a basic skill needed to function in modern society. It is not the only one, of course. Literacy is often mentioned alongside numeracy, the ability to do basic arithmetic, and basic skills courses often cover both skills. They are the basis of the common term "the three rs," meaning reading, (w)riting and (a)rithmetic. This phrase has been around for a couple of centuries. In modern times, the idea has often been extended to include literacy, numeracy, and ICT (information and communications technology, i.e. computers, devices and the internet).

However the phrase is defined, it is clear that the ability to spell is one that is important for literacy and education in general. Spelling is also involved in numeracy, as equations are written using the Roman alphabet. It is also essential in ICT, as this is couched in written language, most often in English.

Exercise

As teachers, we often give learners spelling tests. To get some idea of what goes through learners' minds when this happens, here is a spelling test for you. But before we start, answer this question: "How confident are you that you will get all the words right?"

The exercise is in fact made easier for you, as you are not being asked to spell words from scratch, merely to recognize correct spellings.

Which of the following words are misspelled? What is the correct spelling for the misspelled ones?

accomodation	*hight*	*occassion*	*sacreligious*
calender	*miniscule*	*occurence*	*seperate*
ecstacy	*momento*	*paralell*	*supercede*
harrass	*neccessary*	*questionaire*	*writting*

The answers are at the end of this chapter. The main point to note here is that you were probably not 100% confident of getting the correct answers, or at least had to think twice.

Importance

Is spelling important? That is, is it important that English users and learners spell words correctly? Nowadays with the widespread availability of computers with word-processing programs with spell-checkers, there is little excuse for spelling mistakes. Not using the spell-checker, and not checking written work in general, may at best give an impression of being lackadaisical, and at worst may lead to misunderstandings or failure to understand at all.

One high-stakes situation in which accurate spelling, and other features of good language, are important is in a curriculum vitae when applying for a job. Andrew Hunter, chief executive of Adzuna, a British job search engine, warns, "Spelling mistakes [in CVs] are a huge red flag for potential employers" (Tovey, 2015). *The Guardian* (2009) claims that the problem is worsening because of British language education standards over the last few decades: "Anyone who went to school between the late 60s and the late 90s is part of a 'lost generation' when it comes to any kind of formal education in grammar and punctuation. Both were missing from the UK school curriculum for more than 30 years." Tovey (2015) lists the following ten words, all commonly used in CVs, as the most commonly misspelled: *responsibility, liaise, university, experience, speciality* [BrE], *communication, achievement, management, environment, successful.* In short, spelling may be the difference between getting a job and not getting it, or at least contribute heavily to this decision.

Is punctuation important? There is far more variation and personal taste in punctuation than in spelling (see Chapter 9). So, it is often more difficult to label punctuation as wrong, as opposed to it being unhelpful for the reader. Nevertheless, there are situations where punctuation can have serious consequences. In early 2017, a group of Maine dairy drivers contested the state's law about activities that do not qualify for overtime pay (Rosenblatt, 2017). The legislation states:

> *The canning, processing, preserving, freezing, drying, marketing, storing, packing for shipment or distribution of:*

(1) Agricultural produce;
(2) Meat and fish products; and
(3) Perishable foods.

The ambiguity relates to the phrase "packing for shipment or distribution." This could mean (i) packing for shipment or packing for distribution," which does not include the drivers, or (ii) "packing for shipment, or distribution," which does. The difference lies in what is known as a serial comma. It is also called an Oxford comma, because it is used by Oxford University Press editors. It relates to lists. A serial comma is put before the second-to-last item in the list. This is standard in American English, but less so in British English.

We traveled to Chicago, Ann Arbor, and Detroit. (AmE)

We travelled to Coventry, Leicester and Peterborough. (BrE)

In the above examples, the meaning is clear despite the presence or absence of the comma.

In other situations, a serial comma is necessary in order to convey the intended meaning. Making Light (2010) quotes the following sentence about a documentary film about the American musician Merle Haggard: *Among those interviewed were his two ex-wives, Kris Kristofferson and Robert Duvall.* Without a comma after *Kristofferson*, it reads as if Kris Kristofferson and Robert Duvall were Haggard's ex-wives. In linguistics, this is known as *apposition*.

Vice versa, a serial comma may on occasion create ambiguity. In *I met his mother, Jane Potter, and Simon Robinson*, it is unclear whether he met three people, or whether he met two people, Jane Potter being his mother.

In the case of the Maine dairy drivers, the judge ruled in their favor, and they won the overtime payment. So, a comma may be worth thousands of dollars.

Ghoti

In writings about English spelling, there is often a lot of nonsense written, or over-prescriptiveness, or unsophisticated analysis. One example of the latter is the word *ghoti*.

If you are unfamiliar with the word *ghoti*, that is fine; it does not exist. However, it was used by some people to attempt to illustrate the irregularity of English spelling. It is often associated with the Irish playwright George Bernard Shaw, but it was created before him, and it is disputed whether, despite being an advocate of spelling reform (see Chapter 29), he ever used it as an example.

The argument goes as follows. The word *fish* could just as well be spelled *ghoti*, because:

- *gh* represents the /f/ sound in words like *cough*
- *o* represents the /ɪ/ vowel as in *women*
- *ti* represents the /ʃ/ sound as in *nation.*

While the above three points are true for the words given, they cannot be generalized because the effect of place in the word (in fact, the syllable) has been overlooked.

While *gh* does represent the /f/ sound in words like *cough* (*trough, enough, rough, tough, laugh*), all these examples involve *gh* at the end of a syllable; so it is still /f/ in *laughter*, where the *gh* is at the end of the first syllable. When *gh* occurs at the beginning of a word/syllable, it is pronounced /g/, e.g. *aghast, ghastly, ghee, gherkin, ghetto, ghost, ghoul.* The *h* is silent (see Chapter 12).

While *o* does represent the /ɪ/ vowel in *women*, this is an exceptional case. This word was originally spelled with an *i* letter (as in *wimmen*, among other early possibilities), which was changed by a practice known as minim stroke avoidance (see Chapter 5).

While *ti* does represent the /ʃ/ sound in *nation*, it only does so when part of an ending (suffix) followed by *-al*, *-ent*, *-on*, or *-ous*, e.g. *partial, patient, portion, cautious.*

So, it turns out that, rather than helping to illustrate the irregularity of English spelling, this example in fact demonstrates the regularity, provided you take into account the position of the sound in the word/syllable. It transpires that *fish* is the regular spelling of this word. The regular spelling of word/syllable-initial /f/ is *f*; of /ɪ/ is *i*; and of word/syllable-final /ʃ/ is *sh* (see Appendix 1).

Examples

When analyzing English for the purpose of identifying patterns, it is often the case that a pattern can be identified, but it only applies to a small number of words. The *gh* words just quoted are an example; those are the only words with *gh* at the beginning, and there are only seven of them. Is this enough for us to be able to call it a "pattern"?

Similarly, English words can start with *ps*, but they are mostly learned words deriving from Greek. The only common examples are *psalm, pseudo, psoriasis, psychology, psychic.* However, there are plenty of other, more learned, scientific words, e.g. *psoralen* ("a toxic substance found in plants"), *psammite* ("sandstone"), *psoralea* ("species of plant"), *psilocin* ("a hallucinogenic compound from mushrooms"), *psyllid* ("species of louse"). It is doubtful that readers have ever encountered those words before, and using them as examples of a pattern in a book on teaching English spelling to native-speaking children and non-native learners would seem inappropriate.

Therefore, words used for illustration in this book are mostly common everyday words, as opposed to rare, perhaps scientific terminology.

Summary

- Writing, including spelling, is not "the language."
- The main purpose of a spelling system is to allow users to read and write, and achieve literacy and facilitate education.
- Even English language teachers may have problems with their own command of English spelling.
- Spelling and punctuation may be very important.

Further Reading

On the primacy of spoken language, see Pereltsvaig (2011). Cook (2009) also discusses the differences between first and second language learning.

Answer

In case it was not obvious, all the words were wrongly spelled. Their correct spellings are as follows.

accommodation	*height*	*occasion*	*sacrilegious*
calendar	*minuscule*	*occurrence*	*separate*
ecstasy	*memento*	*parallel*	*supersede*
harass	*necessary*	*questionnaire*	*writing*

The question was also asked, "How confident are you that you will get all the words right?" If, as a teacher of English, you did not answer, "100% confident," you might like to think why not, and whether that is an acceptable answer for a teacher of the subject. This is not an insinuation about your competence as a teacher, but rather a comment about the nature of English spelling.

References

Biber, D., Johansson, S., Leech, G., Conrad, S., & Finegan, E. (1999). *Longman grammar of spoken and written English*. London, UK: Longman.

Bloomfield, L. (1933). *Language*. New York, NY: Holt.

Brown, A. (2014). *Pronunciation and phonetics: A practical guide for English language teachers*. New York, NY: Routledge.

Carter, R., & McCarthy, M. (2006). *Cambridge grammar of English*. Cambridge, UK: Cambridge University Press.

Cook, V. (2009). Questioning traditional assumptions of language teaching. *Nouveaux Cahiers de Linguistique Française 29*, 7-22. Retrieved from clf.unige.ch/files/9014/4102/7479/03_Cook_nclf29.pdf

The Guardian (2009). *Spell it out*. Retrieved from www.theguardian.com/careers/cv-mistakes

Larsen-Freeman, D., & Anderson, M. (2011). *Techniques and principles in language teaching* (3rd edition). Oxford, UK: Oxford University Press.

Making Light (2010). *The return of the final serial comma's vital necessity.* Retrieved from nielsenhayden.com/makinglight/archives/012652.html

Palmer, H., Blandford, F. G., & Kingdon, R. (1976). *A grammar of spoken English* (3rd edition). Cambridge, UK: Cambridge University Press,

Pereltsvaig, A. (2011). *On the primacy of spoken language.* Languages of the World. Retrieved from www.languagesoftheworld.info/language-acquisition/on-the-primacy-of-the-spoken-language.html

Richards, J. C., & Rogers, T. (2001). *Approaches and methods in language teaching* (2nd edition). Cambridge, UK: Cambridge University Press.

Rosenblatt, K. (2017). *Oxford comma defenders, rejoice! Judge bases rulingon punctuation.* Retrieved from www.nbcnews.com/news/us-news/oxford-comma-defenders-rejoice-judge-bases-ruling-punctuation-n734371

Tovey, S. (2015). *Top ten spelling mistakes jobseekers make on their CVs.* Retrieved from www.telegraph.co.uk/finance/jobs/11498666/top-ten-spelling-mistakes-job-seekers-employees-cvs-curriculum-vitae.html

2   Types of Spelling System

Learning Objectives

At the end of this chapter, readers will be able to:

- define logographic, syllabic and alphabetic spelling systems
- list some examples of languages with these systems
- explain why English is a very irregular example of an alphabetic system.

Introduction

This chapter deals with the fact that not all spelling systems are of the same kind. There are three main kinds: logographic, syllabic and alphabetic. While these are the three main categories, we shall see that no spelling system is a 100% example of a category. There is some overlap in spelling systems of languages of the world, and there are irregularities that make languages depart from being 100% logographic, syllabic or alphabetic. Since the English spelling system is alphabetic, the other two categories will be only briefly described.

Logographic

In a logographic system, the individual symbols (often called characters) represent words, phrases, or morphemes (units of meaning). The underlying principle is that the symbols represent concepts rather than sounds. They do not give the reader (such as a foreign learner) the information from which to derive the pronunciation.

Some of the earliest writing systems used logographic writing: the ancient civilizations of the Near East (nowadays called the Middle East), including Egyptian hieroglyphs, Africa, Central American, and China. Present-day Chinese still uses a logographic system; however, its characters also contain some phonetic elements, and many morphemes are written as more than one character.

The 26 letters of the Roman alphabet used for English are not logographic. However, other symbols are used in English writing that are logographic. For instance, the numeral *1* is a symbol that can be written *one*, and represents the pronunciation /wʌn/, but more importantly conveys the meaning "one, singular." Similarly, the symbol *&* can be written *and*, and represents the pronunciation /ænd/, but more importantly conveys the meaning "and, additionally." The symbols *1, &* give no clue to the pronunciation of the word.

Syllabic

In a logographic system, the characters represent words, with no indication of the pronunciation. In syllabic and alphabetic systems, the situation is exactly the opposite, namely that symbols in the spelling represent sounds with no indication of any meaning. In a syllabary, the symbols represent whole syllables of the pronunciation in an indivisible way.

The most obvious modern-day example of a syllabic writing system is the hiragana and katakana systems of Japanese, which were devised around the year 700.

It would be impossible to create a syllabic system for English because English has relatively complex syllable structure possibilities; it can have up to three consonants before the vowel in a syllable, and up to four after it. In contrast, languages that have syllabic writing systems also have relatively simple syllable structures (and thus a manageable number of syllabic symbols). For instance, Japanese syllable structure is (C) V (/n/), that is, no consonant or one consonant before the vowel, and the only possible consonant after the vowel is /n/. Japanese has only about 45 possible syllables, and thus 45 symbols. This is a simplified explanation of Japanese writing, which also uses a logographic system adopted from Chinese.

Alphabetic

Like syllabaries, alphabetic spelling systems work on the principle that the symbols represent sounds. However, while in syllabaries the symbols represent whole syllables, in alphabetic systems, the symbols represent individual vowel and consonant sounds (phonemes). Alphabetic systems are the commonest type of spelling. The symbols are usually called *letters*, although many non-native speakers use the term *alphabet*. In standard English, A to Z is one alphabet consisting of 26 letters, while many non-native speakers refer to this as 26 alphabets.

The difference between logographic, syllabic and alphabetic systems can be illustrated by considering the concept "banana." The logographic spelling of the Chinese for "banana" is as follows, pronounced xiāngjiāo. The two parts are indivisible and give no indication of the pronunciation.

香 蕉

The Japanese for "banana" is in fact a loan of the English word *banana* (see Chapter 16). Its syllabic spelling is as follows. Note that the pronunciation /banana/ has three syllables and there are therefore three symbols in the syllabic spelling (and the final two are the same, representing /na/).

バナナ

The English, alphabetic spelling is of course *banana*. The letters represent individual vowel and consonant phonemes. The letter *b* represents /b/, and the letter *n* represents /n/. The representation of the vowels is more complex; while they are all spelled *a*, the second one, which is stressed, is pronounced /ɑ:/ (BrE) or /æ/ (AmE), while the first and third are unstressed and reduced to the schwa sound /ə/. For this reason, analysts say that, even if the correspondence between English sounds and letters were more regular, the English spelling system would still be irregular in that it does not indicate in a clear, systematic fashion where the stress falls in a word. In many publications, Dickerson (e.g. 1978, 1987, 1989, 2013) has described the use of spelling clues to predict the incidence of stress in multisyllable words.

There are two main advantages of an alphabetic spelling system, against other types. Firstly:

> A feature of the alphabetic writing system that sets it dramatically apart from the preceding systems is the small number of characters it requires. . . . [T]here was a total of about 600 logographic and syllabic signs in the most recent Sumerian writing, about 700 in the Egyptian, and more than 450 in the Hittite, while the letters of various alphabets have characteristically totaled between 20 and 35.
>
> (Balmuth, 2009, p. 29)

This leads to economies of memorization (26 Roman alphabet letters versus 700 Egyptian characters), and efficiencies in typing and printing.

Secondly, since the letters in an alphabetic system represent individual sounds, it is possible to deduce the pronunciation of words newly encountered in spelling. This is impossible in a logographic system, if one does not know the newly encountered characters.

Two further points need to be made about alphabetic systems. Firstly, some systems can use letters to represent both consonants and vowels in spelling, but typically omit the vowel letters, these being predictable to a native speaker from the context. Arabic is an example of this system (known as abjad). The following word contains the letters for the consonant sounds /ktb/. Context allows the user to decide if this represents /kita:b/ "book" or /kuta:b/ "student." This naturally poses a problem for learners of Arabic spelling.

كتاب

Table 2.1 Placement of vowel letters in Thai spelling

Pronunciation	Spelling
/m/	ม
/ma:/	มา
/me:/	เม
/mi:/	มี
/mu:/	มุ
/maw/	เมา

Similarly, in abugida systems, the consonant letters are present, but the vowel sounds are indicated by diacritics (marks written above or below the consonant symbol) or modifications to the consonant letters. As with the difference between logographic, syllabic, and alphabetic systems, so the distinction between alphabetic, abjad, and abugida systems is somewhat fuzzy.

Secondly, the letters of English progress from left to right across the page. However, as in the above Arabic example, there are languages with exactly the opposite direction, namely right to left (the rightmost letter is for /k/). There are languages with a mixture of this. For instance, the Thai spelling system is essentially left to right. However, as Table 2.1 shows, the vowel that follows a consonant in the pronunciation may follow the consonant letter in the spelling, precede it, be placed above it, be placed below it, and even be placed both before and after it.

(Ir)regularity of English Spelling

So the underlying principle of alphabetic spelling systems is that the symbols (letters) represent the individual vowel and consonant sounds (phonemes). However, there is no language where the correspondence between symbols and sounds, and sounds and symbols, is 100%. Often-quoted languages that come close to a 100% correspondence include Bulgarian, Finnish, Italian, Russian, Serbo-Croatian, Spanish, and Turkish. In Chapter 30, we will look at the spelling of Malay, which is also very regular. At the other end of the ranking, English has probably the least regular alphabetic spelling system. There are various ways in which an alphabetic spelling system may be considered irregular, i.e. depart from the one sound-one letter principle:

- A letter may represent more than one sound, e.g. English *c* may represent /k/ (*cat*) and /s/ (*cell*) (and many other possibilities; see Chapter 30).

- Vice versa, a sound may be represented by more than one letter, e.g. the /s/ sound may be spelled with *s* (*sun*) or *c* (*cell*) (and other possibilities).
- A letter may represent a combination of more than one sound, e.g. *x* as in *mix* /mɪks/.
- Vice versa, a sound may be represented by a combination of two letters (digraph), e.g. English *sh* represents the single vowel phoneme /ʃ/.
- A digraph may represent more than one sound, e.g. English *th* may represent the voiceless /θ/ (*thin*) and the voiced /ð/ (*then*).
- There may be silent letters, e.g. in the English word *answer*, there is no /w/ sound (see Chapter 12).
- Dialect variation (see Chapter 15) may mean that different accents pronounce words differently (as in *banana* above), but spell them the same. So, the problem contained in the famous song "You say *tomato*, I say *tomato*" cannot be expressed in conventional writing.
- Language change over the centuries may mean that the pronunciation and the spelling have become out of kilter with each other. In the history of English (see Chapter 4), the introduction of the printing press meant that spellings became standardized; however, the pronunciation of English continued to change inexorably, especially during the Great Vowel Shift. The sounds changed, but the spellings were never updated to reflect this and remained the same.

The long history of English with a written form (see Chapter 5) puts it at a disadvantage, in that it has had a long time in which to turn from a neat garden into a jungle. In fact, as we shall see in Chapter 5, it was never a perfect garden from the beginning. In contrast, languages that have had spelling systems devised for them in the relatively recent past are at an advantage in this respect.

We now come to the question that is the crux of this section: "How regular is English spelling?" The question may sound simple, but giving an answer is difficult. It depends on what is meant by *regular*, and how it is measured. What follows is the attempts of several researchers and writers to quantify this.

If in a language, there were x vowel and consonant phonemes, and x ways of representing them in spelling, we could say that there was a 100% correspondence or regularity between phonemes and graphemes (letters). The English Spelling Society (n.d.) gives figures based on this reasoning. Spanish has 24 phonemes and 29 ways to represent them. This gives a figure of 83% (24 ÷ 29) regularity. For French, the figure would be much lower: 23% regularity (30 phonemes ÷ 130 ways of representing them). And, according to Dewey (1971), English is only 7% regular (41 phonemes ÷ 561 ways of representing them). We may debate the validity of the methodology and the numbers of phonemes and ways of representing them, but few would doubt the conclusion that English is less regular than French and Spanish.

In a seminal study using a corpus of 17,310 English words and AmE pronunciation, Hanna, Hanna, Hodges and Rudorf (1966; also see Hanna, Hodges & Hanna, 1971) concluded that half of the words could be spelled accurately on the basis of sound-letter correspondences. A further 34% had only one irregularity, usually in the representation of vowel sounds. If the meaning of the word (morphology) and its origin (etymology) were taken into account, this figure rose even further. Their bottom line was that only 4% of words were truly irregular.

Confusing Letters With Sounds

In a language with a regular alphabetic spelling system, that is, one with a (near) 100% correspondence between letters and sounds, there is little problem if speakers equate sounds with letters, and letters with sounds. However, as we have just seen, English is a poor example of an alphabetic system, and teachers and learners therefore have to keep the two separate.

The fact that some writers fail to distinguish letters and sounds in English is illustrated by the following two passages, one from a well-known writer, and the other from a primary literacy coordinator. To avoid embarrassment by maintaining anonymity, references to the books in which these passages appeared will not be given.

"We tried *latchstring* on our friends and they passed with flying colours. We believe this word with its six consonants in a row may be the largest consonant cluster in the English language."

When the above author uses the word *consonant*, does he mean consonant letter or consonant sound? When he says that *latchstring* has six consonants in a row, he is clearly referring to letters (*t, c, h, s, t, r*). While there may be six consonant letters here, there are only four consonant sounds (/tʃ, s, t, r/). In short, the three letters *tch* here represent only one sound /tʃ/. However, he then calls this "the largest consonant cluster." The word *cluster* is used to describe two or more consonant sounds occurring either at the beginning or end (in onset or in coda position) in a syllable. This sequence contains only one three-consonant cluster /str/. The /tʃ/ sound occurs at the end of the preceding syllable, and is a single phoneme. The consonantal ending of *latch* /lætʃ/ is no more difficult to pronounce than the ending of *attach* /ətætʃ/, even though *attach* has only two consonant letters in its spelling, while *latch* has three. Obviously, spelling has nothing to do with difficulty here.

Incidentally, there is a rule of English that when /tʃ/, which is normally spelled *ch*, is in syllable-final position and follows a short vowel, a *t* is added, as in *catch, fetch, pitch, scotch,* and *Dutch*. This is a pervasive rule and has only five counterexamples: *attach, rich, which, much,* and *such*. As a result, the verb *attach* is often hypercorrectly written as *attatch*. The irregular word *which* is a homophone with the regular *witch* (apart from speakers who differentiate the initial consonant sound). While *much* and *such* are irregular, there are regularly spelled surnames *Mutch* and *Sutch*.

"Consonants can be used singly or combined (blended) with other consonants. Up to three consonants can be used at the beginning of a word in English (as in *string, splash*) and up to five at the end (as in *twelfths*), although these words are rare. Investigation of three-consonant clusters at the beginnings of words will show that they all begin with /s/.

sch-   *school, scheme*

scr-   *scream, scramble*

shr-   *shred, shrimp*

spl-   *splash, splendid*

spr-   *spring, spray*

str-   *strong, stream*

scl-   *sclerosis* (not likely to be found by children)

squ-   *squirrel, squash* (although the third letter, *u* is not a consonant, *q* is always followed by *u* in English)"

The word *twelfths* may have five consonant letters at the end (*l, f, t, h, s*), but they only represent four sounds. That is, *t* and *h* together represent the /θ/ sound. This author is thus clearly talking about consonant letters when discussing *twelfths*, but she then switches to consonant sounds (as shown by the phoneme brackets: /s/) in the later discussion. The eight spellings she quotes contain five that are unproblematical (*scr-, spl-, spr-, str-, scl-*), as they contain both three consonant letters and three consonant sounds. The word *school* /sku:l/, with three consonant letters, cannot be considered any more difficult to pronounce than *scoop* /sku:p/, with only two. That is, the *h* in *school* is silent (see Chapter 12), and is purely a spelling phenomenon. While *shred* starts with three consonant letters (*s, h, r*), the *s* and *h* work together to represent the /ʃ/ sound (in Chapter 12 we will call the *h* here *auxiliary*). That is, *shred* starts with only two sounds /ʃr-/.

The description of *squirrel* is confusing to any reader. In terms of sounds, there is no problem: the word begins with a /skw-/ three-consonant cluster, and may therefore be difficult for some learners. However, the analysis of how this relates to the spelling is baffling. It is surely simpler to say that *qu* represents /kw/ as in *queen, quick, square* without further analysis. Also, she states that "*q* is always followed by *u* in English." There are words to be found in English dictionaries, where *q* is not followed by *u*, for instance *Qantas, Qatar, Iraq*. And there are many instances of *qu* which do not represent a /kw/ cluster, such as *quiche* /ki:ʃ/, *Quran* /kɔ:rɑ:n/, *unique* /ju:ni:k/.

To sum up, the need to divorce letters from sounds is important in English because of the lack of a (near) 100% correspondence between sounds and letters. Some published writers fail to do this. This confusion has also been going on for many years; de Saussure (1922) notes, "Even [19th century German philologist Franz] Bopp failed to distinguish clearly between letters and sounds. His works give the impression that a language and its alphabet are inseparable."

Similarly, calling some letters consonant letters, and the others vowel letters leads to unnecessary complications, as in the *u* letter of a *qu* letter sequence. The letter *y* can be a consonant letter (representing a consonant sound) in words like *yes, yacht*, but a vowel letter (representing a vowel sound) in words like *crystal, sky*. In short, it does not seem helpful to want to classify letters as consonants or vowels. In contrast, sounds can unambiguously be classified as vowel sounds or consonant sounds.

Devised Spelling Systems

Spelling systems for previously unwritten languages have been devised over the last century by the Summer Institute of Linguistics (n.d.), a Christian not-for-profit missionary organization, one of whose purposes is to translate the Bible into other languages. In order to do so, it has carried out important linguistic work on previously unwritten languages, and devised spelling systems for them.

The spelling systems it has devised have generally been alphabetic, using the Roman alphabet. Gudschinsky (1967) is an early SIL publication explaining the process of identifying the distinctive sounds (phonemes) of a language and assigning symbols to them. As Cahill and Karan (2008) and Cahill and Rice (Eds., 2014) point out, there are many factors that need to be taken into account in devising a spelling system, not all of them linguistic. Apart from being linguistically sound from a scientific point of view, any such system must also be acceptable to all stakeholders from a political perspective, teachable from the educational angle, and easy to reproduce in terms of typewriters and word-processing.

While spelling systems devised for existing unwritten languages have generally been alphabetic (letters representing vowel and consonant phonemes), there are features other than the vowel and consonant phonemes that may need to be represented or considered: "word breaks, punctuation, diacritics, capitalization, hyphenation and other aspects" (Cahill & Karan, 2008, p. 3). Diacritics are marks written above or below the symbol, indicating some aspect of pronunciation, such as *à, ö*, and *ç*.

Non-natural invented languages such as Esperanto (invented in the late 19th century) also use an alphabetic system for writing. Esperanto uses an augmented 28-letter Roman alphabet. It has no *q, w, x,* or *y* letters, but adds diacritics to six letters. Having been invented, its spelling is close to 100% regular.

Summary

- There are three main types of spelling system: logographic, syllabic, and alphabetic.
- Alphabetic systems, where symbols (letters) represent vowel and consonant phonemes, are the most common.
- Like most European languages, English uses the Roman alphabet.
- While the English spelling system is alphabetic, it is perhaps the worst example of an alphabetic system, in terms of sound-letter correspondence.
- Learners of English may come from countries that have languages with non-alphabetic systems, or systems that are much more regular than English.

Exercise

We saw that, despite being alphabetic, English also uses logograms in writing, such as *1* and *&*. List six more logograms in English. (Do not just list six more numbers!)

Further Reading

The spelling systems of languages of the world, including extinct ones, are detailed in Coulmas (Ed., 1996). Languages of the world, including their spelling systems, are contained in Katzner (2002) and Simons and Fennig (Eds., 2017).

References

Balmuth, M. (2009). *The roots of phonics: A historical introduction*. Baltimore, MD: Paul H. Brookes Publishing.

Cahill, M., & Karan, E. (2008). *Factors in designing effective orthographies for unwritten languages*. SIL Working Papers 2008–001. Retrieved from www.sil.org/resources/publications/entry/7830

Cahill, M., & Rice, K. (Eds., 2014). *Developing orthographies for unwritten languages*. Dallas, TX: SIL International.

Coulmas, F. (Ed.) (1996). *The Blackwell encyclopedia of writing systems*. Oxford, UK: Blackwell.

Dewey, G. (1971). *English spelling: Roadblock to reading*. New York, NY: Teachers College Press.

Dickerson, W. B. (1978). English orthography: A guide to word stress and vowel quality. *International Review of Applied Linguistics in Language Teaching, 16,* 127–147.

Dickerson, W. B. (1987). Orthography as a pronunciation resource. *World Englishes, 6,* 11–20. Also in A. Brown (Ed., 1991). *Teaching English pronunciation: A book of readings* (pp. 159–172). London, UK: Routledge.

Dickerson, W. B. (1989). *Stress in the speech stream: The rhythm of spoken English*. Urbana, IL: University of Illinois Press.

Dickerson, W. B. (2013). Prediction in teaching pronunciation. In C. A. Chapelle (Ed.) *The encyclopedia of applied linguistics* (pp. 4638–4645). Hoboken, NJ: Wiley-Blackwell.

The English Spelling Society (n.d.). Retrieved from spellingsociety.org

Gudschinsky, S. C. (1967). *How to learn an unwritten language.* New York, NY: Holt, Rinehart and Winston.

Hanna, P. R., Hanna, J. S., Hodges, R. E., & Rudorf, E. H. (1966). *Phoneme-grapheme correspondences as cues to spelling improvement.* Washington, DC: U.S. Department of Health, Education, and Welfare.

Hanna, P. R., Hodges, R. E., & Hanna, J. S. (1971). *Spelling: Structures and strategies.* Boston, MA: Houghton Mifflin.

Katzner, K. (2002). *The languages of the world* (3rd edition). Abingdon-on-Thames, UK: Taylor & Francis.

Saussure de, F. (1922). *Cours de linguistique générale (Course in general linguistics).* (Compiled by Bally & Séchehaye from notebooks of Saussure's students 1907–11; translated and annotated by R. Harris, 1983. London, UK: Duckworth).

Simons, G. F., & Fennig, C. D. (Eds.) (2017). *Ethnologue: Languages of the world* (20th edition). Dallas TX: SIL International. Online version available at www.ethnologue.com

Summer Institute of Linguistics (n.d.). Retrieved from www.sil.org

3   Spelling, Writing, and Reading

Learning Objectives

At the end of this chapter, readers will be able to:

- define the orthographic depth and dual-route hypotheses
- describe the effect on literacy of the irregularity of English spelling.

Orthographic Depth Hypothesis

So far we have used the term *irregularity* to refer to the extent to which an alphabetic spelling system such as English departs from a one-to-one correspondence between sounds and letters. Other adjectives that have been used to describe this distinction are *deep* vs *shallow*, and *opaque* vs *transparent* orthographies.

This has led to an Orthographic Depth Hypothesis (Katz & Frost, 1992). Regular, shallow, transparent orthographies can be processed solely in terms of the language's phonology (phonemes). Languages that have irregular, deep, opaque orthographies usually do so because they have a long history, and have never been systematically managed; as a result, the spelling may reflect the historical forms of words, may represent the units of meaning (morphemes) in a word as much as its component sounds, and must be processed by a more visual strategy. For instance, the English words *photograph, photographer,* and *photographic* are clearly related morphologically; they are the morpheme *photograph,* with the *-er* and *-ic* endings added, and this is clear from the spelling. However, the pronunciation differs depending on where the stress falls. In *PHOtograph,* it is on the first syllable; in *phoTO grapher,* the second; and in *photoGRAphic,* the third. This difference in stress placement leads to a difference in the vowel sounds represented by the *o* and *a* vowel letters.

Frost (2012) proposes that spelling systems evolve in a non-arbitrary way to reflect the phonological and morphological structure of a language. This presupposes that spelling systems are or should be a case of evolution, rather than a manmade invention eligible for periodical management.

Dual-route Hypothesis of Reading

The process of reading is one of converting the words printed on a page or shown on a computer screen, etc., into either speech (when reading aloud) or into meaning (when reading silently). How do human brains do this? It is intuitive to suppose that we simply convert the letters into sounds either by using individual correspondences (e.g. *v* = /v/) or less individual spelling patterns, e.g. *th* = /θ/ or /ð/. However, that would be an inefficient method for proficient readers to read familiar words. For a long time, writers have suggested that two different pathways are followed. As far back as 1922, Ferdinand de Saussure wrote:

> We read in two ways; the new or unknown word is scanned letter after letter, but a common or familiar word is taken in at a glance, without bothering about the individual letters: its visual shape functions like an ideogram [logogram].
>
> de Saussure (1922, translated 1983, p. 34)

This line of thought led to the dual-route hypothesis, which is captured in Figure 3.1.

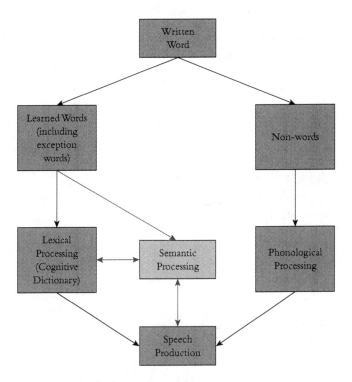

Figure 3.1 The dual-route hypothesis

Two types of processing are contained in the diagram. On the right, phonological processing means that letter-to-sound correspondences are used. Non-words are words that do not exist in the language; they may conform to the spelling and pronunciation patterns of the language (these are also called pseudo-words), or not. Faced with the non-word *pab*, it is not difficult to arrive at the pronunciation /pæb/ by using the regular correspondences p = /p/, a = /æ/ and b = /b/. However, words that are familiar to us are unlikely to be processed this way every time we encounter them. Instead, lexical processing and semantic processing, using our internal dictionary, allows us to bypass the phonological route by recognizing the word as a whole.

Refinements to this original model have involved consideration of familiar words that obey phonological rules (e.g. *can*) and those that do not (e.g. *could*; there is an *l* letter but no /l/ sound); the use of word parts (prefixes and suffixes like *dis-*, *-ment*); and the frequency of words. Nation (e.g. 2013) divides vocabulary into four basic groups. High-frequency words comprise a basic 2,000-word vocabulary that accounts for over 85% of all words in all passages (e.g. *arrive, forward, less*). An academic word list of about 800 words contains words that are common and useful in academia, regardless of the particular subject (e.g. *analyze, maintain, theory*). Technical vocabulary is words that are found only in particular subject areas, although they may be common in those areas; depending on the subject area, this may represent 1,000–2,000 words (e.g. *phoneme, predicate, realia* in English language teaching). And finally, low-frequency words are the remainder; while they are large in number (up to 125,000), on average they represent only 2% of the words in any passage.

Support for the hypothesis comes from at least two sources (Coltheart, 2005). Firstly, speakers with brain damage may have impairments in either the phonological or the lexical route. Those with impairment of the lexical route rely solely on the phonological route, thus pronouncing irregular words like *island* as /ɪzlənd/ and *yacht* as /jætʃt/. Vice versa, speakers with impairment of the phonological route can cope with regular and irregular existing words, because they are familiar with them, but they cannot process non-words, because they do not exist, so are not familiar.

Secondly, computer modeling of the dual-route process has shown that both computers and humans exhibit behavior including the following. High-frequency words are read faster than low-frequency. Existing words are read faster than non-words. Regularly spelled words are read faster than irregularly spelled words. "The later in an irregular word its irregular grapheme-phoneme correspondence is, the less the cost incurred by its irregularity" (Coltheart, 2005, p.15). Thus, *chef*, where the irregularity is the first sound (/ʃ/ represented by *ch*) delays the reading more than *shoe*, where the irregularity is in the second sound (/u:/ represented by *oe*), which delays it more than *crow*, where the irregularity is in the third sound (/oʊ/ represented by *ow*).

The 1996 film *That thing you do!* tells the story of a 1960s pop group. Its frontman and lead singer gives it the name *The Wonders* but, to make it more memorable and give the impression of being #1, spells it *The Oneders*. This leads the compere of a talent show to announce them as *The oNEEders*. The compere, faced with a strange pattern, does not recognize the logographic *one*, but instead reverts to an alphabetic-phonological and analogical strategy, comparing *Oneders* with *impeders, conceders*, etc. (examples of magic *e*; see Chapter 13). Eventually, when they are signed to Play-Tone Records, their A&R representative changes the spelling immediately to a less confusing *The Wonders*, who turn out to be one-hit wonders.

It is suggested that Mxyplyzyk, a store in New York, lost customers because few could spell its name to look up the address. Faced with the unfamiliar store name *Mxyplyzyk*, you probably tried to use a phonological strategy. This may work for the end of the word -*plyzyk*, which can plausibly represent the pronunciation /plɪzɪk/. The problem, however, lies in the first three letters (*Mxy-*) which contravene both spelling and pronunciation rules in English. No English word has *mx* in the spelling, and the usual correspondences for these letters (/m/ and /ks/) cannot occur together in English pronunciation. A phonological strategy has to be used, but in this case, it does not lead to a successful and plausible answer.

The lexical-semantic side of the dual-route hypothesis assumes that the reader already knows the words being read. It is thus of limited use in two contexts: firstly, when teaching foreign learners, perhaps with small vocabularies, who may be encountering the word for the first time, and secondly when competent native speakers encounter an unfamiliar word. In both these situations, a phonological strategy is used, as it allows the reader to pronounce the word even though they do not know the word. In the following example from Hungarian, which has regular spelling-sound correspondences, the speaker uses the phonological route because he/she does not know the technical vocabulary, and is successful because of the regularity.

A Hungarian linguist once told me of a Hungarian physics professor whose grandchild would read scientific papers aloud to him, naturally without understanding, but equally naturally conveying the sense to the listening grandfather. We must ask why we should not expect as much of English-speaking children.

(Upward, 1996, p. 19)

Speed of Literacy

As has already been suggested, the problem with much research into reading is that it is based on research into the reading of English, or at best other similarly irregular European languages such as French and German. The dual-route hypothesis presupposes that there exist words with irregular spellings, that cannot be handled by purely phonological processing. In languages with regular spelling systems and no (or few) irregularly spelled words, the distinction is therefore probably between (i) phonological processing of new, unfamiliar, regularly spelled words, and (ii) lexical processing of familiar, regularly spelled words. Since the focus of this book is the teaching of spelling to foreign learners, for whom most words will be new words waiting to be learned, phonological processing is the more relevant one, and the greater the regularity of spelling correspondences, the quicker and more successful language learning is likely to be.

As we concluded in Chapter 1, the main purpose of a spelling system is to enable literacy. Another measure of the regularity of a spelling system is thus the rate at which literacy is achieved. If a language's spelling system is regular, we would expect speakers of that language to achieve literacy fast. Just such research was carried out by Seymour, Aro and Erskine (2003). They measured the literacy rates of various languages after one year of school instruction (Figure 3.2). The literacy rates of English-speaking children (Scotland being used as the country under consideration, as Seymour, the lead researcher, was based in Dundee) are much lower than for other countries/languages. While other factors may be involved (although Scottish education cannot be that much worse than in the other countries), they conclude (p. 143) "that fundamental linguistic differences in syllabic complexity and orthographic depth are responsible" and "the deeper orthographies induce the implementation of a dual (logographic + alphabetic) foundation which takes more than twice as long to establish as the single foundation required for the learning of a shallow orthography."

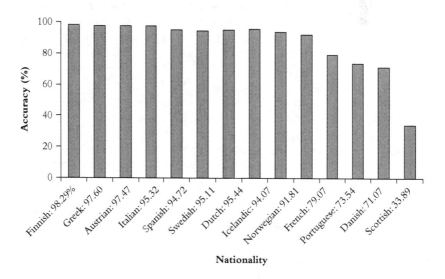

Figure 3.2 Word reading level for various nationalities after one year of instruction (Primary 1)

(Source: Seymour et al, 2003)

The advantages for literacy of a shallow alphabetic spelling system have been acknowledged for many years. Bloomfield (1933, p. 500) observed that "The difficulty of our spelling system greatly delays elementary education, and wastes even much time of adults. When one sees the admirably consistent orthographies of Spanish, Bohemian, or Finnish, one naturally wishes that a similar system might be adopted for English."

Further research supporting the view that regular, shallow, transparent spelling systems lead to faster and better literacy includes the following.

> Data suggest that languages with more regular letter-sound correspondences lead to faster acquisition of decoding skills.
>
> (Oney & Goldman, 1984)

> The English children read fast and inaccurately, whereas the Italian children read slowly and accurately using a systematic, phonological strategy until 10 years, when they read fast and accurately. All the children used a phonological strategy in spelling, but only the Italians were mostly successful. Thus the results suggest that, if the orthography is predictable and invariant, the children use a systematic, phonological strategy and learn to read and spell more quickly and accurately.
>
> (Thorstad, 1991; also see Chapter 29)

> For languages with relatively deep orthographies such as English, French, Arabic, or Hebrew, new readers have much more difficulty learning to decode words. As a result, children learn to read more slowly. For languages with relatively shallow orthographies, such as Italian and Finnish, new readers have few problems learning to decode words. As a result, children learn to read relatively quickly.
>
> (Goswami, 2005)

> The studies so far undertaken in individual countries are building evidence for the hypothesis that shallow orthographies are a real advantage in terms of acquiring reading proficiency for both normal and dyslexic children. Countries with deep orthographies might possibly begin to consider the political and societal feasibility of implementing orthographic reforms.
>
> (OECD-CERI, 2005)

> Both Spanish and English children have demonstrated a great amount of learning in the first two years of reading instruction. However, while the Spanish children have reached [the] ceiling the English children still have some way to go. These are signs of the impact of the orthographic depth of these two writing systems on the learning rate for reading. The transparent nature of Spanish permits children to master the decoding skill necessary for reading quickly soon after the beginning of instruction.
>
> (Quintanilla et al., 2010)

Summary

- Deep orthographies involve less regular sound-spelling correspondences at the phonological level, and may require processing at the morphemic level.
- The dual-route hypothesis proposes two levels of processing for reading English: phonological processing involves letter-to-sound correspondences, while by lexical-semantic processing readers recognize words as a whole.
- Research suggests that shallow orthographies lead to faster acquisition of spelling.

Exercises

1 If you have learned another language other than English (and if your native language is not English), reflect on how regular or irregular the spelling system is, and thus how easy or difficult you found it to learn to spell and read in that language.
2 If you have learned another language, have you had dictation exercises in that language? If so, how easy or hard did you find them? What were the main types of mistake you made?

Further Reading

The orthographic depth hypothesis underlies many of the writings of Ram Frost (n.d. a, b). The dual-path hypothesis underlies many of the writings of Max Coltheart (n.d. a, b).

References

Bloomfield, L. (1933). *Language*. New York, NY: Holt.
Coltheart, M. (2005). Modeling reading: The dual-route approach. In M. J. Snowling & C. Hulme (Eds.) *The science of reading: A handbook* (pp. 6–23). Oxford, UK: Blackwell.
Coltheart, M. (n.d. a). Retrieved from www.cogsci.mq.edu.au/members/profile. php?memberID=53
Coltheart, M. (n.d. b). Retrieved from www.cogsci.mq.edu.au/~max/?page_id=51
de Saussure, F. (1922). *Cours de linguistique générale (Course in general linguistics)*. (Compiled by Bally & Séchehaye from notebooks of Saussure's students 1907–11; translated and annotated by R. Harris, 1983. London, UK: Duckworth).
Frost, R. (2012). Towards a universal model of reading. *Behavioral and Brain Sciences*, *35*, 263–279.
Frost, R. (n.d. a). Retrieved from www.haskins.yale.edu/staff/ramfrost.html
Frost, R. (n.d. b). Retrieved from old.psychology.huji.ac.il/en/?cmd=Faculty.113 &act=read&id=42&page_id=103
Goswami, U. (2005). Orthography, phonology, and reading development: A cross-linguistic perspective. In J. Malatesha (Ed.). *Handbook of orthography and literacy* (pp. 463–464). Mahwah, NJ: Lawrence Erlbaum.

Katz, L., & Frost, R. (1992). Reading in different orthographies: The orthographic depth hypothesis. In R. Frost, & L. Katz (Eds.). *Orthography, phonology, morphology, and meaning* (pp. 67–84). Amsterdam, Netherlands: Elsevier.

Nation, I. S. P. (2013). *Learning vocabulary in another language* (2nd edition). Cambridge, UK: Cambridge University Press.

OECD-CERI (2005). *Shallow vs non-shallow orthographies and learning to read* workshop report. Retrieved from www.oecd.org/edu/ceri/35562310.pdf

Oney, B., & Goldman, S. R. (1984). Decoding and comprehension skills in Turkish and English: Effects of the regularity of grapheme-phoneme correspondence. *Journal of Educational Psychology, 76*(4), 557–568.

Quintanilla, E. O., Citoler, S. D., Caravolas, M., Salas, N., Mousikou, B., & Simpson, I. (2010). Effect of transparency on reading development. Paper at the 5th Enhancing Literacy Development in European Languages (ELDEL) workshop, Bangor, Wales. Retrieved from eldel.eu/sites/default/files/v3%20 Bangor%20Workshop%202010.pdf

Seymour, P. H. K., Aro, M., & Erskine, J. (2003). Foundation literacy acquisition in European orthographies. *British Journal of Psychology, 94*, 143–174.

Thorstad, G. (1991). The effect of orthography on the acquisition of literacy skills. *British Journal of Psychology, 82*, 527–537.

Upward, C. (1996). *English spelling: The need for a psycho-historical perspective.* Birmingham, UK: Aston University, Institute for the Study of Language & Society. Retrieved from spellingsociety.org/uploaded_books/b4aston4.pdf

4   History of English

Learning Objectives

At the end of this chapter, readers will be able to:

- list the main events in the development of English
- explain the Great Vowel Shift.

Introduction

In order to understand why modern English spelling is an alphabetic system, one with poor sound-spelling and spelling-sound correspondences, it is necessary to know something about the history of the English language. This chapter and the next give a brief history of English, concentrating on changes in spelling over the centuries.

When discussing the history of languages, it is important to realize that language change does not take place overnight. Changes are gradual and may take generations, even centuries, to be completed. The Great Vowel Shift, discussed later in this chapter, is a good example of this. One change had a knock-on effect producing other changes, and the whole process took over three centuries to be completed.

It also has to be remembered that, when we discuss spelling, until the 15th century at the earliest, we are talking about scribes laboriously writing manuscripts using quill pens. These scribes lived throughout England, and were simply using whatever letters they thought best represented their own pronunciation of the words. There was accent variation across the width and breadth of England (as indeed there still is), and so the pronunciations being represented differed. Because of the difficulties of travel, there was little contact between scribes and thus no real standardization of spelling until much later, about the 18th century.

The history of English is usually divided into four broad periods: Old English (OE), Middle English (ME), Early Modern English (EModE), and Modern English (ModE).

Old English

Old English is usually dated 450–1100. After the collapse of Roman authority in western Europe (including Britain), Germanic tribes invaded and defeated the Celts around the year 450. These Germanic tribes consisted of the Angles, Saxons, and Jutes (and Franks and Frisians), all from present-day northern Germany (and parts of Denmark and the Netherlands). Together, these tribes are referred to as the Anglo-Saxons, and many British placenames still reflect their influence: *Essex, Sussex, Wessex,* and *Middlesex* (the lands of the east, south, west, and middle Saxons), and *East Anglia* (the lands of the east Angles). Indeed, the words *England* and *English* come from the Angles. The language of the Saxons, known as Old Saxon or Old Low German, thus developed along two separate channels: the Old Saxon of those who stayed on the continent developed into modern German and Dutch, while the language of those who settled in Britain became Old English, developing eventually into Modern English. For this reason, English is called a Germanic language. The Anglo-Saxons gave us the words for basic concepts, many of which are still the most common words in use today, e.g. *man, woman, child, house, meat, eat, drink, fight.*

Old English (Anglo-Saxon) largely supplanted the Celtic languages spoken by the indigenous inhabitants. These Celtic languages still survive today in Welsh (spoken in parts of Wales), Irish (spoken in parts of Ireland), Scottish Gaelic (spoken in parts of Scotland), Cornish (spoken by very few people in Cornwall), and Manx (spoken by very few people on the Isle of Man), as well as Breton (in Brittany, France).

Middle English

Middle English is usually dated 1100–1500, and was brought about when, on 14 October 1066, Duke William of Normandy (in France) invaded England and defeated King Harold the Second at the Battle of Hastings, on the south coast of England. William became king, and is known as William the Conqueror. The invasion is known as the Norman Conquest because William and his army came from Normandy. William spoke French, and thus French became the language of nobility, government, and the law. For the best part of three centuries, subsequent kings of England spoke French as a native language. It is believed that the first subsequent king to speak English was Edward I (reigned 1272–1307). Needless to say, three centuries of French royalty had a profound influence on the English language, including its spelling. This is not to say that all the English spoke French. Since the Norman French were the victorious conquerors, French assumed dominance and prestige not only in royal circles, but also in government, law, education, and the church. For 300 years after the Norman Conquest, English (Anglo-Saxon) was the language of the lower classes. Thus, in England, Anglo-Saxon (a Germanic language) was used alongside French (a Romance language deriving from Latin).

A major author of the Middle English period, whose works are extant, is Geoffrey Chaucer (1343–1400). While he wrote many other works, he is most famous for *The Canterbury tales*.

Two very important episodes in the history of English, and English spelling, occurred in the Middle English period. The first is the invention of the printing press. It was invented by German Johannes Gutenberg around the year 1440 in Mainz, Germany. A Dutchman, Laurens Janszoon Coster, is said to have invented a printing press in Harlem, the Netherlands, at about the same time as Gutenberg, although there is some doubt about this.

This heralded the era of mass communication, as printed copies of works could be produced and distributed relatively easily. For example, Gutenberg produced a printed Latin translation of the Bible. It is known as the Gutenberg Bible, or the 42-line Bible, because each page contained 42 lines of text, in two columns. It sold for 30 florins, which was the equivalent of three years' wages for a clerk. Even so, it was cheaper than a handwritten manuscript copy, which would have taken a scribe over a year to write.

The printing press was brought from Europe to Britain by William Caxton. He learned the trade in Europe, setting up a printing press in Bruges, Belgium, and produced the first printed book in English there in 1473. He returned to England in 1476 to set up a printing shop in Westminster, London. The first book that is known to have been produced at Caxton's press was Chaucer's *The Canterbury tales*. Caxton also produced the first printed verses of the Bible in English translation.

Before Caxton, English was handwritten by scribes in various parts of England, using letters to represent their regional pronunciation. With the establishment of the printing press in London, prestigious London speech was used as the reference accent for spelling English, and variant spellings were gradually standardized. The written standard based on this is known as Chancery Standard and was the spelling of the clerks of Chancery in London, who prepared the king's documents.

The second major event starting in Middle English times is what is known as the Great Vowel Shift (GVS). This was a change in the long vowel sounds of English that started around 1350, and finished around 1600 in the Early Modern English era. Short vowel sounds remained largely unaffected. The major changes that occurred in the GVS can be treated in three groups:

The high vowels /iː, uː/ first lowered and became the central diphthongs /aɪ, aʊ/. This created the room for the non-high vowels to rise. Once all these stages had been completed, the vowel system of English had completely changed.

Table 4.1 The Great Vowel Shift

1 High long vowels became diphthongs				
/iː/	>	/aɪ/	/liːk/	(*like*)
/uː/	>	/aʊ/	/uːrə/	(*our*)
2 Non-high long vowels were raised				
/eː/	>	/iː/	/beː/	(*be*)
/oː/	>	/uː/	/moːnə/	(*moon*)
/æː/	>	/eː/ (> /iː/)	/dæːd/	(*deed*)
/ɔː/	>	/oː/	/hɔːl/	(*whole*)
/aː/	>	/æː/ (> /eː/)	/naːmə/	(*name*)
3 Diphthongs became monophthongs				
/aʊ/	>	/ɔː/	/faʊxt/	(*fought*)
/æɪ/	>	/eː/	/sæɪl/	(*sail*)

Early Modern and Modern English

The English Renaissance was a revival of classical scholarship lasting from the 16th to the 17th century. It is also referred to as the Elizabethan Era, after Queen Elizabeth I (reigned 1558–1603) and the Age of Shakespeare, after the most famous English writer of the time, William Shakespeare (1564–1616). A large number of (now, everyday) words of Latin and Greek origin were introduced into English, e.g. *apparatus, conscious, criterion, critic, education, focus, metamorphosis, specimen.* These words were intentionally introduced into English, not because of any increased contact between English speakers and Latin or Greek speakers.

At around the same time, international trade increased, bringing English speakers into contact with speakers of many other languages, and leading to loanwords from those languages.

Summary

- English has a history dating back to the 5th century.
- It has been influenced at various times in its history by (old versions of) German, French, Latin, and Greek, among others.
- If only printing had been invented a century later, or if the GVS had occurred a century earlier, English pronunciation would have changed before printing standardized the spelling, and present-day spelling would be much more regular than it has turned out to be.
- As a result, the modern spelling of many words reflects more accurately the pronunciation of Chaucer's time, before the GVS.

Exercise

Two of the most famous extant pieces of Old English writing are *Beowulf* and *Judith*, both named after their main characters. While *Beowulf* is a complete poem, *Judith* is an incomplete fragment. To appreciate how much English has changed over the centuries, look at the original versions of these poems, and their modern equivalent. The *Beowulf* original is at Poetry Foundation (n.d., a) and the modern version at Poetry Foundation (n.d., b). The *Judith* original is at University of Virginia (n.d.) and the modern version at Rutgers University (n.d.).

Further Reading

There are many books on the history of English, from the scholarly (Algeo & Hogg, Eds., 2016; Baugh & Cable, 2012; Gramley, 2012; Hogg, 2008; Mugglestone, 2013) to the popular (Barfield, 2002; Bragg, 2011; Crystal, 2005, 2012; Gooden, 2011; Horobin, 2016; Lucas & Mulvey, 2013) and those aimed at students (Burnley, 2000; McIntyre, 2008; Singh, & Singh, 2005).

References

Algeo, J., & Hogg, R. M. (Eds.) (2016). *The Cambridge history of the English language.* Cambridge, UK: Cambridge University Press.

Barfield, O. (2002). *History in English words.* Great Barrington, MA: Lindisfarne Books.

Baugh, A. C., & Cable, T. (2012). *A history of the English language* (6th edition). London, UK: Routledge.

Bragg, M. (2011). *The adventure of English: The biography of a language.* New York, NY: Arcade Publishing.

Burnley, D. (2000). *The history of the English language: A sourcebook.* London, UK: Longman.

Crystal, D. (2005). *The stories of English.* London, UK: Penguin Books.

Crystal, D. (2012). *The story of English in 100 words.* London, UK: Profile Books.

Gooden, P. (2011). *The story of English: How the English language conquered the world.* London, UK: Quercus Publishing.

Gramley, S. E. (2012). *The history of English: An introduction.* London, UK: Routledge.

Hogg, R. M. (2008). *A history of the English language.* Cambridge, UK: Cambridge University Press.

Horobin, S. (2016). *How English became English: A short history of a global language.* Oxford, UK: Oxford University Press.

Lucas, B., & Mulvey, C. (2013). *A history of the English language in 100 places.* London, UK: The Crowood Press.

McIntyre, D. (2008). *History of English: A resource book for students.* London, UK: Routledge.

Mugglestone, L. (2013). *The Oxford history of English.* Oxford, UK: Oxford University Press.

Poetry Foundation (n.d., a). *Beowulf* (Old English version). Retrieved from www.poetryfoundation.org/poems-and-poets/poems/detail/43521

Poetry Foundation (n.d., b). *Beowulf* (Modern English translation). Retrieved from www.poetryfoundation.org/poems-and-poets/poems/detail/50114

Rutgers University (n.d.). *Anglo-Saxon Narrative Poetry Project: Judith* (Modern English translation). Retrieved from anglosaxonpoetry.camden.rutgers.edu/judith

Singh, I., & Singh, G. (2005). *The history of English: A student's guide.* London, UK: Hodder Education.

University of Virginia (n.d.). *Judith* (Old English version). Retrieved from faculty.virginia.edu/OldEnglish/aspr/a4.2.html

5 History of English Spelling

Learning Objectives

At the end of this chapter, readers will be able to:

- list the main events in the development of English spelling
- explain the source of silent letters, and the many-to-one and one-to-many nature of English spelling.

Introduction

Chapter 4 gave a brief history of English. This chapter relates that discussion to the spelling of English. The various influences on English outlined in the previous chapter, especially from German, French, Latin, and Greek, as well as the invention of printing and the Great Vowel Shift (GVS), have all had an effect on the spelling of English that has come down to us today. We shall once again divide the history into three periods: Old English, Middle English, and Early Modern and Modern English.

Old English Spelling

Old English was originally written using the runic alphabet; the individual letters are known as runes. This alphabet was used for Germanic languages from about the 1st or 2nd century. Variations of the runic alphabet have been used in various languages, as late as the 19th century in Sweden. In the present-day, it is only used for traditional or artistic effect. For instance, the German SS (*Schutzstaffel*, literally "Protection Squadron") of World War II used a stylized SS on their uniforms, derived from runes and looking more like lightning strikes. J. R. R. Tolkien used runes in *The Hobbit* (1937), for old-world effect. The 1992 video game *Heimdall*, based on Viking mythology, used runes as magical symbols.

The use of runes changed when Christianity was brought to England in the late 6th century. Christianity had been brought to Britain perhaps as early as the 1st century by the Romans. However, it did not spread outside the areas under Roman control until the 5th century. Saint Patrick brought Christianity to Ireland, and during the 6th century Columba spread Christianity to Scotland and north England. Pope Gregory the Great sent a group of monks to evangelize Britain, led by Augustine, the Italian prior of a monastery in Rome. Æthelberht of Kent was a pagan king, but had married Bertha, the Christian daughter of King Charibert I of Paris. Arriving in 597, Augustine converted the king and many of his subjects, became the first Archbishop of Canterbury and, after his death, was made a saint. Latin had been introduced to Britain centuries earlier by the Romans, but was strengthened by the conversion to Christianity. Over the next four centuries, Britain was gradually converted to Christianity.

From the point of view of language, the conversion of Britain to Christianity is important for three main reasons. Firstly, Christianity at that time meant Roman Catholicism, Protestantism not developing until Martin Luther in the 1520s. As a result, there was an influx of Latin and Greek borrowings, especially for religious concepts, e.g. *abbot, altar, angel, candle, cap, chalice, church, hymn, relic, school.* Secondly, it is difficult to convert people to Christianity without having translated the Bible from its original Hebrew and Greek into their language. The Bible was therefore translated into Old English. Thirdly, the Bible has been re-translated at various times, in order to keep up with changes in the development of English. We therefore have versions of the same document from different stages in the development of English, which allow us to see the changes that have taken place.

Christian missionaries attempted to use their (at that time, 23-letter) Roman alphabet, used for Latin, for the 35 or so phonemes of Old English. The addition of four new letters helped (Table 5.1).

Eth and thorn were used interchangeably in the Old English period. All four letters gradually dropped out of use – eth by about 1300, thorn a century or two later, and wynn also around 1300. It is possible to argue that vestiges of them exist in Modern English. Ash is seen in spellings such as *encyclopaedia*, where the original ash is now spelled with two letters, *a* and *e*. The loop of thorn became less joined, perhaps to distinguish it from *p*, and it became confused with *y*. This is seen in *Ye Olde Tea Shoppe*, where the first word was a spelling of *the*, and pronounced thus. *You* may also have developed from a possible variant spelling of *thou*. Eth, thorn, and ash are all found in the spelling system of modern Icelandic.

Table 5.1 Non-Roman alphabet letters used in Old English

Letter	Name	Phonetic value	Eventually replaced by
æ	ash	/æ/	*a*
ð	eth	/ð/	*th*
þ	thorn	/θ, ð/	*th*
ƿ	wynn	/w/	*w*

Ash and eth derived from Latin, while thorn and wynn came from the runic alphabet. Despite using these extra letters, it still proved necessary to use some letters (such as *c* and *g*) to represent more than one sound, and to represent some sounds by combinations of letters (such as *sc*, the equivalent of present-day *sh*).

In short, from the very beginning, English spelling had a correspondence between sounds and spellings that was far from 100%.

To give a taster of what Old English spelling was like, here is what in Christianity is known as the Lord's Prayer in a version from around the year 1000.

> Fæder ure þu þe eart on heofonum, si þin name gehalgod. Tobecume þin rice. Gewurþe þin willa on eorðan swa swa on heofonum. Urne gedæghwamlican hlaf syle us to dæg. And forgyf us ure gyltas, swa swa we forgyfað urum gyltedum. And ne gelæd þu us on costnungen ac alys us of yfele. Soðlice.

In 865 and 990, there were two waves of invasions by the Vikings. The Vikings came from Scandinavia (modern Denmark, Norway) and spoke a language nowadays called Old Norse. It may have been mutually intelligible with Old English. The Viking invasions had a strong influence on Old English grammar and vocabulary, but little influence on spelling. Both conquests brought Old Norse borrowings, e.g. *birth, sky, trust, take, skirt, disk, give, law, leg*. Old Norse influence also simplified the pronoun and inflexion systems.

Middle English Spelling

Because of the French influence following the Norman Conquest, existing spelling patterns were replaced with French ones. Table 5.2 gives the main changes.

What follows is the first four lines of the General Prologue of Chaucer's *The Canterbury Tales*, with the original spelling on the left, and a modern version on the right.

Table 5.2 Middle English spelling changes

Change	French-influenced new spelling	Original Old English spelling (closest possibility)
cw > qu	*quick*	*cwic*
h > gh	*might*	*miht*
c > ch	*church*	*cyrice*
u > ou	*house*	*hus*
s > c	*cell*	*sell*
u > o	*come, love*	*cume, luve*

Whan that Aprill with his shoures soote	When April with its sweet-smelling showers
The droghte of March hath perced to the roote,	Has pierced the drought of March to the root,
And bathed every veyne in swich licour	And bathed every vein (of the plants) in such liquid
Of which vertu engendred is the flour;	By the power of which the flower is created;

The passage is much easier to understand than the 1100 version of the Lord's Prayer. That is, it is much more similar to modern English. Two points that will be discussed later, are the following. Firstly, many words had a final unstressed (but pronounced) syllable, with an *e* letter (*shoures, soote, droghte, roote, veyne*). This was eventually lost in the pronunciation and in the spelling. Secondly, modern English *flower* is spelled *flour*. These two words were originally the same, in meaning, pronunciation, and spelling (see Chapter 20). The same change from *our* to *ower* has happened with *shoures*.

The final change in Table 5.2 (*u* > *o* in *come, love*) needs further explanation. Scribes used short, vertical strokes for the letters *i* (one stroke, originally without a dot), *n* and *u* (two strokes), and *m* (three strokes). As its name suggests, *w* (double u) was written using two *u* letters. These strokes were known as minims, from the Latin *minimus* "smallest," and because the word *minim* is composed entirely of such strokes. Texts containing these letters were difficult to read because they contained a string of minims. For example, the word *woman/women* comes from Old English *wif* "woman" (not "wife") and *man* "person" (not "man"). Contrary to popular belief, this word has nothing historically to do with the word *womb*. In old English, these were spelled *wimman/wimmen*. Because the first four letters were composed entirely of minims, Middle English scribes arbitrarily changed the *i* to *o*, making the word easier to recognize in writing (minim stroke avoidance). The pronunciation of the first vowel in *woman* changed in ME because of the change of spelling and the influence of the initial *w*.

Similarly, ME scribes used *o* in words like *come, love*, and *honey* for the *u* as in *cup*.

The two major events of the Middle English period were described in Chapter 4: the invention of printing, and the GVS. While the GVS started around 1350 (and perhaps before that) and continued for many decades, the printing press is dated to around 1440. The printing press had the effect of standardizing English spelling before the GVS was complete. So, the sounds (vowels) continued to change. "The spellings of some words changed to reflect the change in pronunciation (e.g. *stone* from *stan, rope* from *rap, dark* from *derk, barn* from *bern, heart* from *herte*, etc.), but most did not" (The History of English, n.d.). It was all a matter of timing. The modern spelling of many words reflects the pronunciation of Chaucer's time, before the GVS. If the GVS had been completed earlier, or if the printing press had been invented later, modern English spelling would have been a much more accurate and regular indication of pronunciation than it is.

Notice that the GVS affected long vowels (long monophthongs and diphthongs). It did not affect short vowels. As a result, many related words nowadays have different vowels, but the same letter in the spelling. For instance, *chaste* and *chastity* are both spelled with a letter *a*, because they were originally long and short versions of the same /æ/ vowel. However, the long vowel in *chaste* underwent the GVS, changing to /e:/, the ancestor of modern /eɪ/, while the vowel in *chastity*, not being affected by the GVS, remained as /æ/.

Caxton learned the printing trade in Belgium and, when he brought the press to England, he also brought printers with him from Europe who spoke no English. They brought European spelling patterns with them. In old English, the Holy Ghost was the *Hali Gast*, with no *h* in *gast*. However, Flemish printers, who spelled the Flemish equivalent of this word *gheest*, inserted an *h* in *ghost*. Similarly, *aghast* and *ghastly* replaced the earlier spellings *agast* and *gastly*. In other *gh-* words, *gh* represents sounds and spellings of foreign origins: *ghee* (Hindi), *ghetto* (Italian), *ghoul* (Arabic). In *gherkin*, the *h* was inserted in the 1800s in order to indicate a "hard" /g/ sound, rather than a "soft" /dʒ/.

As for vowels in the GVS, so some consonant and consonant clusters changed. However, since the spellings of these sounds had been standardized by printing, they did not change and persist to this day.

The voiceless velar fricative /x/ was lost. The word *fought*, originally pronounced /faʊxt/, lost the /x/ (and the vowel changed; see above). Similarly, *night* /ni:xt/ lost its /x/ and the vowel changed (see above).

Some consonant clusters were simplified. The initial clusters /kn-, gn-/ were simplified to /n/, as in *knight* and *gnaw*, originally /kni:xt/ and /gnawən/. The final clusters /-mb, – ŋg/ were simplified to /m, ŋ/, as in *dumb* and *thing*, originally /dʊmb/ and /θɪŋg/.

As a result of the above phenomenon (and others), there are many "silent" letters in modern spelling. "Silent" letters are letters in the spelling that do not represent any sound in the pronunciation (see Chapter 12).

Here is the Lord's Prayer in a 1400 version.

Oure fadir that art in heuenes halowid be thi name, thi kyngdom come to, be thi wille don in erthe es in heuene, yeue to us this day oure bread ouir other substance, & foryeue to us oure dettis, as we forgeuen to oure dettouris, & lede us not in to temptacion: but delyuer us from yuel, amen.

Early Modern English and Modern English Spelling

16th century scholars felt that it was appropriate to try to indicate something of the history of a word in its spelling. In this way, more silent letters were created (Table 5.3).

However, they unwittingly introduced errors (Table 5.4).

Anchor is described as a corrupt spelling of the Latin *ancora*. *Author* was mistakenly thought to come from Greek. *Could* is not analogous to *would* and *should*, both of which had a written and pronounced *l* in Old English (*wolde, sceolde*). *Delight* is not from German; it is not analogous to *light*, which is from German and originally had /x/. *Island* is not from Latin. It is surprisingly not related to *isle*, which is from the Latin *insula*. *Nephew* was mistakenly pronounced with /f/. *Scythe* is not related to *scissors* (from Latin).

The creation of dictionaries had a further normalizing effect on spelling. Readers began to accept the spellings in dictionaries as "correct." While there were many others, two dictionaries in particular had a large influence: Dr. Samuel Johnson's *A dictionary of the English language* (1755) in Britain, and Noah Webster's *American dictionary of the English language* (1828) (see Chapter 15).

English has come into increasing contact with peoples of other languages; for some centuries through colonialization, and more recently through

Table 5.3 Letters inserted in Modern English spelling that correctly reflect etymology

Modern spelling	Previous spelling	Word origin
debt	det	debitum (Latin)
doubt	doute	dubitare (Latin)
fault	faute	fallita (Latin)
reign	reine	regno (Latin)

Table 5.4 Letters inserted in Modern English spelling that incorrectly reflect etymology

Modern spelling	Previous spelling	Word origin
anchor	ancor	ancora (Latin)
author	autor	auctor (Latin)
could	couthe	cuðe (Old English)
delight	delite	delit (French)
haughty	hautif	hautain (French)
island	iland	eyland (Old Norse)
nephew	neveu	nepos (Latin)
scythe	siðe	segitho (Proto-Germanic)

economic and cultural activity, and international education. Words have entered English from this contact. However, unlike loanwords in other languages, the spelling or transliteration from the original language has usually been retained, giving un-English-looking spellings. For instance, French gave *ballet, bizarre, brusque, gazette, genre, intrigue, moustache*. Other examples include *bamboo* (Malay), *bazaar* (Persian), *bravado* (Spanish), *buoy* (Dutch), *geisha* (Japanese), *geyser* (Icelandic), *macaroni* (Italian), *maelstrom* (Norwegian), *sauna* (Finnish), *waltz* (German), *yoghurt* (Turkish).

In the present day, there is still borrowing of words from various languages or inventions, e.g. *intifada* (Arabic), *perestroika* (Russian), *squaerial* ("square aerial").

Here is the Lord's Prayer in a version from around 1700.

Our father which art in heaven, hallowed be thy Name. Thy kingdome come. Thy will be done, in earth, as it is in heaven. Giue vs this day our dayly bread. And forgiue vs our debts, as we forgiue our debters. And leade vs not into temptation, but deliuer vs from euill: For thine is the kingdome, and the power, and the glory, for euer, Amen.

And a contemporary version.

Our Father, who is in heaven, may your name be kept holy. May your kingdom come into being. May your will be followed on earth, just as it is in heaven. Give us this day our food for the day. And forgive us our offenses, just as we forgive those who have offended us. And do not bring us to the test. But free us from evil. For the kingdom, the power, and the glory are yours forever. Amen.

See Chapter 7 for an even more modern version.

Summary

- English spelling has never contained a good correspondence between sounds and letters. From the beginning, the 23-letter Roman alphabet was not suitable for the 35 or so phonemes of Old English.
- Throughout its history, English spelling has come under the influence of the spelling patterns of various foreign languages.

Exercise

The following pairs of related words contain long and short vowels. The long vowels underwent the GVS; the short vowels did not. However, they are both spelled with the same vowel letter. Fill in the blanks with appropriate examples. The first pair, *chaste* and *chastity* are given as a sample. (Note that an /r/ sound affects the nature of the long vowel. *Hilarious* is thus /hɪleəriəs/ in BrE not /hɪleɪriəs/.) (This exercise is based on one by Carney, 1997, p. 15).

- *a* spelling for /eɪ/ – /æ/ (including /eə(r)/ – /æ(r)/)

Long V	Short V	Long V	Short V	Long V	Short V
chaste	chastity	....	gratitude	hilarious	....
....	humanity	mania	....	....	opacity
shade	....	tenacious	....	....	valley

- *e* spelling for /iː/ – /e/ (including /ɪə(r)/ – /e(r)/)

Long V	Short V	Long V	Short V	Long V	Short V
austere	....	....	credulous	severe	....
serene	....	hero	....	....	legislate
female	....	obscene	....	supreme	....

- *i* and *y* spelling for /aɪ/ – /ɪ/ (including /aɪə(r)/ – /ɪ(r)/)

Long V	Short V	Long V	Short V	Long V	Short V
....	biblical	....	criminal	....	definitive
five	....	line	....	satire	....
mime	....	....	mineral	....	typical

- *o* spelling for /oʊ/ – /ɒ, ɑ/ (including /ɔː(r)/ – /ɒ, ɑ (r)/)

Long V	Short V	Long V	Short V	Long V	Short V
....	atrocity	....	closet	phone	....
floral	....	holy	....	omen	....
provoke	....	....	solitude	....	tonic

Further Reading

The runic alphabet is explained in Page (2006). The history of the Roman alphabet is explained in Haley (1995), Man (2001). The history of English spelling is covered in many books, e.g. Balmuth (2009), Crystal (2012), Scragg (2011), Upward and Davidson (2011), Venezky (1999).

References

Balmuth, M. (2009). *The roots of phonics: A historical introduction.* Baltimore, MD: Paul H. Brookes Publishing.

Carney, E. (1997). *English spelling.* London, UK: Routledge.

Crystal, D. (2012). *Spell it out: The singular story of English spelling.* London, UK: Profile Books.

Haley, A. (1995). *Alphabet: The history, evolution and design of the letters we use today.* London, UK: Thames & Hudson.

Man, J. (2001). *Alpha beta: How 26 letters shaped the western world.* New York, NY: Barnes & Noble.

Page, R. I. (2006). *An introduction to English runes.* Woodbridge, UK: The Boydell Press.

Scragg, D. G. (2011). *A history of English spelling.* Manchester, UK: Manchester University Press.

The History of English (n.d.). *Early Modern English.* Retrieved from www.thehist oryofenglish.com/history_early_modern.html

Tolkien, J. R. R. (1937) *The Hobbit, or there and back again.* London, UK: George Allen & Unwin.

Upward, C., & Davidson, G. (2011). *The history of English spelling.* Chichester & Malden, UK: Wiley-Blackwell.

Venezky, R. L. (1999). *The American way of spelling: The structure and origins of American English orthography.* New York, NY: The Guildford Press.

Section 2

Technology

6 A Computer Is Not a Typewriter

Learning Objectives

At the end of this chapter, readers will be able to:

- give details of the history of the QWERTY keyboard
- list at least six differences between typewriting and word-processing
- describe smart quotation marks, and the choice of fonts
- explain why nowadays, underlining and all capitals is avoided.

Introduction

It is important to realize that most young people nowadays have hardly seen, let alone used, a typewriter. However, being older, many teachers have used a typewriter, and some continue using a computer for word-processing in the same way they used a typewriter many years ago. There are really only two similarities between the two: they both use the QWERTY keyboard, and they are both used to produce pages of text. But the similarities end there. A computer is a vastly more sophisticated machine capable of producing much higher-quality text than a typewriter ever was. Each successive version of word-processing software incorporates more and more features to allow users to produce more attractive text more easily.

In the past, computer-based word-processing was referred to as desktop publishing. Whether you think the word *publishing* is the right one to use in non-professional situations such as a student producing an assignment, someone writing a letter of complaint to a company or an informal email to their grandmother, they have features at their disposal to produce documents that are as attractive, readable, and legible as those that professionals could produce.

This chapter covers two topics: the QWERTY keyboard, and ways in which a computer surpasses a typewriter.

The QWERTY Keyboard

The keyboard is named QWERTY after the first six keys on the top row of letters. You may wonder why this layout was established for typewriters, and subsequently persisted for computers. The QWERTY layout was devised and patented by American newspaper editor and printer Christopher Latham Sholes in the 1870s, and sold to the Remington company. The characters on the keyboard were mounted on metal arms which would jam if adjacent keys were typed in rapid succession. The layout of the characters therefore aimed to avoid this, partly by using left and right fingers for alternating strokes, as far as possible. Nevertheless, it is still the case that the left hand is used more than the right for typing. While it is often thought that the QWERTY arrangement was designed to slow typists down, the fact that it was aimed at avoiding jams in fact meant that it sped them up, by avoiding delays caused by jamming.

The number of keys on the keyboard was fewer than for later typewriters, again in an attempt to optimize the layout and avoid jams. For example, the numbers 1 and 0 were missing, these being typed as a lowercase L, and a capital O respectively. Similarly, the exclamation mark ! was created by typing an apostrophe, backspacing, and then typing a full stop under the apostrophe.

The QWERTY layout has been enhanced over time. Also, alternative designs to the QWERTY layout have been proposed at various times. However, none of these has achieved widespread adoption, for two main reasons. Firstly, any non-QWERTY keyboard would involve retraining in the new system for those typists trained in QWERTY – and indeed everyone who uses a computer, which is most people. Secondly, the devisers of new layouts have claimed improved typing speeds, but this has not been conclusively proven empirically; typists seem to be able to adapt to any layout of the keys and achieve similar speeds.

The QWERTY computer keyboard is a very enhanced version of the QWERTY typewriter layout. The layout of the three rows of letters is the same. However, the top row of function keys (F1, etc.) has been added, as have the numberpad, direction arrows, and various other keys such as Ctrl, Print Screen, and Delete.

In view of the fact that young people are likely to use computers for word-processing and other functions almost every day, if not every hour, of their present-day lives, and for the rest of their lives, it is surprising that keyboard skills are not seen as a vital life skill nowadays, to be taught from primary school level.

Only the best typists make no typing errors. Certainly, most teachers and learners, who have usually received no training in keyboard skills, make typing errors. As a result, it may not be clear from typed assignments whether a spelling mistake is the result of a learner not knowing the correct spelling, or a simple typing error.

Computer vs Typewriter

As already pointed out, a computer is a far more advanced and sophisticated machine than a typewriter was. In this section are outlined some features of a computer that were impossible on a typewriter. The kind of typewriter we are using for comparison is the traditional, standard, desktop or portable typewriter, rather than golfball typewriters or later models that included a small screen and limited memory, and were thus a transitional phase between typewriters and computers. While it would be possible to list a large number of differences, six simple and useful ones are highlighted here.

Choice of Font

Typewriters came with one font, and it was usually Courier.

```
This sentence is in Courier font.
```

Two things can be said about Courier. Firstly, it was a non-proportional, monospaced font. This means that each letter was the same width as every other letter. In contrast, computer fonts are proportional, that is, the width of a letter depends on the particular letter. So, for instance, an *m* is about five times the width of an *i*. Secondly, Courier therefore looks like an old-fashioned typewriter font, and publishers and other people do not choose it unless that is the effect they are aiming for.

Computer word-processing programs come with many fonts. It is also possible to download extra fonts from the internet – legally and free of charge. And they are all proportional. This means that the computer-user has lots of fonts to choose from, and does not need to use the default font.

How do you choose which font to use? It depends on the type of document you are preparing, and the effect you want to have. There are two main distinctions between types of font.

Firstly, fonts can be divided into serif and sans serif. *Serif* refers to the little extensions at the ends of the strokes of a letter. A sans serif font has no such extensions. An easy way to tell the difference is to look at the letter *l*. In a sans serif font, it is simply a vertical line, e.g. l (Arial), while in a serif font it has those extensions, e.g. l (Times New Roman). As Williams (1990, p. 55) says, "Serif type is more readable and is best for text; sans serif type is more legible and is best used for headlines." Similarly, unless you have training in design and typography, a good rule of thumb is not to use more than two fonts in one document, e.g. one serif and one sans serif.

Secondly, there are fancy fonts, and non-fancy fonts. Fancy fonts are whimsical ones that can have great effect in advertisements and the like, but should be used very sparingly, if at all, in more formal documents.

This sentence is in Magneto font.

This sentence is in Vivaldi font.

This sentence is in Old English MT font.

THIS SENTENCE IS IN STENCIL FONT.

Note that some fancy fonts are cursive, some are italic, some are all capitals, etc. A paragraph in one of these fonts would be difficult to read. Fancy fonts should therefore only be used for the occasional letter or word, if at all.

Special mention might be made of one particular sans serif font that seems to be popular with teachers: Comic Sans.

This sentence is in Comic Sans font.

Debate rages on the internet about contexts in which it is appropriate. Its designer, Vincent Connare, produced it primarily as a fun font for young children. "Comic Sans isn't complicated, it isn't sophisticated, it isn't the same old text typeface like in a newspaper. It's just fun." (Strizver, n.d.). So, it is an informal font appropriate for learners at primary level, but probably not above.

To summarize, you don't have to stick with the default font. Choose fonts that give you the look you are aiming for.

Headings

Using a typewriter, how could the writer show that a piece of text was a heading?

In fact, there were only two things the writer could do in such circumstances: use underlining and/or all capital letters. Neither of these is considered good practice on a computer. Some people used quotation marks although, since the text was not a quotation, this seems inappropriate.

If you open a book from a reputable publisher, you will probably see no instances of underlining. It is generally considered an old-school typewriter feature, and avoided.

All capitals is avoided for a different reason. In lowercase, some letters extend above the line (have ascenders: *b, d, f, h, k, l, t*) and some below the line (have descenders: *g, j, p, q, y,* and italic *f*). Two letters have dots above the line: *i* and *j*. Words are recognized partly by the arrangement of ascenders, descenders, and dots. That is, the overall shape of the word (coastline) helps readers to recognize the word and read more quickly. This information is missing in all capitals, where each letter has the same height (but may vary in width). In short, text written in all capitals is harder and slower to read.

Now let us consider computers. How can the writer show that a piece of text is a heading?

While underlining and all capitals are still available on computers, there are a whole host of other, more attractive features that can be exploited:

- change of font
- change of size of font
- color of font
- centering
- bold
- italic
- various other effects, such as outline.

All of these computer features lead to a professional look; however, they should not be overdone. Only use one or two (or three) of them; don't go overboard.

Tabs, Indents; Including Hanging Indents

Style manuals usually state the rule that if a quotation is 40 words or longer, it should be put in block format, which involves indenting the left-hand margin of each line. How could you do that on a typewriter? This involved adding a tab after each (manual) carriage return, which was fine provided you got everything right first time.

Computers, however, have memory, as well as rulers with indent markers. There are three markers: (i) first line of each paragraph, (ii) subsequent lines of each paragraph, and (iii) both first and subsequent lines of paragraphs together. If you need to indent a whole block quotation, you can simply (highlight the text and) move the third of these markers. This is preferable to adding tabs, even though it may seem to give the same effect on screen. Imagine you wanted to add a phrase, or delete a phrase, or change the font, or change the size of the font, etc. If you have used the indent markers on the rulers, this will not affect the block format; if you have used tabs, everything will need to be redone.

How do you show a new paragraph? There are two ways. Firstly, you could leave a blank line. Secondly, you could indent the first line of each paragraph. But you don't need both. This is known as the belt and braces rule: if you wear a belt to keep your trousers up, you don't need braces as well, and vice versa. So, if you leave a blank line, you don't need to indent, and if you indent, you don't need to leave a blank line. It is overkill. If you decide to indent the first line of each paragraph, simply move the first of the markers described above. Again, use the ruler, not a tab; if you decide to add or remove a paragraph break, it will automatically be correctly indented.

A particular form of indent is used for things like reference lists, as at the end of each chapter of this book. Style guides usually tell you to have the first line of each entry not indented (left-flush) but all subsequent lines indented. This is known as a hanging indent. Again, use the ruler rather than a tab. Move the second marker listed above; if you add or delete text, the handing indent will still be correct.

Finally, while tabs may be appropriate in rare circumstances, make sure you use a tab (on the ruler) and not a series of spaces. If you make changes, the tab will always remain a tab, whereas the spaces may lead to problems.

A Single Space Between Sentences

Some typists will insist that you have to leave two spaces between sentences. When asked why, they typically reply that that is how they were taught (many years ago, on a typewriter) and that is what they have always done.

As already explained, computer fonts are proportional, as opposed to the non-proportional fonts (e.g. Courier) of typewriters. With non-proportional typewriter fonts, a double space may have been a good idea; with proportional computer fonts, it is unnecessary.

In some circumstances, typed double spaces may lead to unwanted problems. For example, in fully (left and right) justified text in narrower line width (e.g. in columns), the spaces between words will be stretched in order to achieve right-hand justification. Stretched double spaces will then create unacceptably large gaps in the text.

Dashes

As will be explained in Chapter 9, some punctuation marks are dropping out of fashion, and others are coming into fashion. The dash is one that is currently fashionable, especially in informal writing.

It is important to distinguish a dash from a hyphen. There are also two types of dash that should be distinguished.

A hyphen is located on the keyboard next to the number 0. The various uses of the hyphen are given in Chapter 10.

A dash is not located on the keyboard. Instead, you need to find it using Insert > Symbol. Depending on your word-processing software, typing two hyphens (followed by a space) may automatically be converted into a dash, because two hyphens was the only way to express this on a typewriter.

There are two types of dash, known as an en-dash and an em-dash. The en-dash is the width of a capital N, roughly twice the width of a hyphen. The em-dash is the width of a capital M, roughly three times the width of a hyphen. American writers tend to use the em-dash without surrounding spaces, while British writers tend to use the en-dash with surrounding spaces.

Smart Quotation Marks

Quotation marks are used, among other things, to mark word-for-word quotations. They used to be referred to in school as 66s and 99s, because opening quotation marks were shaped like 6s, and closing ones like 9s. This was impossible on a typewriter, where both opening and closing quotation marks were the same vertical strokes.

However, this is possible on computers because of what are known as smart quotation marks. The computer allocates 66s and 99s appropriately; if there is a space before and text after, it is an opening quotation mark and thus a 66, and if there is text or punctuation before and a space or punctuation after, it is a 99. Or at least the opening quotation marks are different in some way from the closing. The same applies to single quotation marks or apostrophes. This is true of all but a few sans serif fonts. Depending on your word-processing software, smart quotation marks may be the default.

Conclusion

These six differences are ones that will add a professional look to any document without a great deal of technical knowledge of typography. There are many other such features, but that would be delving too far into the field of typography for this book on spelling.

There are, of course, other major differences between a typewriter and a computer. Some of these are covered in the next chapter.

Summary

- A computer is far more sophisticated than a typewriter.
- While both typewriters and computers may use the QWERTY keyboard layout, the computer keyboard has many extra keys.
- A few simple features found in word-processing software will add a professional look to printed work.
- Children nowadays would benefit from training in QWERTY keyboard skills.

Exercises

1   Rate your personal typing skills on a scale of 1 to 10. Have you ever tried to improve them? How would you go about improving them?
2   Take an audit of your practices when typing text on a computer. Is it set to use American, British, or some other variety of English? Does it automatically correct typing errors? Do you correct typing errors as you go, or do you type the whole draft and then go back and correct?
3   Open a book from a reputable publisher and look for instances of underlining, and all capitals. Also take note which fonts are used, and how headings and subheadings are shown.

Further Reading

The history of the QWERTY keyboard, and discussion of its various keys is found in Lundmark (2002). The explanation of typographical devices is based largely on the writing of Williams (1995, 2003, 2014).

References

Lundmark, T. (2002). *Quirky QWERTY: The story of the keyboard @ your fingertips.* Sydney, Australia: University of New South Wales Press.

Strizver, I. (n.d.). *The story behind Comic Sans.* Retrieved from www.fonts.com/content/learning/fyti/typefaces/story-of-comic-sans

Williams, R. (1995). *The PC is not a typewriter.* San Francisco, CA: Peachpit Press.

Williams, R. (2003). *The Mac is not a typewriter* (2nd edition). San Francisco, CA: Peachpit Press.

Williams, R. (2014). *The non-designer's design book* (4th edition). San Francisco, CA: Peachpit Press.

7 Technology

Learning Objectives

At the end of this chapter, readers will be able to:

- evaluate the impact of spell-checkers and auto-correct on spelling
- list a dozen examples of SMS text language
- justify claiming that SMS text language is not all-good or all-bad.

Introduction

Forty years ago, there were only two methods available to the general public for writing a document: handwriting or a typewriter. Technology has of course progressed enormously in the intervening four decades. Originally, all typewriters were mechanical. Then in the 1970s, electric typewriters became available. In the 1980s, electronic typewriters were invented. These had two important features for spelling: memory and spell-checkers. Memory meant that documents did not need to be printed at the same time as they were typed. The text could be inspected, proofread, and corrected if necessary, before printing. Initial memories were small, but gradually grew exponentially. Spell-checkers could be applied to text stored in memory, and misspellings and mistypings corrected before printing. The huge advantage that these two features brought to typing is obvious to anyone old enough to remember correction fluid.

Starting in the 1970s, dedicated word-processors were produced for the general public, which only performed the composing, editing, formatting, and printing of documents. By the 1990s, these had been replaced by word-processing programs running on personal computers. PCs could handle word-processing and a wide variety of other tasks.

It is important to realize that people make mistakes when typing for two reasons. Firstly, they may not know the correct spelling of the word. Secondly, they may simply not be perfect typists, and press the wrong key. "Fat finger" syndrome is a term used to refer to the fact that some people's fingers may find keys small, especially, for instance, on a touchscreen on a smartphone. When typing words, people do not type letter by letter but use familiar sequences of letters, e.g. *-ation*. However, some sequences conflict; for example, two common words for language teachers are *communication* and *pronunciation*, and these are often mistyped as *communciation* and *pronunication*. Similarly, *commercial* and *clerical* may be mistyped as *commerical* and *clercial*.

Are these two types of misspelling serious? Clearly, if the writer does not know the correct spelling of the word, it is likely to be misspelled every time the writer uses the word, whatever medium the writer is using, e.g. handwriting.

Typos may have serious consequences, as the following episode illustrates. On 6 July 1962, the U.S.A. carried out a nuclear test in the Nevada desert. It created a huge crater 390 m by 100 m, known as the *Sedan Crater*, after the codename of the experiment. However, this was unfortunately reported in 2005 in the Congressional Record by a Californian Democratic member of the US House of Representatives as *Sudan*. This led to an international incident, with accusations of causing rising cancer rates among Sudanese, in which

> The Sudanese Foreign Ministry has summoned the US charge d'affaires in Khartoum and requested clarification regarding statements that the United States had carried out nuclear tests in Sudan. Sudanese Foreign Minister Mustafa Uthman Isma'il said his country has embarked on an investigation into the issue: "The Sudanese Government takes this issue seriously and with extreme importance."
>
> (Federation of American Scientists, n.d.)

The following section considers the implications for spelling of technological advances, especially spell-checkers and auto-correct.

Spell-checkers and Auto-correct

Spell-checkers (also called spelling-checkers) are embedded in almost every program and device we use: smartphones, email, Facebook, chatrooms, etc. However, they used not to be so ubiquitous nor as sophisticated as they are nowadays. At their simplest, spell-checkers try to match words in a document with words stored in a list in the program. In this way, they are similar to looking words up in a dictionary. Early spell-checkers did this, and no more. As a result, they had limited success. This was captured in the following poem, originally written in 1992 by Jerrold H. Zar, professor of biology at Northern Illinois University, inspired by lines by Mark Eckman.

I have a spelling checker,

It came with my PC.

It plane lee marks four my revue

Miss steaks aye can knot sea.

Eye ran this poem threw it,

Your sure reel glad two no.

Its vary polished in it's weigh.

My checker tolled me sew.

The poem is entitled "Candidate for a Pullet Surprise" (Pulitzer Prize), and appears on many websites. The original nine-verse version is at Zar (1994). It depends on homophones; that is, words that are pronounced the same, but spelled differently (Chapter 20).

Clearly, spell-checkers at this level of sophistication have limitations, and cannot correct every spelling that is wrong. In fact, there are many reasons why a wrong spelling may not be detected and corrected by a spell-checker.

1   The text may be marked "Do not check spelling or grammar" in the word-processing program.
2   If the "No proofing" setting is made in a particular "style" in the program, any text written in the same style in the document will also be skipped.
3   The language set for proofing may not be the one the writer wants. For instance, choosing British English as the proofing language will allow both *realise* and *realize*, whereas choosing American English will only allow *realize* (see Chapter 15).
4   A word may have been added, perhaps wrongly, to the program's internal dictionary, by previously clicking the "Add" button when spell-checking.
5   The word may be typed in all capital letters, and the program is set up to ignore such words.
6   The word may have a number in it, perhaps as the result of a typo, and the program is set up to ignore such words.
7   The spell-checker may overlook the word, because what was typed represents a different, correctly spelled, word. Common problematical English pairs are *form* and *from*, and *use* and *sue*. Homophones (words that are pronounced the same, but spelled differently; see Chapter 20) such as *there* and *their* are also a common problem here.
8   In typos, letters can be misplaced, but so can spaces. Spell-checkers will typically not detect misplaced spaces such as *cut sin* (for the intended *cuts in*), *firs tone* (*first one*), *joint he* (*join the*), *make sup* (*makes up*), *thin kit* (*think it*), *thing shave* (*things have*), *toy our* (*to your*).

The first six cases described here may be rectified by adjusting settings in the word-processing program.

It must be remembered that the dictionaries in spell-checkers are not totally comprehensive. They contain regular everyday words of English but have a limited list of names (of places, people, etc.) and do not contain technical and specialist words.

In summary, it is important that writers use the spell-checker, but also then give the text a thorough proofread before finalizing it.

Fortunately, spell-checkers have become more sophisticated over the years, and current ones use algorithms incorporating far more information than simply a list of correctly spelled words, such as subject-verb agreement and apostrophes. They may also identify words which, while correctly spelled words of English, are probably not the intended words in the context.

A further, more recent development is auto-correct, whereby the program automatically corrects certain misspellings to what it thinks the intended word was. As might be expected, the correction may sometimes be as wrong as the typo. Such mistakes are referred to as the Cupertino Effect, because European Union staff found that slight misspellings of the common word *cooperation* (without a hyphen) were autocorrected to *Cupertino*, a city in California that is the location of the headquarters of Apple Inc. computers. Note that both words contain the consonant letters c – p – r – t – n. An amusing example, loaded on the internet in 2000 but still accessible in an Italian food recipe at Yahoo Groups (2000) is the following:

> Crumble bread sticks into a mixing bowl. Cover with warm water. Let soak for 2 to 3 minutes or until soft. Drain. Stir in prostitute, provolone, pine nuts, 1/4 cup oil, parsley, salt, and pepper. Set aside.

If you are wondering what a prostitute has to do with the recipe, it is the word *prosciutto* (Italian for *ham*) presumably slightly mistyped by the author, and auto-corrected to *prostitute*.

The Effects of Spell-checkers and Auto-correct

The view has often been expressed that spell-checkers are making students lazy by not bothering to learn the correct spellings of words (because the spell-checker will correct it anyway) and not bothering to proofread written work carefully (because the spell-checker will correct misspellings anyway).

The dangers of slavishly accepting suggested corrections are even worse for grammar-checkers, but they are not the focus of this book.

There are arguments on both sides of the debate as to whether spell-checkers are a Good or Bad Thing, and have made students, and writers in general, better or poorer spellers. In an early study, Galletta, Durcikova, Everard, and Jones (2005) found that accuracy in spelling and grammar was better when spell- and grammar-checkers were turned off by students.

"They attribute power and trust to the language-checking software rather than search the document for errors" (p. 86).

Similarly, the UK learning disability charity Mencap (formerly The Royal Society for Mentally Handicapped Children and Adults) investigated the effect of spell-checkers (BBC News, 2012). It found that one-third of respondents (without learning disabilities) could not spell *definitely*, and two-thirds could not spell *necessary* (see Chapter 21). Only 9% responded that they never used a spell-checker. The danger is that the other 91% may not bother to proofread their writing apart from passing it cursorily through a spell-checker. The Mencap president Mark Goldring concluded, "With over two-thirds of Britons now having to rely on spellcheck, we are heading towards an auto-correct generation."

Commentators have also pointed out that typing while the word-processing program immediately identifies incorrectly spelled words breaks the flow of the writer's thought. They feel that they need to immediately correct the spelling, rather than continue with the train of thought and come back to correct typos later. In light of this, it may be beneficial to turn off the spell-checker while writing a first draft.

There is little evidence that spell-checking has had a positive effect on spelling. Word-processing in general may, however, have had a positive effect on general language and literacy skills, by making writing more available to the general public, as well as increasing the amount of information and learning that they can access.

In general, spell-checkers seem to have had a negative effect of the spelling skills of most users. As was pointed out earlier in this chapter, mistypings occur for two main reasons. If the writer has simply made a slip on the keyboard, a spell-checker will usually detect and correct this. If, however, the writer does not know the correct spelling, then the typed version may be so far from the correct spelling that a spell-checker will be unable to suggest the correction. Similarly, if the spell-checker does suggest alternatives, the writer may not be able to choose the correct one.

Spell-checkers are a feature of most language-based programs nowadays: smartphones, computers, email, Facebook, etc. Indeed, it is difficult to think of a circumstance in which students are required to produce written work without the availability of a spell-checker, apart from traditional handwritten examinations. The possibility of conducting such examinations in computer labs should be explored, as should the necessity to incorporate spell-checking skills into writing classes.

Text Language

Text language, known by many other names, refers to the features of language used by people when texting. The idea of short message service (SMS) texting began in the early 1980s, but it was not until the turn of the millennium that it really took off, because of advances in technology.

In the early days, users resorted to various language features because of the limitations of pre-smartphone technology. Firstly, messages were originally limited to 160 characters in length; for comparison, the previous paragraph contained 287 characters, including spaces. So, messages had to be short, and longer messages had to be sent as more than one message. Secondly, letters were keyed in using the numberpad; thus, for example, the letter A was created by pressing the 2 button once, B twice, C three times, all quickly enough for the phone not to time-out and move to the next letter in the message. Given that the process of typing letters was so complex, it is not surprising that users started using shortcuts in order to speed up their typing.

Both the above limitations have disappeared; messages are no longer limited to 160 characters, and a QWERTY keyboard appears on the screen of a smartphone. Nevertheless, many of the original features of text language persist. Crystal, in his book *Txting: The gr8 db8*, written in 2008 before smartphones, summarizes the reasons for text language: "It's easier. And it's fun" (Crystal, 2008, p. 65).

In terms of spelling, there are several features of text language but, as we shall see, none of them are new. They all existed before texting.

Initialisms and Acronyms

Text language uses initials for the words of a phrase, or the elements of a compound.

OMG "Oh, my God!"   *LOL* "laughing out loud"   *IMHO* "in my humble opinion"

Initialisms and acronyms are discussed further in Chapter 11.

Contractions

Contractions involve omitting some letters, usually from the middle of a word.

msg "message"   *txtin* "texting"   *kybrd* "keyboard"   *plz* "please"

Clippings

Clippings involve omitting letters from the end of the word.

diff "different/ce"   *poss* "possible"   *perh* "perhaps"   *rad* "radical"

Nonstandard Spellings

As we have already seen with *plz* above, texters sometimes use nonstandard spellings that nevertheless unambiguously represent the pronunciation of the word and thus allow readers to recognize it.

coz "because"   *fone* "phone"   *luv* "love"   *shud* "should"

sum "some"   *thanx* "thanks"   *thru* "through"   *wot* "what"

Many of these text spellings are spellings proposed by spelling reformers (see Chapter 29).

Other Informal Elements

Other informal elements found in text language include the following.

muahaha (the sound of diabolical laughter)

Yes!!! (with repeated exclamation marks)

Logograms

Logograms are single symbols used to represent whole words.

b "be"   *4* "for"   *u* "you"   @ "at"

These can be used in combination with other letters.

b4 "before"   *gr8* "great"   *2morrow* "tomorrow"

Pictograms

While the pronunciation of logograms is important in deciphering the meaning (e.g. both the letter *b* and the word *be* are pronounced /biː/), pictograms are purely pictorial. In pre-smartphone days, emoticons were produced by creatively using different letters and symbols. Thus, a smiley was a colon, plus a hyphen, plus a closing bracket, thus :-), to be viewed sideways. On smartphones, a whole range of smileys and other emoticons are available, e.g.☺.

Punctuation

Punctuation in text language is in general very light, and often almost completely absent. This occurs in terms of the punctuation of sentences, e.g. the absence of commas, but also in individual words.

english (without an initial capital)   *theres* (without an apostrophe)

Discussion

Crystal (2008) looks very sympathetically on text language, for three reasons.

Firstly, the features of text language are not used anywhere near as frequently as some people suggest. On average, fewer than 10% of the words in text messages are abbreviated.

Secondly, most of the features of text language have been around in English for decades, if not centuries, long before texting. The song entitled "Nothing Compares 2 U" (spelled that way), written by Prince and popularized by Irish singer Sinéad O'Connor, was a global hit in 1990, before the texting era. The British multinational telecommunications company Vodafone was founded in 1991, its spelling perhaps influenced by the British Telecom Freefone service that predated it. *OMG* was used by British admiral John Arbuthnot Fisher in a letter to Winston Churchill in 1917 (Allen, 2012). The initialism *pm* for "post meridiem" dates to the 17th century. The @ symbol (known as the "at sign," but also by many other names; Italie, 2010) dates back to at least the 16th century. Pictorial elements (logograms, pictograms) have been used in word play for centuries. The coat of arms of the Bowes-Lyon family (Elizabeth Bowes-Lyon was the wife of George VI and mother of Elizabeth II) features (archery) bows and lions (Wikimedia Commons, n.d.). Rebus puzzles, like *neafriended* ("A friend in need") have been around for centuries.

Thirdly, Crystal argues that texting makes young people better communicators, because it engages them with reading and writing much more than would otherwise be the case. The argument of detractors is that the features of text language (initials, abbreviations, nonstandard spellings, etc.) would appear in non-texting contexts, such as writing an academic essay, and lead to a generation growing up not knowing standard spelling. However, Crystal points out that you have to be able to spell correctly before you can send a text message, and nonstandard spellings make up a small proportion of text messages. In addition, adults, who can spell perfectly well, nevertheless use abbreviations and other features of text language when texting. Also, Crystal (Peters, 2009) explains that the distinction between informal text language, and more formal language has not been blurred with school-aged children.

> I ask the kids themselves would they ever use textisms in their writing. They look at me as if I'm nuts. "Why would you ever want to do that?" said one to me. "That would be stupid." Quite so. You'd have to be pretty dumb to not see the difference between texting style and essay style.
>
> (Peters, 2009)

In conclusion, while many disparagers initially talked about texting sounding the death knell of proper spelling and good English in general, this does not seem to have happened. Crystal (2008) gives the final chapter of his book the title "Why all the fuss?"

Most of the comments made here about texting apply equally to other informal electronic forms of written communication, including chatrooms, email, etc.

Summary

- Spell-checkers are becoming more and more sophisticated, incorporating grammatical, contextual, and predictive information. At the very minimum, students should put their writing through a spell-checker.
- Many errors are missed, or incorrectly flagged, by spell-checkers. It is therefore important that learners also proofread their work themselves.
- Text language incorporates features that make texting easier and fun. Most of these features have been used in English for centuries.
- A clear distinction needs to be maintained between language that is appropriate for texting, and other, more formal language.

Exercises

1   Using an etymological dictionary, look up the following features of text language and discover when they were first used.

&   ("ampersand")
luv ("love")
NIMBY ("not in my back yard")
SWAK ("sealed with a kiss")
thanx ("thanks")
thru ("through")
TTFN ("tata for now")
wot ("what")

2   The following version of the Lord's Prayer, in text language, won a competition by the online Christian magazine *Ship of Fools* (n.d.). Work out how it represents the Lord's Prayer (see Chapter 5).

dad@hvn
urspshl
we want wot u want
&urth2b like hvn
giv us food
&4giv r sins
lyk we 4giv uvaz
don't test us!
save us!
bcos we kno ur boss
ur tuf
&ur cool 4 eva!
ok?

Further Reading

The importance of, and techniques for, proofreading are taught in many books, some technical (e.g. Anderson, 2006) and some more practical (e.g. Evans, 2013). Crystal (2008) examines the language of SMS texting. Rebuses and other forms of language play are discussed in Augarde (2003) and Crystal (1998).

References

Allen, E. (7 August 2012). O.M.G it's so old! Phrase loved by today's teenagers was first used 100 YEARS AGO in letter to Winston Churchill (who thought it was LOL!). *Daily Mail.* Retrieved from www.dailymail.co.uk/news/article-2184777/O-M-G-old-Phrase-loved-todays-teenagers-used-100-years-ago-letter-Winston-Churchill-thought-LOL.html

Anderson, L. (2006). *McGraw-Hill's proofreading handbook* (2nd edition). New York, NY: McGraw-Hill Education.

Augarde, T. (2003). *The Oxford guide to word games* (2nd edition). Oxford, UK: Oxford University Press.

BBC News (22 May 2012). *Poor spelling of 'auto-correct generation' revealed.* Retrieved from www.bbc.com/news/education-18158665

Crystal, D. (1998). *Language play.* Chicago, IL: University of Chicago Press.

Crystal, D. (2008). *Txting: The gr8 db8.* Oxford, UK: Oxford University Press.

Evans, D. (2013). *Don't trust your spell check: Pro proofreading tactics and tests to eliminate embarrassing writing errors.* Good Content Company (goodcontentcompany.com).

Federation of American Scientists (n.d.). *US envoy summoned over House remarks on US nuclear tests in Sudan (Al Jazirah* Arabic newspaper, 9 March 2005). Retrieved from fas.org/irp/news/2005/03/sudan.html

Galletta, D. F., Durcikova, A., Everard, A., & Jones, B. M. (2005). Does spell-checking software need a warning label? *Communications of the ACM (Association for Computing Machinery),* 48(7), 82–86. Retrieved from pdfs.semanticscholar.org /68f5/562f0361b82436a6a56ec88183e2cee74847.pdf

Italie, L. (19 November 2010). *In other parts of the world, @ isn't where it's 'at'.* Associated Press. Retrieved from www.columbian.com/news/2010/nov/19/ in-other-parts-of-the-world-isnt-where-its-at

Peters, M. (26 January 2009). *Text-pocalypse Now?* The Daily Good. Retrieved from www.good.is/articles/text-pocalypse-now

Ship of Fools (n.d.). Retrieved from ship-of-fools.com

Wikimedia Commons (n.d.). *Arms of Elizabeth Bowes-Lyon.* Retrieved from commons.wikimedia.org/wiki/File:Arms_of_Elizabeth_Bowes-Lyon.svg

Yahoo Groups (2000). *All about Italian food and cooking.* Retrieved from groups. yahoo.com/neo/groups/italianfood/conversations/topics/1281

Zar, J. H. (1994). Candidate for a pullet surprise. *The Journal of Irreproducible Results,* 39(1), 13, and 45(5–6), 20. Retrieved from www.jir.com/pullet.html

8 Rules of English Spelling

Learning Objectives

At the end of this chapter, readers will be able to:

- explain how rules of language are different from rules of, for example, football
- demonstrate why the most commonly quoted spelling rule ("*i* before *e* except after *c*") has more exceptions than examples
- list, with examples, two spelling rules that are more reliable.

Definition

Before we can discuss rules of English spelling, we need to be clear exactly what kind of rules they are. Dictionaries distinguish two types: a strict one and a not-so-strict one. The strict sense is given in the following entries:

- a prescribed guide for conduct or action (*Merriam-Webster online dictionary*, n.d.)
- Rules are instructions that tell you what you are allowed to do and what you are not allowed to do (*Collins English dictionary online*, n.d.)
- an official instruction that says how things must be done or what is allowed, especially in a game, organization, or job (*Longman dictionary of contemporary English online*, n.d.).

Collocations involving *rule* in this sense include *following / obeying / observing the rules*, of *breaking rules*, and of things being *against the rules*.

The less strict sense is given in the following entries:

- a usually valid generalization (*Merriam-Webster online dictionary*, n.d.)
- The rules of something such as a language or a science are statements that describe the way that things usually happen in a particular situation (*Collins English dictionary online*, n.d.)
- something that is normal or usually true (*Longman dictionary of contemporary English online*, n.d.).

Collocations involving *rule* in this sense include *as a rule, the exception rather than the rule.*

The difference between the two senses is shown by the choice of words in the definitions. The first type is called an instruction that tells, while the second type is a statement or generalization that describes. This is the distinction between prescription (using words such as *must* and *allowed*) and description (with hedges such as *usually, normally* and *in a particular situation*).

Strict and Less Strict Rules

The difference between types of rule can be explained by contrasting the rules of a sport like football with the rules of language, by asking four questions. Let us start with football.

1   ***Who makes the rules?***
     For football, there is a world governing body, FIFA (Fédération Internationale de Football Association).

2   ***Where can I see the rules?***
     FIFA publishes a *FIFA Handbook*, with updates and changes from time to time.

3   ***Who enforces the rules?***
     On the pitch, referees enforce the rules. Off the pitch, local authorities, and FIFA worldwide, enforce them.

4   ***What penalties are there for breaking a rule?***
     If, for example, a player other than the goalkeeper handles the ball, their team is penalized with a free kick, or a penalty kick if it is inside the penalty area. The player can also be cautioned (yellow card) or sent off (red card) if the referee thinks the offence was serious.

So, for football, the questions are simple to answer. However, for language there are no simple answers.

1   ***Who makes the rules?***
     There is no governing body for English language, as there is for football. For some languages – especially those spoken in single countries – there is, but not for English which is spoken in many countries around the world. Such a body would have to be global, prestigious, and accepted as authoritative by English users. Microsoft software is common in computers, and when users want to check spelling, they use the Microsoft spell-checker. Oxford and Cambridge University Presses are parts of old, prestigious universities, and they publish dictionaries and other reference works for English. The British Council has branches worldwide, and is respected for its English language teaching.

These are all possible candidates for such a governing body, but at present no such authority exists.

2 *Where can I see the rules?*

For correct spelling, most writers would "look it up in the dictionary" (or use the computer's spell-checker). However, dictionaries differ from one another, albeit in minor ways; otherwise, there would be no need for more than one definitive reference for English spelling.

In any case, dictionaries only tell you the correct spelling of individual words. For more general rules, you would have to consult a book on spelling; often, however, these contain lists of words and therefore are little better than dictionaries.

3 *Who enforces the rules?*

Teachers enforce spelling rules by correcting spelling. Examiners may enforce them by marking down incorrect spelling. In a sense, Microsoft enforces the rules by automatically correcting (or suggesting changes to) misspelled words. However, in everyday life, nobody enforces rules of language.

4 *What penalties are there for breaking a rule?*

You may suffer consequences (rather than penalties) by, for instance, having your CV ignored. You may lose face because a reader may take poor spelling as a sign of lack of education. At worst, a reader may simply not be able to decipher what you have written. However, nothing more serious than that (and nothing comparable to being sent off in football) occurs.

In short, a rule of spelling is little more than a generalization about the way users of the language spell (and do not spell) words. Because this is the less strict sense of rule, exceptions may be found, whereas a referee will definitely send off a player for a serious foul (or at least they should, if they saw it clearly, etc.).

The Archetypical Spelling Rule of English

If you ask an English speaker to quote a rule of English spelling, chances are they will reply, "*i* before *e* except after *c*." Chances are too that they will find it difficult to quote any other rule. So, let us examine this rule.

Exercise

For each of the following words, state what they are an example of:

- *i* before *e* not after *c* (follows the rule)
- *i* before *e* after *c* (does not follow the rule)
- *e* before *i* after *c* (follows the rule)
- *e* before *i* not after *c* (does not follow the rule)

albeit	eighty	Keith	seeing
ancient	fancied	leisure	seize
atheism	feisty	lie	sheikh
being	field	Neil	Sheila
believe	foreign	neither	shriek
bingeing	frieze	perceive	sleigh
brief	geisha	piece	society
caffeine	glacier	Policies	species
ceilidh	grieve	priest	sufficient
ceiling	happier	protein	their
conceited	Heidi	receipts	therein
deceit	height	relief	vein
deity	icier	Rottweiler	weight
eider	kaleidoscope	science	weird

That exercise should have convinced you that:

- There are very few examples of "*i* before *e* except after *c*." In fact, if the spirit of the rule is that *ie* is the normal spelling, but that this "becomes" *ei* after *c*, there are very few words that exemplify *cei*: *ceilidh* (a clearly Gaelic loanword), *ceiling*, and *-ceive* words (*conceive, deceive, perceive, receive*) and related forms (e.g. *conceit, inconceivable, deceit, receipt*).
- There are as many counterexamples.
- The rule as phrased ("i before e except after c") needs to have a number of ifs and buts added to it. The following rewrite seems to account for most of the many exceptions:

i before *e* except after *c*, except:

- o   when the vowel is not /iː/, e.g. *weight*
- o   when the *c* letter is pronounced /ʃ/, e.g. *ancient*
- o   in *science* and related words, e.g. *conscientious*
- o   when the *e* letter is required for a "soft" *g* (/dʒ/), e.g. *singeing*
- o   when the *e* letter is part of an ending (suffix), e.g. *fancied*
- o   when the *i* letter is part of an ending (suffix), e.g. *seeing*
- o   when the *e* and *i* letters in the spelling are parts of two separate syllables, e.g. *atheism*
- o   in words of foreign origin, e.g. *sheikh, Heidi*
- o   in some names, e.g. *Keith, Sheila*.

And even then there are exceptions that cannot be explained, e.g. *caffeine, seize.*

As a result, "*i* before *e* except after *c*" has been abandoned as a rule to be taught in British primary schools: "Advice sent to teachers says there are too few words which follow the rule and recommends using more modern methods to teach spelling to schoolchildren. The document, entitled *Support for spelling*, is being distributed to more than 13,000 primary schools" (BBC News, 2009).

More Reliable Rules of English Spelling

So, if the archetypical rule of English spelling that everyone knows, does not work because it has more exceptions than examples, are there any rules that are reliable? Fortunately, the answer is yes. However, many of these more reliable rules are not known consciously by native English speakers, even though they may use them productively in new words. Here we will look at two such rules.

Bulking Up of Content Words

In order to explain the first, we must distinguish content words from function words.

Content words are nouns (e.g. *tree*), main verbs (*remember*), adjectives (*happy*), and adverbs (*quietly*). Function words, on the other hand, are all the other grammatical categories, such as articles (*a, the*), auxiliary verbs (*be, have, can*), conjunctions (*and, but*), prepositions (*at, with*), and pronouns (*she, us*).

Content words are the kind of words teachers might tell a learner to look up in a dictionary. For instance, a teacher might tell a learner to look up the word *expedite* in the dictionary. But the teacher would be unlikely to tell the learner to look up a word like *of*.

It is usually easy to give a definition for content words, and their entries in dictionaries are short. For example, *expedite* is given a one-line definition in the *Longman Dictionary of Contemporary English Online* (n.d.): "to make a process or action happen more quickly." The entry for *of*, however, extends to 25 subentries. The "meaning" of *of* depends on its context of use. A teacher might ask a learner to give the phrase in which the word is used, and paraphrase *the house of a celebrity* as "the house belonging to a celebrity," but *a bottle of milk* as "a bottle containing milk."

For this reason, content words are also called lexical words, because they convey real inherent meaning. Function words are also known as grammatical words, because their meaning depends on their function of relating parts of sentences.

So, the spelling rule relating to content and function words is:

Content words have at least three letters in spelling, whereas function words can be shorter.

This is sometimes referred to as "bulking up" of content words, a process presumably started originally in order to emphasize their lexical importance. This bulking up often takes the form of doubling consonant letters, or adding silent letters (see Chapter 12), often *e*. It is thus possible to find pairs of words – one content, the other function – such as the following.

Grammatical function	Lexical content
an	*Ann*
be	*bee*
by	*buy*
I	*eye*
in	*inn*
no	*know*
oh	*owe*
or	*ore, oar*
so	*sew, sow*
to	*two*
we	*wee*

Are there exceptions to this rule, that is, content words that have only two letters in spelling? The answer seems to be only three: *ax* (AmE), *go, ox*. While there are other examples, they are clearly foreign words like *pi, qi, re, xu* (the kind of word loved by Scrabble enthusiasts precisely because they are only two letters long). Similarly, long words may be abbreviated to two-letter versions (known in linguistics as clippings), e.g. *ad* (*advertisement*), *ed* (*edited* or *education*), *op* (*operation*).

The American two-letter *ax* is three-letter *axe* in British spelling. Similarly, *ox* was spelled *oxe* in Middle English (11th – 15th century).

That leaves the word *go*. English speakers do not think of the word *go* as having an exceptional spelling. But it is an exceptional spelling. As this rule has shown, it is the only content word with only two letters in spelling. (In older forms of English, it had a final *n*; a vestige of this is the participle *gone*.) If *go* were to bulk up, how would it look? Other one-syllable content words ending in /oʊ/ are bulked up by one of two processes:

- adding a (silent) final *w* letter: *bow* (and arrow), *low, mow, sow* (seeds)
- adding a (silent) final *e* letter: *doe, foe, hoe, woe*.

Indeed, it is possible to find homophones (words that are spelled differently but pronounced the same; see Chapter 20) with *w* and *e* final consonant letters: *row, roe; flow,* (ice) *floe; slow, sloe* ("blackthorn"); *tow, toe.*

Which is the more regular spelling of /oʊ/: *ow* or *oe*? We can consider content words that are longer than three letters because of clusters (two sounds at the beginning of the word, e.g. /st-/, digraphs (two letters representing one sound e.g. *sh-*) or other silent letters; they all have *ow: blow, crow, glow, grow, know, show, snow, stow, throw.* So, if it were regular, *go* would probably be *gow.*

Marking Surnames

The second rule that has more examples and fewer exceptions than "*i* before *e* except after *c*" relates to surnames. English speakers know that surnames, like given names, have initial capital letters. However, there are other features of the spelling of surnames that may not be so obvious.

The first is to do with the representation in spelling of final consonant sounds.

> *Where a final consonant sound follows a short vowel in a one-syllable surname, the consonant letter is usually doubled.*

There are many examples of this. The following list is of fairly common such surnames. A final *e* and/or *s* does not affect this rule; so, for example, *Bigg(e)(s)* subsumes *Bigg, Bigge, Biggs,* and *Bigges.*

Batt	*Dobbs*	*Hamm*	*McNutt*
Benn	*Dodd(s)*	*Higg(e)(s)*	*Mimm(s)*
Bigg(e)(s)	*Donn(e)*	*Hobb(e)s*	*Nobbs*
Brett	*Dunn(e)*	*Hudd*	*Nunn*
Brigg(e)(s)	*Finn*	*Hutt*	*Pegg(e)*
Budd	*Flynn*	*Judd*	*Penn*
Bunn(e)	*Fripp*	*Kidd*	*Pimm(e)*
Butt	*Gadd*	*Knott*	*Pitt*
Chubb	*Gibb(s)*	*Ladd*	*Platt*
Clegg(e)(s)	*Gigg(s)*	*Legg(e)*	*Pott(s)*
Cobb	*Glynn(e)*	*Lynn*	*Pratt*
Crabb(e)	*Gunn*	*Matt*	*Rhett*
Dann(e)(s)	*Gwynn(e)*	*McCann*	*Rigg*

Robb	*Stott*	*Topp(s)*	*Wyatt*
Rudd	*Stubb(e)s*	*Twigg(e)*	*Wynn*
Scott	*Tibbs*	*Watt(s)*	
Simm(s)	*Timm(s)*	*Webb*	
Stagg	*Todd*	*Wrenn*	

English accents can be divided into those that pronounce final /r/ sounds (most Americans, Canadians, Scots, Irish, etc.) and those that do not (most speakers in England, Wales, Australia, New Zealand, etc.). The former are known as rhotic, and the latter non-rhotic accents. A final *r* letter follows this doubling rule, regardless of whether it is pronounced or not.

Barr	*Carr*	*Garr*	*Parr*
Burr(e)	*Corr*	*Kerr*	*Storr*

The rule of doubling the final consonant letter is most often found in one-syllable surnames. However, it also applies in some multi-syllable surnames, where the final syllable is unstressed and has the schwa vowel /ə/ or /ɪ/ followed by /t/ or /l/.

Barrett	*Buffett*	*Hamill*	*Moffatt*
Beckett	*Campbell*	*Kendall*	*Revell*
Bennett	*Cavill*	*Leggatt*	*Russell*
Bentall	*Everett*	*Marshall*	
Boxall	*Faithfull*	*Mitchell*	

There are many pairs of words, where one is an ordinary word, with a lower-case first letter and a single final consonant letter, and the other a surname, with an initial capital and a doubled final consonant letter: *bat/Batt; buffet* (verb)/ *Buffett; car/Carr; fin/Finn; kid/Kidd;* etc. A fuller list of less common such surnames is given in Appendix 2.

A second rule relating to surnames, which again has a reasonable number of examples, is that surnames are often shown to be surnames by having a silent (empty; see Chapter 12) *e* letter added at the end.

Bowes	*Brooke*	*Clarke*	*Coombe(s)*
Bowles	*Browne*	*Coates*	*Deere*
Boyle	*Byrne*	*Cooke*	*Eyre*

Forde	*Lowe*	*Poole*	*Waite*
Frye	*Moore*	*Rowe*	*Wilde*
Greene	*Oakes*	*Sharpe*	*Younge*
Howe	*Oates*	*Steele*	
Locke	*Penney*	*Trollope*	

We noted in Chapter 5 that English spelling was variable until the 18th century. An example that is often quoted is that William Shakespeare's surname was represented in spelling and in his own signature in a variety of ways (Wikipedia, n.d.), including *Shackspeare, Shakespear, Shakespere, Shakspeare, Shaksper,* and *Shakspere. Shakespeare* was the most common spelling in his time, but it does not seem coincidence that this spelling has persisted as the modern spelling, following the rule of final silent *e*.

The third, and least pervasive, of these rules relating to surnames is that what would otherwise be an *i* letter changes to a *y* in surnames.

Hyde	*Pye*	*Smythe*	*Wylde*

There are other given names and surnames, where both the *i* and *y* versions can be found.

Brian/Bryan

Simon/Symon

All the above (in addition to the initial capital letter) are spelling features that help a reader to appreciate immediately that the word is a surname, where this might not be obvious in speech.

These rules (in the sense of generalizations) not only apply to surnames with many examples, but also seem to be becoming more common with English first names too. For instance, Russell Crowe is a famous New Zealand-born Australian actor. His surname *Crowe* follows the rule that surnames often have silent final *e*s. His given name *Russell* follows the rule (primarily for surnames) of doubled consonant letters. Perhaps this is simply a consequence of the fact that many given names nowadays are what used to be surnames, e.g. *Brett, Matt, Rhett, Todd.*

One way in which linguists sometimes determine whether a rule is valid or not is to see if it applies to nonsense words, that is, words that do not exist in the language. Similarly, we may look at invented surnames.

In 1962 Richard Starkey joined the Beatles as the new drummer and the rest, as they say, is history. He is of course much better known by his stage name, Ringo Starr. Presumably he chose the name because he hoped to become a pop star. While Starr has been an English surname since Anglo-Saxon times, it is rare. The interesting point is that Ringo Starr spelled his new name with a double *r* at the end, thus following this rule. The same is true of British comedian Frederick Fowell, better known by his stage name, Freddie Starr. (Again, notice the double *l* letter in his original name.)

Likewise, Joan Larkin became a pop star with the stage name Joan Jett (and the Blackhearts). Like Starr, Jett has been an English surname for centuries, but is rare. Joan chose the spelling with doubled *t*.

Rapper Cordozar Calvin Broadus Jr. is better known by his stage name Snoop Dogg. While Dogg may not really be considered a surname here, the doubled *g* letter seems to be another example of this rule. Similarly, the rule is being applied increasingly by parents to given names, such as *Brett*.

The rule even applies to fictional characters. When Jules Verne wrote *Around the world in eighty days* in French in 1873, his main character was an Englishman, Phileas Fogg. Again, the surname, with a doubled *g*, has been in English since Anglo-Saxon times, but is rare.

Since the 1950s, the cartoon character Andy Capp has appeared in British newspapers, notably the *Daily Mirror* and *Sunday Mirror*. The invented name is a play-on-words of *handicap*, and Andy always wears a cap over his eyes, symbolizing his outlook on life. The English surname Capp, with a doubled *p*, has a history of a thousand years, but is rare.

In Britain, a common expression for a hypothetical average man is Joe Bloggs (occasionally Fred Bloggs). In this respect, it is similar to the American John Doe, except that there is no female equivalent, as in Jane Doe. Like Capp, the surname Bloggs with a doubled *g*, has been in English for a thousand years, but is rare.

In similar vein, the plot of a 1980s television series involved a private detective (played by Stephanie Zimbalist) who found clients hard to come by, because she was a woman. So she hired a fictitious male superior (played by Pierce Brosnan) and business improved. The real name of Brosnan's character, a former con man, is not revealed, and he, and the detective agency, is given the name *Remington Steele*, presumably a play-on-words of the shaver manufacturer. Note that a silent final *e* is added to this as a surname.

Summary

- There are two types of rules: strict ones, and less strict ones. Spelling rules, like other language rules, are of the less strict variety.
- While "*i* before *e* except after *c*" is a well-known rule, it simply has too few examples and too many exceptions to be of practical use.

- "Content words have at least three letters in spelling, whereas function words can be shorter" is a much more reliable rule.
- Surnames are often marked by three spelling devices: doubled final consonant letters, final silent *e* letters, and/or changing *i* to *y*.

Exercises

1 Here are some illustrative sentences for the word *rule*, given in *Merriam-Webster online dictionary* (n.d.), *Collins English dictionary online* (n.d.) and *Longman dictionary of contemporary English online* (n.d.). Decide whether each one uses *rule* in the strict or not-so-strict sense.

   1 *Anyone who violates this rule will be severely punished.*
   2 *As a general rule, burglars are wary about gaining entry from the front or side of a building.*
   3 *There's an unwritten rule that you never call an actor before 10 a.m.*
   4 *I understand the basic rules of chess.*
   5 *Hanson's golden rule is to add value to whatever business he buys.*
   6 *Under the rules, the company must publish its annual accounts.*
   7 *Early marriage used to be the rule in that part of the world.*
   8 *As a rule of thumb, a cup of filter coffee contains about 80 mg of caffeine.*
   9 *There are no hard and fast rules about what to wear to classes.*
   10 *It is a rule of English that adjectives generally precede the noun they modify.*

2 Make a list of grammatical function words (articles, auxiliary verbs, conjunctions, prepositions, pronouns, etc.). How many of them are long words (longer than one syllable in pronunciation; longer than two letters in spelling)?

3 Give 20 examples of famous people with the surnames listed in this chapter, e.g. Warren Buffett (American businessman and investor), Lee J Cobb (American actor), Robert Fripp (British guitarist of King Crimson), Roger Moore (British actor), John Oates (of Hall and Oates, American singing duo), Paul Potts (British singer).

Further Reading

The nature of spelling rules in English is explored by Cook (2004).

References

BBC News (20 June 2009). *Schools to rethink 'i before e'.* Retrieved from news.bbc. co.uk/2/hi/uk_news/education/8110573.stm
Collins English dictionary online (n.d.). Retrieved from www.collinsdictionary.com/ dictionary/english
Cook, V. (2004). *The English writing system.* London, UK: Hodder Education.

Longman dictionary of contemporary English online (n.d.). Retrieved from www.ldoce online.com

Merriam-Webster online dictionary (n.d.). Retrieved from www.merriam-webster. com/dictionary

Wikipedia (n.d.). *Spelling of Shakespeare's name*. Retrieved from en.wikipedia.org/ wiki/Spelling_of_Shakespeare's_name

Section 3

Punctuation

9   Punctuation

Learning Objectives

At the end of this chapter, readers will be able to:

- list the main events in the history of English pronunciation
- explain why English pronunciation is governed "two-thirds by rule and one-third by personal taste"
- teach the main functions of English punctuation marks
- describe current trends in English punctuation.

Introduction

You may think that we are straying from the topic of this book, namely spelling, by having a chapter on punctuation. However, there are some features of written language, such as the use of capital letters, that could be called punctuation (capital letters occur at the beginning of sentences after full stops) but equally could be called spelling (*March* the month is different from *march* the noun/verb). Similarly, if this book is about conveying a message by marks on paper (screen, etc.) in the written medium, then punctuation is certainly part of that medium.

This chapter covers the history of English punctuation (see Chapter 5 on the history of the English spelling system), some discussion of how important punctuation is, and current trends in English punctuation. While it is important that learners understand the main uses of English punctuation marks, these may correspond closely to the way the same punctuation marks are used in their native language, and they are therefore listed in Appendix 3 for ease of reference.

A Brief History of Punctuation

Most readers, including teachers, are likely to know little, if anything, about the history of punctuation. Teachers do not need to know this in order to be able to teach and correct punctuation, but it may be considered important in showing that punctuation, like many other aspects of language, has never been managed by formal rules; that is, punctuation rules are very much the not-so-strict rules (generalizations) outlined in Chapter 8.

As with the history of English spelling in Chapter 5, this history of punctuation will be brief, only touching on the main episodes in a 30-century story.

The Mesha Stele is considered to be the first extant historical document using punctuation. It is an inscribed basalt stone dating to the period of King Mesha of Moab, a kingdom in modern Jordan, around 840 BC. It is written in the Moabite language using the Phoenician alphabet. It uses points and horizontal strokes to separate words.

In the 5th century BC, Greek playwrights including Aristophanes and Euripides used three punctuation symbols in their plays, to help actors know when to pause: the *comma* (a centered dot), *colon* (a dot on the base line), and *full stop* (a raised dot). However, most Greek writing used no punctuation, not even spaces between words.

The practice of not using spaces between words continued (in various languages, in various locations) for many centuries. This naturally led to difficulties in reading, and mistakes in reading and writing. To appreciate the problems caused, Lundmark (2002, p. 42) gives the following ingenious, invented example for modern English:

ANDSOAKINGWASHEVERYTHINGAUNT

Depending on the spaces – that is, the word breaks – this could represent two sentences with totally different meanings:

And so, a king was he: very thin, gaunt.

And soaking! Wash everything, Aunt!

This is similar to the present-day situation in some languages, such as Thai, where spaces are not used between words, but to show the ends of sentences, and pauses.

In the 1st century BC, the Romans adopted the Greek practice of indicating where readers should pause. The full stop (called the interpunct) was used to separate individual words in a passage. The message of the previous invented example would then have been clear:

AND•SO•A•KING•WAS•HE•VERY•THIN•GAUNT

Still, this practice was eventually abandoned, and the full stop was used instead to mark the end of a grammatical stretch (sentence). However, this use was inconsistent; punctuation was not yet standardized.

Greater standardization was achieved around 400 when the Bible started to be translated into English, with large numbers of copies. As with the Greek playwrights centuries before, punctuation was introduced to help readers when reading aloud. St. Jerome and his colleagues, who produced the Vulgate translation of the Bible into Latin, introduced a system of punctuation marks, including indentation, and an early version of initial capital letters. This system was refined by Alcuin of York in the 8th century, who introduced the slash (known as a virgule), and dots that were centered in the line, raised or in groups. Initial letters of sentences were capitalized by the 13th century, but this was not consistently applied until the 16th century.

Prior to the invention of printing (by Gutenberg around 1440; see Chapter 4), punctuation was light and haphazard, "decidedly unsystematic and at times virtually absent" (About Education, n.d.).

William Caxton, who brought the printing press to England in 1476, used three punctuation marks: the stroke (/) for marking word groups, the colon (:) for marking distinct syntactic pauses, and the full stop (.) for marking the ends of sentences and brief pauses.

The thyrde temptation that the deuyl maketh to theym that deye. is by Impacyence: that is ayenste charyte/ For by charyte ben holden to loue god abouve alle thynges.

(In modern English:

The third temptation that the Devil makes to them that die is by impatience; that is against charity. For by charity be holden to love God above all things.)

Some writers used a double slash to signal a longer pause or the start of a new section of text.

Aldus Manutius of Venice (1449–1515) standardized the system, by ending sentences with a full stop or colon, creating the semicolon, parentheses and italics, and changing the slash (virgule) into the modern comma. The comma signaled the shortest pause, the semicolon next, then the colon, with the full stop terminating the sentence. At this stage, their purpose was still for reading aloud (elocutionary), not for showing grammatical boundaries (syntactical).

George Puttenham, in his treatise *The Arte of English Poesie* (1589), and Simon Daines, in *Orthoepia Anglicana* (1640), specified a pause of one unit for a comma, of two units for a semicolon, and of three for a colon, thereby explicitly bringing order into a previously confused situation. Apostrophes were first used around this time.

Ben Jonson, in his *English grammar*, a work composed about 1617 and published posthumously in 1640, first recommended syntactical punctuation (indicating grammar rather than pauses) in England.

For, whereas our breath is by nature so short, that we cannot continue without a stay to speake long together; it was thought necessarie, as well as for the speakers ease, as for the plainer deliverance of the things spoken, to invent this meanes, whereby men pausing a pretty while, the whole speech might never the worse be understood.

After Jonson, the main functions of several punctuation marks were standardized: capital letters at the beginning of a sentence or a proper name, spaces between words, the comma, parentheses, full stop (AmE period), colon, question mark and exclamation mark, and indenting the first line of a paragraph.

It is not known for certain when the question mark (originally called the note of interrogation) was created – possibly as late as the late 17th century. It is thought to derive from the letter Q. Similarly, with the exclamation mark (originally called the note of admiration): one theory is that it comes from the Latin word for joy, *Io*, written with the *I* above the *o*.

By the 18th century, it was common to use excessive punctuation, sometimes using commas with every subordinate clause and separable phrase. As a reaction to this, Timothy Dexter wrote a 24-page pamphlet entitled "A Pickle for the Knowing Ones" featuring creative spelling and an absence of any punctuation. The first edition sold out, but readers demanded that he should make some changes for the second edition. His response was to add a page of punctuation marks, inviting his readers to scatter them as they wished: "the fust edition had no stops I put in A nuf here and thay may peper and solt it as they please."

Quotation marks were used, at first to call attention to aphorisms or pithy sayings. However, they soon came to be used for direct quotations.

Fowler and Fowler's *The King's English* (1906) established the current British practice of light punctuation. By contrast, American spelling uses a number of punctuation marks where British spelling has nothing. Compare the following two versions.

At 9 p.m., Mr. and Mrs. Smith flew to the U.S.A., S. E. Asia, etc. on S.I.A.

At 9 pm, Mr and Mrs Smith flew to the USA, S E Asia, etc on SIA.

In the 1960s and 1970s, when electric typewriters used carbon-film ribbons, writers started to omit what they considered to be optional punctuation marks, for economy.

Bullets for lists were introduced in the late 20th century. Smilies and emoticons (☺) may also be considered a newly invented form of punctuation, as may the double slash as in *http://*. The advent of email led to a resurgence in use of the @ symbol, known by a number of different names (Italie, 2010); before the 1970s, it was used almost exclusively by grocers and accountants (e.g. *3 boxes @ £5 each*), but quickly became ubiquitous in separating usernames from server names for email addresses.

Needless to say, this has been a brief account of the main developments in the 30-century history of punctuation.

The Importance of Punctuation

How important is punctuation in a written text? Answers that writers have suggested range from very important to very unimportant. Most such writers have used invented examples to prove their point.

To show that punctuation can be very important, here are some sentences that contain no punctuation and are consequently difficult to understand on first reading.

Exercise

The following sentences are given with no punctuation. Insert whatever punctuation you think is necessary.

1 I told the girl that the boy kissed a story
2 These two dogs are my parents
3 Lets eat grandpa
4 The boy and the girl in jeans were late
5 If you understand the instructions clearly there's no problem
6 The secretary remembered that in addition to the printer she had been asked to order a number of other items needed replacing
7 The children the doorman admitted were a nuisance
8 John said the teacher is stupid
9 You've left too much space between fish and and and and and chips
10 We had one problem only Janet knew we faced bankruptcy

The answers are given in Appendix 4.

These examples show that in some circumstances, punctuation is vital in order to understand a sentence being read.

From the opposite point of view, many writers have shown that texts can still be understood with 100% or close to 100% intelligibility, even if all punctuation is deleted apart from capitals to show the beginnings of sentences and names. An earlier paragraph would thus be as follows.

> Greater standardization was achieved around 400 when the Bible started to be translated into English with large numbers of copies As with the Greek playwrights centuries before punctuation was introduced to help readers when reading aloud St Jerome and his colleagues who produced the Vulgate translation of the Bible into Latin introduced a system of

punctuation marks including indentation and an early version of initial capital letters This system was refined by Alcuin of York in the 8th century who introduced the slash known as a virgule and dots that were centered in the line raised or in groups Initial letters of sentences were capitalized by the 13th century but this was not consistently applied until the 16th century

As with many arguments, the truth is probably somewhere in the middle. Punctuation is important in some contexts, unimportant in others, but overall some punctuation is necessary or desirable for easy reading.

The Main Uses of Punctuation Marks

The intended readership of this book is pre- and in-service teachers. If you are an in-service teacher, you are probably well aware of the uses of English punctuation marks. If you are a native-speaker pre-service teacher, you probably need little clarification of their uses. If you are a non-native-speaker pre-service teacher, you probably were taught punctuation when you learned English, and may use the same punctuation marks in your native language. Whichever group you belong to, you do not need a list of the main uses of punctuation marks disrupting your reading of the body of this book. A reference list is therefore included as Appendix 3.

Trends in Punctuation

As in many fields, things come into fashion and go out of fashion. The same is true of punctuation marks.

Punctuation marks that seem to be on the way out include the following.

Opinions are divided on the semicolon. Some writers feel that it has a place, as it fulfils a valid function. Others disagree. "Just as there are writers who worship the semicolon, there are other high stylists who dismiss it – who label it, if you please, middle-class" (Truss, 2003, p. 107). George Orwell wrote his book *Coming up for air* (1939) without any semicolons, remarking "I had decided about this time that the semicolon is an unnecessary stop and that I would write my next book without one."

Commas also seem to be on the way out, or at least used less frequently than before. Peter Carey won the Booker Prize in 2001. His book *True history of the Kelly gang* (2000) contained no commas.

Apostrophes are increasingly omitted. Surprisingly, G. V. Carey in *Mind the stop* (1971), devoted only one paragraph to the use of the apostrophe, because he felt there was so little to say about it. "If only all marks were so easy." Clearly, many English speakers do not find apostrophes so simple. A phenomenon known informally as the greengrocer's apostrophe involves

Table 9.1 Apostrophes in American and British shop names

	With apostrophe	*Without apostrophe*
U.S.A.	Bloomingdale's	Barneys
	Boscov's	Bealls
	Dillard's	Halls
	Kohl's	Younkers
	Macy's	
U.K.		Beales
		Bentalls
		Boots
		Debenhams
		Harrods
		Selfridges

using *'s* incorrectly to make the simple plural of nouns, e.g. *potato's*. Shops that bear the (given or family) name of the founder may or may not carry an apostrophe in the U.S.A., but usually do not in the U.K. (Table 9.1).

Punctuation marks that seem to be in fashion include the following.

Dashes are in fashion (see Chapter 6 for the difference between dashes and hyphens). However, commentators often note that dashes are sometimes used in inappropriate contexts. Dashes are informal and therefore should not appear in more formal forms of writing. In more formal forms, a colon or brackets are generally considered more appropriate.

Bulleted lists are also in. Their use seems to have taken off with the advent of word-processing, and especially PowerPoint. Before this, asterisks, hyphens or dashes, or lowercase *O*s used to be used. On a computer, bullets can take many shapes; while the default is a small filled circle •, they can be squares ■, diamonds ♦, arrows ⇨, etc. A number of other symbols, such as pointing fingers ☞ or ticks ✓, can be used for this function too.

A phenomenon known as a comma splice or run-on sentence is becoming increasingly common. Often viewed as an error, it involves two separate, grammatically and semantically complete stretches of writing (sentences) being joined with just a comma, e.g. *It is half past five, I think we should finish now*. Commentators who object to this make appeal to a rule that commas cannot join sentences. Instead they suggest (i) keeping the two sentences as two sentences with a full stop, question mark, or exclamation mark, (ii) using punctuation marks that can join two sentences into one, such as colons, semicolons or dashes, or (iii) using linking expressions such as *and, so, because, therefore*. Comma splices are sometimes acceptable when the clauses are short and alike in form, e.g. *I came, I saw, I conquered*. However, as Truss (2003, p. 88) observes:

So many highly respected writers [including Samuel Beckett, E. M. Forster and Somerset Maugham] observe the splice comma that a rather unfair rule emerges on this one: only do it if you're famous. . . . Done knowingly by an established writer, the comma splice is effective, poetic, dashing. Done equally knowingly by people who are not published writers, it can look weak or presumptuous. Done ignorantly by ignorant people, it is awful.

Conclusion

The purpose of this chapter has not been to teach about punctuation. As a reader of English, you are already aware of punctuation and its main uses. Rather, the purpose was to explain that punctuation has been variable over the centuries. It is still not standardized, although if you are writing for a particular publisher, they may produce a style guide with instructions to follow, including for punctuation. Punctuation is flexible, and trends come and go, such that, as G. V. Carey observed in *Mind the stop* (1971, p. 15), punctuation is governed "two-thirds by rule and one-third by personal taste."

Summary

- Punctuation is important because it can, in some cases, disambiguate sentences.
- Punctuation has had a long and mixed history. A common debate throughout has been whether the function of punctuation is to indicate where people reading out loud should pause etc., or to indicate grammar.
- There is a lot of individual preference. Punctuation is governed "two-thirds by rule and one-third by personal taste."
- Just as punctuation has changed through the centuries, so it is likely to change in future; think of recent innovations caused by email, SMS texting, etc.

Exercises

1   The following letter is given with no punctuation, apart from capitals for names and *I*. Insert whatever punctuation you think is necessary.

dear John I want a man who knows what love is all about you are generous kind thoughtful people who are not like you admit to being useless and inferior you have ruined me for other men I yearn for you I have no feelings whatsoever when we're apart I can be forever happy will you let me be yours Jane

2   The following passage is from *Harry Potter and the Philosopher's Stone* (Rowling, 1997). In it, Harry meets for the first time some of his new classmates on the train to Hogwarts, the school of wizardry and witchcraft. It has been deliberately printed here without any punctuation. Add the punctuation.

want a hand it was one of the redhaired twins hed followed through the ticket box yes please harry panted oy fred cmere and help with the twins help harrys trunk was at last tucked away in a corner of the compartment thanks said harry pushing his sweaty hair out of his eyes whats that said one of the twins suddenly pointing at . harrys lightning scar blimey said the other twin are you he is said the first twin arent you he added to harry what said harry harry potter chorused the twins oh him said harry I mean yes I am the two boys gawped at him and harry felt himself going red then to his relief a voice came floating in through the trains open door fred george are you there coming mum with a last look at harry the twins hopped off the train harry sat down next to the window where halfhidden he could watch the redhaired family on the platform and hear what they were saying their mother had just taken out her hand-kerchief ron youve got something on your nose the youngest boy tried to jerk out of the way but she grabbed him and began rubbing the end of his nose mum geroff he wriggled free aaah has ickle ronnie got somefink on his nosie said one of the twins shut up said ron wheres percy said their mother hes coming now

Further Reading

Truss (2003) discusses many of the recent trends in English punctuation.

References

About Education (n.d.). *A brief history of punctuation.* Retrieved from grammar. about.com/od/punctuationandmechanics/a/PunctuationHistory.htm

Carey, G. V. (1971). *Mind the stop.* Cambridge, UK: Cambridge University Press.

Carey, P. (2000). *True history of the Kelly gang.* Brisbane, Australia: University of Queensland Press.

Fowler, H. W., & Fowler, F. G. (1906). *The King's English.* Oxford, UK: Clarendon Press.

Italie, L. (19 November 2010). *In other parts of the world, @ isn't where it's 'at'.* Associated Press. Retrieved from www.columbian.com/news/2010/nov/19/in-other-parts-of-the-world-isnt-where-its-at

Jonson, B. (1640). *The English grammar.* New York, NY: Sturgis & Walton (1909). Retrieved from archive.org/details/englishgrammar00jons

Lundmark, T. (2002). *Quirky QWERTY: The story of the keyboard @ your fingertips.* Sydney, Australia: University of New South Wales Press.

Orwell, G. (1939). *Coming up for air.* London, UK: Victor Gollancz.

Rowling, J. K. (1997). *Harry Potter and the philosopher's stone.* London, UK: Bloomsbury.

Truss, L. (2003) *Eats, shoots and leaves: The zero tolerance approach to punctuation.* London, UK: Profile Books.

10 Spaces and Hyphens

Learning Objectives

At the end of this chapter, readers will be able to:

- explain (i) compounds, and (ii) compound premodifiers
- illustrate how hyphens can be used to disambiguate.

What Is a "Word"?

While this may seem like a simple question, if one delves into it from a linguistic point of view, it turns out to be a complex question.

Exercise

How many words are there in the following passage? (Ignore the reference.)

> Fossil-bearing rocks are dated in various ways. Sometimes the fossils themselves are used to date the rocks in a relative way. Some fossil species had short time-spans, but were so widely distributed and common that their remains can be used as reliable indicators of a rock's age over very wide areas. However, this dating method only works well in marine rocks, and dinosaurs mostly occur in non-marine rocks, usually formed in rivers and lakes.
>
> (Martill & Naish, 2000, p. 9)

There are three different three types of "word" that linguists distinguish:

1   *Orthographic word*: a sequence of characters (letters) on the page with spaces before and after, ignoring punctuation. By this definition, there are 74 words in the passage, and this is the answer you probably gave.
2   *Word-form*: The criterion is the same as 1, but ignoring repetitions. Word-forms are types; orthographic words are tokens. In the above passage, *rocks* occurs four times, and *and* three.

3   *Lexeme/lemma*: The criterion is the same as 1 and 2, but ignoring grammatically related word-forms. Thus in the passage *are, were*, and *be* belong to the same lexeme, as do *date, dated* and *dating*, and *way* and *ways*.

So, for most people, a word is something with spaces or punctuation either side. Indeed, this is the way that a computer's word count works: in fact, it doesn't count words, it counts spaces (and adds one, because the first word does not have a space before it).

This works well enough for English, but will not work for other languages. Other spelling systems, including Arabic and Thai, do not leave spaces between words. The spacing rules for these languages may be quite complex. This leads to problems for foreign learners in knowing where one word ends and the next starts.

There are also problems in English. Martill and Naish (2000) spell *timespan* as one hyphenated word, but you may feel it could also be spelled *timespan* or *time span*. Can we say that *fossil* is one word and *fossil-bearing* also one word? What about *marine* and *non-marine*? Hyphenation problems are explored further in the section below.

It is also worth reiterating at the outset that there is no need to leave two spaces after full stops (periods), and a hyphen is not the same thing as a dash (see Chapter 6).

Spaces

There is not a lot more that needs to be said about spaces. Writers leave spaces between things that they consider to be words. See the next section about compounds.

Spaces may or may not be left before and/or after punctuation marks. The following list shows the rules normally followed by typists.

No space before; one space after

- colon
- semicolon
- comma
- full stop / period
- question mark
- exclamation mark
- closing bracket
- closing quotation mark

One space before; no space after

- opening bracket
- opening quotation mark

No space before or after

- apostrophe
- AmE dashes (i) are usually M dashes (see Chapter 6), and (ii) have no spaces either side
- hyphen

One space before and after

- BrE dashes (i) are usually N dashes (see Chapter 6), and (ii) have spaces either side.
- ellipsis

However, with many of these there is variation possible, and other punctuation marks immediately preceding or following the above marks may override the rule. If you are writing for a publisher, use whatever guidelines they recommend.

Punctuation in Compounds

A compound is a word that is composed of two existing words. Most compounds in English are noun phrases that are composed of a noun preceded by another element, usually another noun or adjective, e.g. *bedroom, greenhouse*. There are three ways in which compounds are shown to be compounds. Firstly, in terms of meaning (semantics), the compound has more meaning than the sum of its parts. Thus, a *whiteboard* is more than a board that is white; it is a particular type of board used in classrooms.

Secondly, in terms of pronunciation, the stress usually falls on the first element of a compound. Thus we say *BEDroom, GREENhouse, WHITEboard*. This may seem counterintuitive, in that a bedroom is a type of room; nevertheless, that is how compounds are pronounced in English.

Thirdly, and this is of relevance to spelling, including punctuation, compounds are often written as one word, as in *bedroom, greenhouse*, and *whiteboard*. However, this pattern is not as regular as you might think. There are in fact three ways in which compounds may be spelled/punctuated. They may be written as one word (solid), as in *toothpaste*. They may be written as one word with a hyphen in the middle, e.g. *six-pack*. And finally, they may be written as two words, with a space in between (spaced), as in *bus stop*.

Whether compounds are written solid, hyphenated, or spaced does not seem to conform to any clear rules or patterns, as is shown in the following exercise.

Exercise

Do you write the following compounds as solid, hyphenated or spaced? Choose one alternative each time.

Solid	Hyphenated	Spaced
carpark	*car-park*	*car park*
drycleaning	*dry-cleaning*	*dry cleaning*
firefly	*fire-fly*	*fire fly*
onlooker	*on-looker*	*on looker*
orangutan	*orang-utan*	*orang utan*
riffraff	*riff-raff*	*riff raff*
saddlebag	*saddle-bag*	*saddle bag*
sledgehammer	*sledge-hammer*	*sledge hammer*
taperecorder	*tape-recorder*	*tape recorder*
trainspotting	*train-spotting*	*train spotting*
troubleshooter	*trouble-shooter*	*trouble shooter*
wellbeing	*well-being*	*well being*

The spelling given by six dictionaries (three British and three American) is in the Answers (Appendix 4). As can be seen, some dictionaries are more prescriptive, giving only one spelling, while others are more descriptive, suggesting that English speakers vary in their habits. One compound that illustrates this point well is *spellchecker/spell-checker/spell checker*. The *Oxford learner's dictionary online* (n.d.) gives only the solid spelling, the *Merriam-Webster online dictionary* (n.d.) only gives the hyphenated spelling, and the *Random House dictionary online* (n.d.) only gives the spaced spelling. There is clearly a lot of variation here, and some dictionaries acknowledge this. Both the *American Heritage dictionary online* (n.d.) and the *Collins English dictionary online* (n.d.) give the solid and spaced versions as alternatives, while the *Longman dictionary of contemporary English online* (n.d.) gives all three: solid, hyphenated, and spaced.

It is difficult to discern any clear patterns here, even with compounds where the first element is the same, as the following exercise shows.

Exercise

Do you write the following compounds as solid, hyphenated, or spaced?

Solid	Hyphenated	Spaced
windowbox	*window-box*	*window box*
windowpane	*window-pane*	*window pane*
windowseat	*window-seat*	*window seat*

windowshopping	*window-shopping*	*window shopping*
windowsill	*window-sill*	*window sill*

Again, the spellings given by dictionaries are in the Answers (Appendix 4). They show that there is variation between the dictionaries, and no obvious pattern here.

Hyphens

The rules for use of the hyphen are given in Appendix 3. A more comprehensive list of uses of the hyphen is given in GrammarBook (2018). However, three extra points will be emphasized here.

Firstly, hyphens are common in compound premodifiers such as *a five-dollar note*. *Five-dollar* comes before (pre) and describes (modifies) the noun *note*. It is compound because it contains more than one element (*five* and *dollar*). Note that, as a premodifier, it is hyphenated, but not if the same elements occur after the verb: *This note is worth five dollars*. This also illustrates the general rule that premodifiers are singular (*dollar*) even if they are plural (*dollars*) in meaning, e.g. a brush for your teeth is a *toothbrush* (not a *teethbrush*). Hyphenation does not occur if the first element is an adverb: *a very valuable painting* (not *a very-valuable painting*).

In compound premodifiers, hyphens are used to show which elements belong together. Thus, *twenty five-dollar notes* refers to twenty notes, each worth $5; *twenty-five dollar notes* refers to twenty-five notes, each worth $1; and *twenty-five-dollar notes* refers to some notes, each worth $25.

The second, and perhaps the most important, rule is that hyphens should be used wherever they help to avoid confusion. GrammarBook (2018) gives the following examples. *Springfield has little-town charm* unambiguously means that Springfield has charm as a little town. However, *Springfield has little town charm* may mean this, but may also mean that Springfield has little charm as a town; *little* may modify *town* or *charm*. Similarly, *She had a concealed-weapons permit* can only mean that she had a permit for a concealed weapon, whereas *She had a concealed weapons permit* may additionally mean that she had a concealed permit for a weapon.

The same rule about avoiding confusion applies to prefixes and suffixes. Writers generally use hyphens when the stem after the prefix starts with a capital letter, e.g. *pan-African, mid-March*. A hyphen is also helpful to avoid two identical letters, e.g. *pre-empt, re-evaluate, co-operate, graffiti-ism*. A hyphen is also useful to show whether a prefix or suffix has just been added to a stem, or is part of an established word, e.g. *recover* ("regain health") vs *re-cover* ("cover e.g. a sofa again"); *recreation* ("fun or sport") vs *re-creation* ("creating again"); *unionized* ("formed into a union") vs *un-ionized* ("not separated into ions"). Even where there is no competing meaning, a hyphen may be useful to avoid misreading, e.g. using *coworker* instead of *co-worker* may lead readers to think of someone who orks cows.

A hyphen may occasionally be necessary to avoid sequences of three identical letters, e.g. *shell-like*.

Finally, the rules surrounding hyphenation are flexible, and the hyphenation of words may change over time as they become more established as words in the language in their own right. Cook (2009, p. 211) makes the generalization, "The longer a word has been in English, the more likely it is to have lost its space and its hyphen. The *Oxford English dictionary* records a progression from *tea bag* 1898 to *tea-bag* 1936 to *teabag* 1977." A similar process seems to be occurring with *anti-Semitism*. The word was originally coined by European Jews around 1880, as the German adjective *antisemitisch*; German does not require a hyphen or capital letter. This was translated directly into English as *anti-Semitism*. However, confusion arose over the people against whom there was prejudice; Semites include Arabs, Assyrians and even Maltese. Two things happened: the capital letter was dropped (*anti-semitism*) and nowadays it is commonly spelled without the hyphen (*antisemitism*).

Summary

- Different definitions of a "word" exist.
- The most common definition involves spaces, but writers' uses of spaces may vary.
- Likewise, there is flexibility in the use of hyphens.
- The wisest advice regarding spaces and hyphens is to use whatever avoids confusion for the reader.

Exercises

1 Which type of "word" is referred to in the following sentences?

- The five commonest words in written English are *the, of, to, and,* and *a*.
- Write an essay of about 1,000 words.
- The *Longman dictionary of contemporary English* contains entries for over 80,000 words.
- A picture is worth a thousand words.
- At age 4, native speaker children know an average of 700 words.
- *Forewent* is a rare word in English.
- There are two words *bank*: one meaning a place where you deposit money, the other the side of a river.
- A good typist can reach over 100 words a minute.
- I can't read the doctor's handwriting – what is this word?

2 The situation in Arabic, Thai, etc, where spaces are not left between words is similar to internet addresses (URLs), where spaces are usually avoided. This may lead to comical and often suggestive misreadings.

For instance, a company recycling IT material has the internet address *itscrap.com*. In full, this can be read correctly as *IT scrap* or incorrectly as *It's crap*. The following are similar examples that have appeared on the internet. Many of them have been taken down or changed because of the potential for comical misreading. Some of them may have been hoaxes in the first place. Explain the correct and incorrect readings each time.

- A website encouraging viewers to book holiday rentals in Spain is choosespain.com
- Teachers Talking Spanish is a language booster course for teachers and teaching assistants, website: teacherstalking.org
- The Speed of Art promotional videos website is speedofart.com
- Similarly, the BITEF (Belgrade International Theatre Festival) Art Café has a website bitefartcafe.rs
- The website for IHA, a holiday rentals company in Las Vegas, is ihavegas.com
- A data trawling site for experts covering jobs, real estate, insurance, etc. is expertsexchange.com
- An online newsletter website about Winters City, California, U.S.A. is wintersexpress.com
- Via Grafix, a graphics company subsequently acquired by Learn 2, had a website viagrafix.com
- For accommodation at Lake Tahoe, California/Nevada, U.S.A., access gotahoenorth.com
- To search for the business agents representing celebrities, try whorepresents.com
- Pen Island custom-made pens can be found at penisland.net

Further Reading

Any book on punctuation should contain guidelines for spaces and hyphens. When writing for a publisher, use whatever style guide it prescribes. GrammarBook (2018) contains a comprehensive list of uses of the hyphen.

References

American Heritage dictionary online (n.d.). Retrieved from ahdictionary.com
Collins English dictionary online (n.d.). Retrieved from www.collinsdictionary.com/dictionary/english
Cook, V. (2009). *It's all in a word.* London, UK: Profile.
GrammarBook (2018). *Hyphens.* Retrieved from www.grammarbook.com/punctuation/hyphens.asp
Longman dictionary of contemporary English online (n.d.). Retrieved from www.ldoceonline.com
Martill, D., & Naish, D. (2000). *Walking with dinosaurs: The evidence.* London, UK: BBC Books.

Merriam-Webster online dictionary (n.d.). Retrieved from www.merriam-webster. com/dictionary

Oxford learner's dictionary online (n.d.). Retrieved from www.oxfordlearners dictionaries.com

Random House dictionary online (n.d.). Retrieved from www.dictionary.com

11 Capital Letters

Learning Objectives

At the end of this chapter, readers will be able to:

- list some languages that do not have the distinction between capital and lowercase letters
- teach the main functions of capital letters in English
- explain the difference between initialisms and acronyms
- describe the stages in acronyms becoming regular words, e.g. *radar*.

Capital Letters in Languages

In the days of manual printing of English texts, letters were kept in boxes (cases) and the printer took the letters from the cases and compiled the text in a block. Capital (large) letters are also known as uppercase letters because they were kept in the upper case (a partitioned drawer), while small letters are also called lowercase, because they were in the lower drawer. The terms *uppercase* and *lowercase* have nothing to do with type-writers or the Shift key.

An important first point in this chapter is that the distinction between uppercase capital letters and lowercase small letters exists in English (that is, in the Roman alphabet) and in some other alphabets, but the distinction does not exist in many other alphabets.

There are essentially five modern alphabets that have the distinction, and they are all historically related. The ancestor of all these alphabets is the Greek alphabet, produced around the 8th or 9th century BC, which itself came from the Phoenician alphabet which dated to three centuries before that. The Greek alphabet is still used for present-day Greek.

The Cyrillic alphabet, used in Russia and neighboring countries, is a descendant of the Greek alphabet. So is the Coptic alphabet, used in Egypt until the 17th century, but now only found in use by the Coptic churches in Egypt. Another descendant is the Armenian alphabet, used in Armenia and Armenian diasporic communities.

The predominant one is the Roman alphabet, also called the Latin alphabet. This is the familiar one used in English (as in this book), and many other European languages. It is also the basis for International Phonetic Association (IPA, 1999) transcription, and spelling systems devised for previously unwritten languages (Summer Institute of Linguistics, n.d.).

While it may seem that a distinction that exists in only five historically-related alphabets should not carry much weight worldwide, it is important to appreciate how many people speak languages using those five alphabets. In particular, English is spoken by 320–380 million people as a native language, 150–300 million as a second language, and 100–1,000 million as a foreign language (Crystal, 1997). In Eurasia, 252 million people use the Cyrillic alphabet or variants of it.

In contrast, there are plenty of languages that use alphabets with no distinction between capital and lowercase letters: Arabic, Devanagari (used in many Indian languages), Hebrew, Korean, Thai. Syllabic and non-alphabetic writing systems, as in Japanese and Chinese, have no such distinction.

The upshot of this discussion is that learners of English may well come from languages that have no distinction between capital and lowercase letters. It is therefore a feature that has to be taught and learned, and errors are likely to occur.

History

Readers might be tempted to ask, "When did the Roman alphabet develop capital letters?" In fact, the question is the wrong way round: "When did the Roman alphabet develop lowercase letters?" In ancient Roman times, Latin was written in capital letters, because their shapes were easy to carve in stone. However, when writing with a pen, the capital letter shapes were awkward and smaller versions were therefore developed. Nevertheless, rather than writing in all small letters, scribes added capital letters in order to add prestige and importance to particular words, such as names and titles. This is the origin of the modern English practice.

Rules for English Capitals

The rules for capital letters in English are relatively straightforward. They are used:

- for the letter *i* when you are referring to yourself, e.g. *I don't know.*
- in acronyms (initials), e.g. *UNICEF* (see below)
- in Roman numerals, e.g. 2018 is MMXVIII
- when mocking something, e.g. *Ray thought it was a Good Idea to go skinny-dipping.*
- for the first letter of:

o   a sentence, e.g. *My head aches.*
o   a quoted sentence, e.g. *She said, "My head aches."*
o   the names of:

    o   people (first and last names), e.g. *Sally Higgins*
    o   places (cities, states, counties, roads), e.g. *Washington, Alabama, Surrey, Pall Mall*
    o   continents, countries, languages, nationalities, and religions, e.g. *Europe, Australia, Arabic, Indian, Buddhism*
    o   buildings, monuments, e.g. *the White House, Buckingham Palace, the Taj Mahal*
    o   planets, stars, constellations, e.g. *Saturn, the Great Bear*
    o   companies, trademarks, and products, e.g. *Hoover* but *vacuum cleaner*
    o   transport such as ships, trains, and spacecraft, e.g. *the Jolly Roger, the Flying Scotsman, Soyuz*
    o   wars and historical periods, e.g. *the Korean War, the Bronze Age*

* the titles (only content words, namely nouns, verbs, adjectives, and adverbs) of:

    o   covers of books, e.g. *A Practical Guide for Language Teachers*
    o   films, e.g. *The Hobbit: The Desolation of Smaug*
    o   plays, musicals, e.g. *Waiting for Godot, Joseph and the Amazing Technicolor Dreamcoat*
    o   songs, e.g. *Bohemian Rhapsody*
    o   poems, e.g. *The Rime of the Ancient Mariner*
    o   companies, organizations, and associations, e.g. *Kentucky Fried Chicken, the Red Cross, the Chartered Institute of Management Accountants*
    o   days, months, holidays, and competitions, e.g. *Tuesday, July, National Day, Ryder Cup*

These are rules in the sense described in Chapter 8, namely generalizations about what English speakers and writers do and consider to be correct. As with many rules of language, they can be played with and broken, for effect. For instance, the German sportswear manufacturer Adidas regularly spells its name with a lowercase first letter; thus, *adidas*. Similarly, the American poet Edward Estlin Cummings often wrote his name without capitals, and sometimes without the full stops (periods) that would be normal in AmE; thus, *e e cummings*. Likewise, the Canadian singer Kathryn Dawn Lang spells her stage name all in lowercase: thus, *k.d. lang*. Nowadays, and especially in IT, there is a use of capitals, called camel case, where a capital is used in the middle of a compound word without spaces, such as *PowerPoint, FedEx,* and *HarperCollins*. Apple has named many of its recent products this way with the prefix *i-* (originally in *iMac*, but then in *iPod, iBook, iPhone, iPad, iTunes*, etc); there are differing views as to whether the prefix stands for *internet, individuality*, or *innovation*. In order to emphasize the camel case used for *Mac, Pod*, etc, the initial *i* is lowercase. The same applies to *eBay*. Obviously, these unconventional uses of capital and lowercase initials have the desired publicity effect, as they have all just been mentioned in this book.

As with most spelling rules, there are fuzzy edges, and some variation. As *The Economist style guide* (n.d.) states, "A balance has to be struck between so many capitals that the eyes dance and so few that the reader is diverted more by our style than by our substance." A rule of thumb is to write the passage in lowercase letters, and then capitalize only those words that look wrong. "Useless capitals can quickly make your writing look idiotic" (Trask, 1997, p. 53).

Titles and designations are one such arguable case. Should a word like *president* have an initial capital? Style guides typically say that it should if it precedes the president's surname (*President Trump*), but not if it is used in a sentence (*Trump is the president*). The designation of job positions within companies is a questionable case. "In some organizations, job titles like *managing director* are given initial capitals but this is poor practice – at what rank do you stop?" (Cutts, 1995, p. 87). That is, if you capitalize *Managing Director*, would you also capitalize *Deputy Marketing Manager, Secretary* and *Cleaner*?

The word *government* is often given an initial capital, but only if it refers to the government of the country in which the writing takes place (*The Government has raised taxes*). Many style guides state that this is unnecessary, e.g. "The *government*, the *administration* and the *cabinet* are always lower case" (*The Economist style guide*, n.d.).

As a result of these rules, there exist in English pairs of words (known as capitonyms) where one word has an initial capital, and the other does not. For instance, *Cancer* (the astrological sign) versus *cancer* (the disease); *Lent* (the Christian festival) versus *lent* (past tense of *lend*); *Mercury* (the Roman god) versus *mercury* (the metal). Some capitonyms involve a change in pronunciation, e.g. *August* (the month) versus *august* ("venerable"); *Polish* (from Poland) versus *polish* ("shine").

While these rules may seem uncomplicated, they do not necessarily correspond to the way capital letters are used in languages closely related to English.

In German, all nouns have initial capital letters. So the German for *house, book, mother* are *Haus, Buch, Mutter*. The regular capitalization of nouns can be found in older forms of English. In modern German and Luxembourgish, it is standard. Until a spelling reform in 1948, it was also standard in Danish.

Vice versa, initial capitals are used in English in some situations where they are not used in other related languages. For instance, the French equivalents of *Monday* and *June* are *lundi* and *juin*, without initial capitals.

Initials

One common feature of writing where capital letters are found is initials. Initials are abbreviations and thus make the expression shorter. Five stages can be distinguished in the treatment of initials and eventually integrating them into the language as regular words.

The first is for the longer expression to be expressed as initials, with capital letters, and with full stops (periods) after them, to show that they are initials. Thus, *the United Kingdom* becomes *the U.K.* and *Mister John Smith* becomes *Mr. J. Smith*. (*Mister* is not initialized, but it is an example of the same use of the full stop, to show an abbreviated form.)

The second stage is for the full stops to be omitted; thus *the UK* and *Mr J Smith*. This contributes to what is known as light punctuation and is standard practice in Britain. In the U.S.A., however, the periods are usually retained (a feature of heavy punctuation). Ambiguity is rarely possible with omitted full stops. A counterexample is headlines, provided they are written in all capitals, e.g. INTEGRATING IT IN THE CLASSROOM (Information Technology), WHO TO RESEARCH EBOLA OUTBREAK (the World Health Organization). However, as we saw in Chapter 6, it is unnecessary and unusual nowadays to use all capitals for headlines (indeed for anything).

Note that some initials do not use capital letters, e.g. *i.e.* (Latin *id est* "that is"), *e.g.* (Latin *exempli gratia* "for the sake of example"), *et al.* (Latin *et alii* "and others"). Notice also that *et* is not an abbreviation in this last example.

The third stage is when the word comes to be pronounced as a word rather than as a set of initials. This seems more likely to happen, the longer the expression; for instance, UNESCO is pronounced as a word /juːneskoʊ/, not as the names of the letters /juː en iː es siː oʊ/. The word is quicker to say: /juːneskoʊ/ is three syllables, whereas /juː en iː es siː oʊ/ is six. Some shorter expressions are pronounced as words, such as RAM: /ræm/ (one syllable) versus /ɑːr eɪ em/ (three) versus *random access memory* (seven).

Some writers reserve the term *acronym* for initials that are pronounced as words, like *UNESCO*. Those that are not pronounced as words are *initialisms*.

It would seem to be a prerequisite for an initialism to become an acronym, i.e. to be pronounced as a word, that it contains a vowel as an initial, such as the *A* in RAM. However, vice versa, there seem to be expressions that could easily become acronyms, i.e. be pronounced as words, but nevertheless are still pronounced as initials. Examples include *URL* /juː ɑːr el/ (rather than /ɜː(r)l/ for "Uniform Resource Locator," and *doi* /diː oʊ aɪ/ (rather than /dɔɪ/) for "digital object identifier."

In the fourth stage, only the first letter is a capital, the rest being lowercase. The acronym AIDS (for "acquired immune deficiency syndrome") is often spelled Aids (e.g. Science Daily, n.d.). Similarly, while the Association of Southeast Asian Nations refers to itself as ASEAN, Air Asia (n.d.), a Malaysian low-cost airline, advertises an AirAsia Asean Pass.

Cutts (1995, p. 87) asserts that "Acronyms that can easily be spoken as words need only have an initial capital: *Nato, Unicef, Unesco.*" The final stage is for the initial capital letter to disappear. This means that the word is spelled and pronounced like a regular word of English. Indeed, speakers of the language may not realize that the word was originally derived from initials. This has happened with *scuba* and *radar*; many people are unaware that *scuba* stands for "self-contained underwater breathing apparatus," and *radar* for "radio detection/direction and ranging."

Jackson (2002, p. 14) uses the term *syllabic acronym* for examples where it is the first syllable, rather than the first letter, of each word that is used, sometimes with slight changes of spelling or pronunciation; for instance, *modem* (*modulator-demodulator*), *pixel* (*picture element*), and *wi-fi* (the popular term for a high-frequency wireless local area network, from *wireless fidelity*, modeled after *hi-fi* (*high fidelity*)).

Teaching

As the rules listed in this chapter show, the use of capital letters in English is not overly complex. However, it may be different from the way capital letters are used in learners' native languages. Also, many learners will speak languages that have no such distinction. As a result, the standard use of capital letters in English is a feature that should be covered early in a learner's study of English. Extensive reading of English texts, and the guided noticing of the spelling feature of capital letters should also be encouraged.

Summary

- Most alphabets in use in the modern world do not have a distinction between capital and lowercase letters.
- Even languages that use the Roman alphabet may use capital letters differently from English.
- Texts are, in general, understandable even with incorrect capital letters, showing that they are not a barrier to intelligibility. They may, however, be taken as indicative of poor proficiency.

Exercise

The following passage (adapted from Seddon, 2010, pp. 279–280) has been printed all in lowercase letters, but with other punctuation. Decide where capital letters are needed.

bertram 'bert' albert patenaude passed to the great dressing room in the sky certain that a place in fifa world cup history had been unfairly denied him, for he always claimed that on 17 july 1930 he had scored a hat-trick – two days before argentinian guillermo stabile bagged a famous 'first' with three goals against mexico. in his own version of events the historic feat was achieved when the united states beat paraguay 3-0 in the inaugural world cup. bert opened the scoring in the 10th minute and also notched the final goal in the 50th minute. yet for some reason, bert had not been officially credited with a second goal in the 15th minute. one source gave it to the us player tom florie and another tagged it an own goal by paraguay's aurelio gonzalez. nothing would have changed but for a group of dogged statisticians unearthing the original sources. first they checked the 1930 world cup report submitted to the united states football association by manager alfred cummings – it credited patenaude with all three goals. then they found three survivors of the game who backed bert to the hilt. some 1930 newspaper reports were equally convincing – the argentinian daily la prensa not only gave bert the hat-trick, but issued diagrams of how the goals were scored. so that is how bert patenaude finally secured world cup immortality and found his way into the guinness world records book to boot. he will remain forever the scorer of the world cup's first hat-trick.

References

Air Asia (n.d.). *AirAsia Asean Pass*. Retrieved from www.airasia.com/my/en/book-with-us/asean-pass/overview.page

Crystal, D. (1997). *English as a global language*. Cambridge, UK: Cambridge University Press.

Cutts, M. (1995). *The plain English guide: How to write clearly and communicate better*. Oxford, UK: Oxford University Press.

International Phonetic Association (1999). *Handbook of the International Phonetic Association: A guide to the use of the International Phonetic Alphabet*. Cambridge, UK: Cambridge University Press.

Jackson, H. (2002). *Lexicography: An introduction*. London, UK: Routledge.

Science Daily (n.d.). *Reference terms: AIDS*. Retrieved from www.sciencedaily.com/terms/aids.htm

Seddon, P. (2010). *The World Cup's strangest moments*. London, UK: Portico.

Summer Institute of Linguistics (n.d.). Retrieved from www.sil.org

The Economist style guide (n.d.). Retrieved from www.economist.com/style-guide/capitals

Trask, R. L. (1997). *The Penguin guide to punctuation*. Harmondsworth, UK: Penguin.

Features of Present-day English Spelling

12 Silent Letters

Learning Objectives

At the end of this chapter, readers will be able to:

- explain the distinction between empty, auxiliary, and inert silent letters.

Introduction

As was explained in Chapter 4, the Great Vowel Shift (GVS) was a wholesale change in the sounds of the London accent of English, between roughly 1350 and 1600. This was not an overnight change, and the sounds of English continued to change after the GVS, as they still do. The GVS mostly affected vowel sounds; however, various changes in consonant sounds occurred during the same period. Mostly, they involved the dropping of consonant sounds that had been previously pronounced. The fly in the ointment is that the printing press was invented in the 15th century, and spellings were quickly standardized. Thus, after the GVS, English was left with pronunciations that had changed, but spellings that had not. It was all a matter of timing.

English teachers are familiar with the concept of silent letters; that is letters that do not represent any sound in the pronunciation. If learners, whether native or non-native, do not hear a sound in their pronunciation, why should they expect to need to use a letter for a non-existent sound? Likewise, teachers are used to pointing out omitted silent or misplaced letters, and may wish that they could all be done away with.

Categories of Silent Letter

The situation is in fact more complex than this. Carney (1994) distinguishes three different types of silent letter.

Empty Letters

Empty letters are ones that do not represent a sound and do not have any other function. They could therefore be omitted, leaving a plausible, more regular spelling for the word.

The *i* in *friend* is an example of an empty letter. It represents no sound; there is no /ɪ/, for instance, in the pronunciation of the word. Neither does it have any other function.

So, why is there an *i* in *friend?* As with many strange English spellings, the answer is in the history of the word (etymology). It comes ultimately from Proto-Germanic *frijand*, which is also the source of modern Dutch *vriend*. While there is no vestige of an /ɪ/ sound in modern English pronunciation, the *i* letter has persisted in the spelling. In Old English, it was *freond*, and the spelling *frend* occurred in Middle English, alongside *frende* and *freond*.

If it were spelled *frend*, it would still be pronounced the same. Indeed, it would not only rhyme with other words but also look like them too: *bend, blend, fend, lend, mend, send, spend, tend, trend,* etc. In short, it would be more regular. The letters *ie* are not a regular way of representing the /e/ vowel; if you were to suggest that *bend, blend,* etc. could be spelled *biend, bliend,* etc., nobody would take you seriously. Indeed, with *fend,* this would lead to problems, as *fend* is a distinct word from *fiend.*

The spelling *frend* already occurs in three other contexts. It has been an English surname for centuries. Famous recent people with the surname spelled this way include Charles Frend (1909–1977), English film director; William Frend (1916–2005), English ecclesiastical historian; and Ted Frend (1916–2006), British competitive motorcyclist. Secondly, *frend* may be used as the name of commercial products. The New Zealand Vanish company produces a carpet-cleaning powder named *Frend.* Thirdly, there are acronyms FREND, presumably emphasizing that the item is user-friendly. The South Korean-US NanoEnTek company produces immunodiagnostic products called FREND. It can also stand for Front-end Robotics Enabling Near-term Demonstration.

By continuing to have an empty *i* in *friend,* it is not surprising that learners often misplace it and spell the word as *freind.*

In short, empty letters have no sound or function, and could be omitted leaving a plausible, more regular spelling for the word.

Auxiliary Letters

Auxiliary silent letters are ones that represent no sound but work in conjunction with other letters. As a result, they cannot be omitted leaving a plausible spelling for the word.

We have just discussed the empty letter *i* in *friend.* It can be omitted without loss. However, in the word *fiend,* it cannot. *Fend* cannot represent the pronunciation of *fiend* /fiːnd/. Instead, it happens to correspond to another English word with a different pronunciation with a different vowel sound /fend/. So, in *fiend,* the *i* and *e* letters work together to represent the /iː/ vowel, and this pattern is found in other words such as *belief, achieve, field, piece, siege.*

The phenomenon known as "magic *e*" is another example of an auxiliary letter. It is discussed at greater length in the next chapter.

Inert Letters

Morphology refers to the way that words are composed of smaller units of meaning (morphemes). These morphemes carry their own lexical meaning or grammatical function (Table 12.1).

Morphemes that have a grammatical function are called inflections. There are eight in English, they are all suffixes (occur after the stem), and they do not change the grammatical category (noun, verb, etc.) (Table 12.2).

All other prefixes (before the stem) and suffixes (after the stem) are derivations. They change the lexical meaning (rather than the grammatical function) of a word, and usually (but not always) change the grammatical category.

Table 12.1 Component morphemes of some English words

Word	*unhappiness*	*disability*	*dehumidifiers*
Component morphemes	*un-* (negative) *happy* (the stem, an adjective) *-ness* (turns an adjective into a noun)	*dis-* (negative) *able* (the stem, an adjective) *-ity* (turns an adjective into a noun)	*de-* (removal) *humid* (the stem, an adjective) *-ify* (turns an adjective into a verb) *-er* (turns a verb into an agent noun) *-s* (makes a noun plural)

Table 12.2 The eight inflectional suffixes of English

Inflection	*Added to a . . .*	*Example*	*Function*
-s	noun	*boys*	plural
-'s, -s'	noun	*boy's, boys'*	possessive
-er	adjective	*quicker*	comparative
-est	adjective	*quickest*	superlative
-(e)s	verb	*(he) helps, fetches, proves*	3rd person singular present tense
-ed	verb	*(he) helped, fetched, proved*	past tense
-ed	verb	*(he has/was) helped, fetched, proved*	participle (for perfect tense or passive)
-ing	verb	*(he is) helping, fetching, proving*	participle (for continuous)

Examples include the prefixes *un-*, *dis-*, and *de-*, and the suffixes *-ness*, *-ity*, *-ify*, and *-er* in *unhappiness, disability,* and *dehumidifiers.*

We are now in a position to answer a question such as, "Why is there a *g* letter in *sign?*" There is no /g/ sound (so it is, in this sense, silent), and it is pronounced the same as (i.e. is a homophone of) *sine,* the mathematical term. However, it has some function, because we cannot omit the *g* (*sin*) and be left with a spelling that is plausible for the pronunciation. There are two answers.

Firstly, historically speaking, the modern word comes from Latin *signum,* via Old French to Middle English *signe.* As has happened with many English words, the pronunciation has changed through time (the /g/ sound has been dropped) but the spelling has remained the same (the *g* letter has not been dropped).

The second answer relates to morphology. The word *sign* is related to *signal, signature, signatory, signify,* and (less obviously) *signet, significance* by the adding of morphemes (*-al,* etc.). In all these related words, there is a /g/ sound. Carney (1994) proposes the term *inert* for this situation. All these morphologically-related words contain a *g* letter, but in *sign* it is inert (not pronounced, but useful to show the morphological connection with *signal,* etc.).

Discussion

It is not always obvious whether silent letters should be analyzed as empty, auxiliary, or inert. Some letters can be silent in all three categories. The case of *h* illustrates this well, and highlights some problems in analysis.

The letter *h* is often an empty letter, having no sound or function. It can occur initially on its own in words like *hour, heir* (thus homophones with *our* and *air*), *honest,* etc. It can occur after *r,* as in *rhapsody, rhetoric, rheumatism, rhinoceros, rhubarb, rhyme,* and *rhythm.* Elsewhere in the word, it can be empty in *silhouette, cheetah, messiah.*

The letter *h* is often an auxiliary letter, combining with *c, p, s,* and *t.* Thus, the two-letter combinations (digraphs) *ch, ph, sh,* and *th* occur in words like *chase, phew, shock,* and *thinker,* distinguishing them from the unrelated words *case, pew, sock,* and *tinker.*

The case of *wh* needs further examination. In *what, when, where, whether, why,* it is silent for most speakers, who pronounce *what, where,* and *whether* the same as (their homophones) *watt, wear,* and *weather.* However, many Scots and Americans do not pronounce these the same, and distinguish other pairs such as *whales/Wales, which/witch,* etc., so for those speakers it is auxiliary. Also, note that in a handful of words (*who/whose/whom, whole, whooping, whore*), it is the *w* that is silent, not the *h,* as these are pronounced with /h/.

In the word *vehicle* (which has no /h/ sound), it is inert because of the existence of the adjective *vehicular* (which does have an /h/ sound).

For the word *herb*, the /h/ is pronounced in British English (so, not silent) but not in American English (so, empty).

There are various words with the *h* letter after *ex*: *exhale, exhaust, exhibit, exhilarate, exhort, exhume*. The pronunciation of these words, with or without an /h/ sound, varies. It usually has the /h/ in *exhale* (so, not silent); it does not usually have the /h/ sound in *exhaust, exhilarate, exhort* (so, empty); and it may or may not in *exhume* (so its status as a silent letter depends on the speaker's pronunciation). *Exhibit* is historically and morphologically related to *inhibit* and *prohibit*, where the /h/ is always pronounced, so may be considered inert.

Similar problems in analysis occur with *gh*. In *ghastly, ghost,* and *ghoul*, the *h* is silent and could be omitted. However, given the rule that *g* before *e* is "soft" (/dʒ/), it could not be omitted from *ghee, gherkin,* or *ghetto*; this is perhaps best analyzed as auxiliary, as it has a function. In *though, through, thorough, thought, fought, sought, bough, borough, daughter, slaughter, weigh*, etc., the *gh* digraph has no sound or function, so is empty. However, in *laugh, cough, tough, rough, trough*, the *gh* digraph is pronounced /f/, so the *h* is auxiliary with *g*.

The word *doughnut* is also interesting. This is often spelled *donut* nowadays. If so, are such donuts made of *do* (rather than *dough*)?

Similar problems occur with *ch*, usually in words of Greek origin. In *anchor, chaos, character, charisma, chlorine, chorus, Christian, monarch*, the *h* could be omitted, leaving a plausible spelling; in short, it is empty. However, because of the rule that *c* before *e* and *i* is "soft" (/s/), it could not be omitted from *ache, architect, chemist, scheme*, in order to maintain the /k/ sound (so, is auxiliary). *Ache* is different from *ace*.

The purpose of this section about *h* was to illustrate that, while silent letters can be categorized into empty, auxiliary, and inert, in some cases, this categorization is difficult to apply, as it may depend on particular words rather than groups of words, the pronunciation of individual speakers, differences between British and American English, and other factors.

Summary

- Silent letters are those that do not represent any sound in the pronunciation.
- There are three types of silent letter.
- Empty letters have no other function and can be omitted leaving a plausible spelling for the pronunciation.
- Auxiliary letters work with other letters to represent sounds; they therefore cannot be omitted.
- Inert letters represent no sound in the word, but represent a sound in morphologically-related words.

Exercises

1   Can you complete an alphabet of silent letters? That is, for each letter, can you think of a word of English where that letter is silent? For
instance, *a* is silent in *bread* (because it has no sound, and if we leave it
out, the resulting spelling (*bred*) would still be pronounced the same).
2   Are the underlined letters in the following words empty, auxiliary, or
inert?

bom*b*, de*b*t, colum*n*, has*t*en, lam*b*, recei*p*t, hav*e*, hu*ge*, t*w*o

Further Reading

The explanation given here of types of silent letters is from Carney (1994).

References

Carney, E. (1994). *A survey of English spelling*. London, UK: Routledge.

13 Doubled Consonant Letters

Learning Objectives

At the end of this chapter, readers will be able to:

- explain the phenomenon known in teaching circles as "magic *e*" (*hop, hope*)
- describe how magic *e* originated historically
- show how magic *e* is related to doubled consonant letters, e.g. *hope/hoping* vs *hop/hopping*
- list some exceptions to this basic rule.

Let us start this chapter with an exercise in order to establish a basic principle.

Exercise

Which of the following letters and letter combinations can be doubled? For instance, the letter *e* can be doubled, as in *sleep*. Ignore double consonants in compounds where one consonant ends a morpheme and the other starts a new one, e.g. *glowworm*. (So, doubled *w* does not exist.) Also ignore words that are clearly foreign loanwords, e.g. *aardvark*. (So doubled *a* does not exist.)

a	*g*
b	*h*
c	*i*
ch	*j*
d	*k*
e	*l*
f	*m*

n	*th*
o	*u*
p	*v*
q	*w*
r	*x*
s	*y*
sh	*z*
t	

Answers and discussion are in the Appendix 4.

Magic e

In Chapter 12, we distinguished three different types of silent letter. Empty letters have no sound, and have no function, so they can be omitted with no effect, e.g. the *a* in *bread*. Auxiliary letters have no sound in themselves, but cannot be omitted because they work with other letters, e.g. *thank*. Finally, inert letters have no sound in the word being considered, but have a sound in morphologically-related words, e.g. *sign* (cf. *signal*).

A very pervasive example of an auxiliary letter is *e*, as in *mate* (vs *mat*). In American circles this is known as silent *e*. However, it is not silent in the way that the *e* in the surname *Browne* is silent. In *Browne*, the *e* can be omitted without changing the pronunciation. In *mate*, it cannot; the *e* thus performs a function. For this reason, the *e* in *mate* is known in British circles as magic *e*.

The phenomenon of magic *e* dates back to the Great Vowel Shift (GVS) described in Chapter 4. Between roughly 1350 and 1600, the long vowels of English changed. Before the GVS, they had long monophthongal pronunciations; that is, they were long vowels in which the tongue and lip position did not move. After the GVS, they had changed into different long monophthong vowels, or into diphthongs (vowels with a change in tongue and/or lip position). Subsequently, some of the long monophthongs became diphthongs. The main vowel changes of relevance to this chapter are shown in Table 13.1.

Why is there an *e* letter at the end of the spelling of these words? Because in the Middle English pronunciation of these words, there was a vowel at the end (a schwa) which was eventually lost. However, since the spelling had been standardized, by the advent of the printing press, it remained in the spelling.

The modern state of affairs is that the examples in Table 13.1 form pairs where one word has the final *e*, and the other does not: *mat* vs *mate;*

Table 13.1 Vowel changes in the Great Vowel Shift

Example word	Before the GVS	After the GVS, Modern English
bite	/iː/	/aɪ/
mete	/eː/	/iː/
mate	/aː/	/eɪ/
robe	/ɔː/	/oʊ/
huge	/oː/ (hoge)	/(j)uː/

Table 13.2 The effect of magic *e* in Modern English

Without magic e			With magic e		
Word	Pronunciation (BrE)	Vowel sound (BrE)	Word	Pronunciation (BrE)	Vowel sound (BrE)
mat	/mæt/	/æ/	mate	/meɪt/	/eɪ/
met	/met/	/e/	mete	/miːt/	/iː/
bit	/bɪt/	/ɪ/	bite	/baɪt/	/aɪ/
rob	/rɒb/	/ɒ/	robe	/roʊb/	/oʊ/
hug	/hʌɡ/	/ʌ/	huge	/hjuːdʒ/	/(j)uː/

met vs *mete; bit* vs *bite; rob* vs *robe; hug* vs *huge*. The pronunciation of the word without the final *e* contains a short vowel, as in Table 13.2.

If you read down the vowel sounds in the final column, you will notice that these post-GVS vowels happen to correspond to the Modern English names of the vowels: *a, e, i, o, u* (see Chapter 17 on the names of letters). For this reason, the slogan used in British literacy circles is "Magic *e* makes the vowel say its name." That is, magic *e* is an auxiliary letter, in that it has no sound of its own, but it has the function of working with the other vowel letter to represent the vowel sound.

Magic *e* has another function. Where the final letter is *g* or *c*, it changes this as follows. As in *hug* vs *huge*, magic *e* changes /ɡ/ to /dʒ/. As in *Mac* vs *mace*, it changes /k/ to /s/. In non-technical vocabulary, it changes a "hard" sound into a "soft" one.

In 1971, Tom Lehrer wrote a song "Silent *e*" for the children's program *The Electric Company* (available on YouTube: Lehrer, 1971). It teaches what we have been calling "Magic *e*." A similar British "Magic *e*" version is KidsTV123 (n.d.).

A complication for American English is that the vowel of *rob* is usually a long /ɑː/.

Doubled Consonant Letters

Again, let us start this section with an exercise, your answers to which will guide the discussion.

Exercise

The following words do not exist in English. But if they did exist, how would they be pronounced?

blunnish	*quiggen*	*spedder*
buny	*rotish*	*swibes*
fammy	*sheggle*	*thritted*
fruded	*skable*	*tropers*
pladded	*snoppy*	*wabing*

Answers are in Appendix 4, but you could continue to the following paragraph.

A further phenomenon associated with pairs like *mat* and *mate* relates to the spelling when suffixes or other syllables are added that start with a vowel sound (*-ing, -ed, -en, -er, -est, -y, -ish*). A schoolboy howler goes, "In olden days, people lived in small huts and there was rough mating on the floor." That is, *mat* becomes *matting*, while *mate* becomes *mating*. That is, for the short vowel word without magic *e* (*mat*), the final consonant letter is doubled (*matting*). On the other hand, for the long/diphthong vowel word with magic *e* (*mate*), the *e* is dropped and the final consonant is not doubled (*mating*). The same is true for examples like *better* vs *Peter; pinning* vs *pining; poppy* vs *ropy; cutter* vs *cuter*. This accounts for the answers to the previous exercise.

Examples and Exceptions

So far, so good. Table 13.3, and the answers to the exercise, show that this is the underlying rule. However, as with many English spelling rules, it has many exceptions. These lead Bell (2001) to the following conclusion.

> Consonant doubling is the most difficult aspect of English spelling. The highest single category of errors committed by students in examinations or spelling tests is caused by uncertainty about consonant doubling, either omitting them or inserting them where none is required. When to double or not to double consonants requires more learning than any other aspect of English spelling, and is never completely mastered by most people.
>
> (Bell, 2001, p. 4)

We have already used as illustrations various English words that are problematic because of doubled letters (*accommodation, necessary*), and it is easy to think of others (*millionaire, millennium, parallel*).

Table 13.3 The spelling of magic *e* and non-magic *e* examples with suffixes in Modern English

Without magic e			With magic e		
Word	Vowel sound (BrE)	Spelling of -ing form	Word	Vowel sound (BrE)	Spelling of -ing form
mat	/æ/	matting	mate	/eɪ/	mating
bet	/e/	betting	mete	/iː/	meting
hit	/ɪ/	hitting	bite	/aɪ/	biting
rob	/ɒ/	robbing	robe	/oʊ/	robing
hug	/ʌ/	hugging	fuse	/(j)uː/	fusing

It is also important to emphasize that we are talking about doubled consonant letters; that is, words that have two identical letters in the spelling but only one sound in the pronunciation. We are not talking about words with two letters representing two sounds. For instance, in compounds, the first element may end in a consonant and the second begin with the same consonant, e.g. *lamppost* /læmppoʊst/. There are two /p/s in the middle, and they are usually pronounced as one double-length articulation. This differs from a single-morpheme word like *lampoon*, which has only one *p* letter and one /p/ sound (/læmpuːn/). Similar examples are *bombmaker* vs *pomade, penknife* vs *Pennine, backcomb* vs *Jacko*. The same is true of words with prefixes and suffixes, e.g. *unnerve* vs *unearth, disservice* vs *discern, drunkenness* vs *governess*.

Word-final Doubling

The historical picture in a nutshell is as follows.

> . . . originally in English and probably at one stage in French, there was a distinction between short and long consonants. For example, in early Middle English *sune* "son" was distinct from *sunne* "sun". When the following consonant was long or doubled, the vowel sound before it was – or became – short, and quite often when the consonant was short or single, the vowel sound before it was – or became – long.
>
> (Oxford Dictionaries, n.d.)

That is, the length of the consonant affected the length of the preceding vowel, so that together they remained a similar length. However, this distinction between long and short final consonant sounds disappeared in Middle English, and a doubled consonant letter became a convenient way of showing that the preceding vowel was short. Coupled with the GVS that followed, the eventual outcome was magic *e* and doubled consonant letters, as in *mate, mating, mat,* and *matting*.

Table 13.4 Spellings of final /s/ and /z/

Consonant sound	After vowel	Spelling pattern	Examples	Exceptions
/s/	short	-ss	*mess, kiss*	*bus, gas*
	long	-ce	(French) *piece, price*	*lease, cease*
			(Not French) *twice, fleece*	
/z/	long	-s or -se	*raise, ease*	*freeze, booze*

Table 13.5 Word-final doubled consonant letters

Consonant letter	Examples	Exceptions
z	*jazz*	*quiz*
f	*puff, off*	*if, chef*
k	*neck, sick* (where *ck* counts as doubled *k*)	*tic, sac*
l	*still, bell*	*gel*, -*all* words (*ball, call,* etc.)

English regularly makes nouns plural by adding an -*s* ending. Originally, this was only pronounced /s/ but in early Modern English became /z/. So now, both /s/ and /z/ could occur between vowels and at the ends of words, and for the plural ending, the *s* letter was no indication of whether the preceding vowel was long or short. A doubled -*ss* came to be used to represent /s/ after a short vowel (e.g. *mess*), with -*s* or -*se* representing /z/ after a long vowel (e.g. *raise*). For final /s/ after a long vowel, the French pattern -*ce* was used, both for words from French (e.g. *piece*) and for words with no French connection (e.g. *twice*). However, there is still irregularity and unpredictability here (Table 13.4).

Most consonant letters are single at the end of a word, regardless of whether they follow a long or short vowel, e.g. *rid, read; gem, gleam; dip, deep*. However, four consonant letters double after short vowels in stressed syllables (Table 13.5).

In fact, there are very few words exemplifying the -*zz* pattern, and they all have an informal, slang, perhaps onomatopoeic, feel to them: *buzz, fizz, fuzz, pizazz, razzmatazz*. One example can be spelled both ways: *whiz/whizz*.

Another curious exception is the name of the American cartoonist Bil Keane (born William, 1922–2011), famous for *The Family Circus*. As he explained, "I didn't always spell my name *Bil*. My parents named me *Bill*, but when I started drawing cartoons on the wall, they knocked the 'L' out of me." His spurious explanation is a play on the word *hell*.

Examples that are abbreviations such as *croc*(*odile*), *choc*(*olate*) do not double their final consonant, but have the same spelling as in the full form.

Word-medial Doubling

In word-medial position, many words are counterexamples to the rule that a stressed short vowel is followed by a doubled consonant letter, before

Table 13.6 Non-doubling of consonant letters in GVS examples

Long vowel or diphthong post-GVS example	*Short vowel post-GVS example*	*If it followed the consonant doubling rule, it would be spelled . . .*
shade	shadow	shaddow
hilarious	hilarity	hilarrity
serene	serenity	serennity
extreme	extremity	extremmity
crime	criminal	crimminal
define	definitive	definnitive
holy	holiday	holliday
tone	tonic	tonnic

another vowel. Some of these relate to the effect of the GVS. As a result of the GVS, short vowel sounds did not change. However, long versions of the same vowel sounds changed, becoming higher vowels or diphthongs. From the point of view of spelling, the important point is that the spelling had been standardized by the printing press, and did not change despite the change in vowel sounds. In Modern English, we thus have short vowels on the one hand, and long vowels or diphthongs with different sounds, both being represented by the same letter. Similarly, the consonant letter following this vowel sound did not change, by doubling after the short vowel. Examples in Table 13.6 make the point.

Further Exceptions

There are other words that do not follow the consonant letter doubling rule, for no good reason.

In the next chapter, we shall see that Dr. Samuel Johnson, in his pioneering dictionary of 1755, had to decide which spellings of words to use and implicitly sanction. He was influenced by the Latin spellings of English words that had come originally from Latin, ignoring the consonant letter doubling rule, e.g. *copy*. He also used double consonant letters for words of Latin origin containing an initial prefix, e.g. *apply* from *adplicare*.

In the next chapter, we shall also see that words with unstressed final syllables ending in *-l* double the *l* before endings starting with a vowel consonant in BrE, but have a single *l* in American English, e.g. *cancelled* (BrE), *canceled* (AmE).

That still leaves a large number of words (397, according to Bell, 2004) that have the pattern of (i) a short vowel sound spelled with a single letter, (ii) a consonant letter, and (iii) a following vowel letter, that do not follow the rule of doubling the consonant letter. Some examples are given in Table 13.7.

Table 13.7 Exceptions to the consonant letter doubling rule (adapted from Bell, 2001, 2004)

Example	If it followed the rule, it would be spelled . . .	Then it would resemble the regular . . .
agony	aggony	maggot
body	boddy	shoddy
galaxy	gallaxy	gallery
heron	herron	herring
lateral	latteral	latter
leper	lepper	pepper
limit	limmit	simmer
manor	mannor	manner
melon	mellon	mellow
parish	parrish	parrot
planet	plannet	planner
profit	proffit	offer
proper	propper	popper
radish	raddish	daddy
robin	robbin	bobbin
study	studdy	muddy
very	verry	merry
wizard	wizzard	blizzard

Summary

- Magic *e* is an example of an auxiliary letter. Its effect is to "make the vowel say its name."
- The doubling of consonant letters is connected to the phenomenon of magic *e*.
- The consonant doubling rule is that where short vowel sounds are followed by a consonant letter and a vowel letter, the consonant letter is doubled.
- There are exceptions to this rule. Nevertheless, the above is the rule, as shown by usual pronunciations of non-words.

Exercises

If you are a teacher, look at the last class set of essays you marked. How many of the spelling mistakes are related to the doubling of consonant letters?

Further Reading

The explanation given here of types of silent letters, including magic *e*, is from Carney (1994). The problem of doubled consonant letters is discussed in Bell (2001, 2004), which contain appendices with lists of examples and exceptions.

References

Bell, M. (2001). *Types and magnitude of English spelling problems and their significance for reform.* English Spelling Society, Personal View #13. Retrieved from spelling society.org/uploaded_views/pv13bell-personal-view-1419714516.pdf

Bell, M. (2004). *Understanding English spelling.* Cambridge, UK: Pegasus Educational.

Carney, E. (1994). *A survey of English spelling.* London, UK: Routledge.

KidsTV123 (n.d.). *The "Magic e" song.* Retrieved from www.youtube.com/watch?v=bZhl6YcrxZQ&list=RDbZhl6YcrxZQ#t=0

Lehrer, T. (1971). *Silent e.* Retrieved from www.youtube.com/watch?v=91BQqd NOUxs

Oxford Dictionaries (n.d.). *Why do some words end in double consonants?* Retrieved from en.oxforddictionaries.com/explore/why-do-some-words-end-in-double-consonants

14 Spelling of Unstressed Vowels

Learning Objectives

At the end of this chapter, readers will be able to:

- explain the occurrence of unstressed vowels, especially /ə/, in speech
- list some guidelines for dealing with frequently confused spellings involving unstressed vowels.

Stress in Spoken English

Before we can start discussing the representation of unstressed vowels in spelling, we need to briefly explain the function of stress in English pronunciation (Brown, 2014, ch. 19).

English words may be composed of only one syllable (e.g. *white, car, drive*), two syllables (e.g. *teacher, student, exam, today*), three syllables (e.g. *register, monitor, assignment, computer, absentee*), four syllables (e.g. *exercises*), five syllables (*vocabulary*), and so on. If words have only one syllable, and the word is stressed, then clearly that syllable is stressed (e.g. *WHITE*). If words have more than one syllable, then one of those syllables is usually stressed, and the others unstressed (e.g. *TEACHer, toDAY, REgister, asSIGNment, absenTEE*). In some words of English, the only difference in the pronunciation is the placement of stress, all the consonant and vowel sounds remaining the same, for example *insight* (*INsight*) versus *incite* (*inCITE*), *an import* (*IMport*) versus *to import* (*imPORT*).

The placement of stress within the word is in many cases predictable but, in many other cases, is not. Roach (2009, p. 76) states that "in order to decide on stress placement, it is necessary to make use of some or all of the following information:

(i) Whether the word is morphologically simple, or whether it is complex as a result either of containing one or more affixes (that is, prefixes and suffixes) or of being a compound word.
(ii) What the grammatical category of the word is (noun, verb, adjective, etc.).

(iii) How many syllables the word has.
(iv) What the phonological structure of those syllables is."

These rules are obviously more complex than is desired by the average English language learner. There are also counterexamples to most of these rules.

Vice versa, is it possible to predict, from the spelling of words, where the stress falls? Dickerson (e.g. 1978, 1987, 1989, 2013) provides rules for predicting from (American) English spelling the placement of stress within words; again, the rules are quite complex.

Whether syllables within multisyllable words are perceived as stressed is related to four factors:

- Stressed syllables are usually louder than unstressed ones.
- Stressed syllables are usually longer than they would be if they were unstressed.
- Stressed syllables are usually pronounced on a different pitch (usually a higher one) than surrounding syllables.
- Stressed syllables are never weak syllables, but have a full quality. Weak syllables are those that contain /ə/ (known as schwa) or /i, u/. The vowel /ɪ/ is also very common in unstressed syllables (e.g. *disCUSS*), but may also occur in stressed syllables (e.g. *DISC*).

It is the final point that is the most relevant for spelling. Schwa only occurs in unstressed syllables, where it is very common and, as a result, it is the commonest vowel in connected spoken English. However, schwa has no regular spelling correspondence. The following list of words all in /ə/ (with a following /r/ in rhotic accents such as AmE, and Scottish and Irish English), but the schwa may be represented by any vowel letter.

beggar, teacher, Yorkshire, doctor, murmur, martyr

It is therefore no surprise that spelling mistakes such as *calender* for *calendar* are made, both by native-speaking children, and by learners. In some cases, the correct letter in the spelling is obvious from morphologically-related words (see Chapter 22); for instance, a learner who is unsure whether it is *accidant* or *accident* need only think of the adjective *accidental*, with a stressed /e/ vowel in the third syllable that must be spelled *e*. They thus arrive at the corresponding correct spelling with *e* for the noun *accident*.

The remainder of this chapter looks at four similar instances of unstressed vowels, that affect a large number of words.

-er *vs* -or

This ending usually shows a person or thing that does an action; for example, a teacher is someone who teaches. Regardless of the spelling, it is pronounced /ə(r)/. There are no rules about whether it is spelled *-er* or *-or*. However, one can say that the *-er* ending is much more common, and the more productive, in that new words always take it, e.g. *blogger*.

Since *-er* is the more common of the two spellings, Oxford Dictionaries (2017a) gives a list of words with *-or*.

There is a third, even less common, possibility: *-ar*. There are a handful of such nouns, e.g. *beggar, burglar, liar*.

Occasionally, words can be spelled either way, e.g. *convener / convenor*.

-ary *vs* -ery *and* -ory

A similar problem occurs in words such as *dictionary, battery*, and *preparatory*. How can a learner remember the vowel letter in the ending? If the learner has American English (AmE) as the reference accent, then there may be no problem in many cases: *-ary* words are often pronounced with final /eri/, *-ery* words with /əri/, and *-ory* words with /ɔːri/. However, in British English (BrE), weakening of this unstressed syllable takes place, and it is pronounced as schwa, or elided altogether; for instance, *battery* is /bætəri/ (three syllables) or /bætri/ (two).

Oxford Dictionaries (2017b) gives some rules (in the sense of generalizations that hold in many, but usually not all, cases:

- If the stem is not an English word, the ending will often be spelled *-ary*, e.g. *vocabulary*.
- If the stem is an English word, the ending will often be spelled *-ery*, e.g. *trickery*.
- Words ending in *-ery* are often related to words ending in *-er* or *-e*, e.g. *shivery, bravery*.
- Words ending in *-ory* are often related to words ending in *-or*, or nouns ending in *-ion*, e.g. *contributory, introductory*.

As is often the case with English spelling, these are generalizations, but have exceptions, e.g. *wintry*. Some pronunciations can be spelled either way, such as *stationary / stationery*. In BrE pronunciation, these pairs of words pose a problem, in that they are homophones (see Chapter 20).

-able *vs* -ible

Exercise

In order to put you in the same position as learners, try this exercise. Is the missing letter in each word *a* or *i*?

accept_ble

aud_ble

avail_ble

break_ble

comfort_ble

ed_ble

feas_ble

gull_ble

horr_ble

measur_ble

navig_ble

neglig_ble

permiss_ble

plaus_ble

practic_ble

The answers are given at the end of this chapter. But again, let us ask the question, "How confident are you that you have them all correct?"

Notice that the meaning is usually the same: "that can be [verb]ed." Thus *acceptable* means "that can be accepted." However, there are some *-able/-ible* adjectives where the meaning is more one of suitability, deserving, or leading to something. Thus, a *readable* book is one that is easy or enjoyable to read, rather than one that can be read; that is *legible*. A *lovable* or *likeable* person is one who is easy to like, or deserving love. A *regrettable* event is one that gives rise to regret.

Also notice that the rules already outlined apply here, motivated by the fact that the *-able/-ible* ending starts with a vowel letter and vowel sound. Firstly, if the syllable before the ending is stressed, and contains a short vowel sound followed by a final consonant sound, the letter representing the final consonant sound is doubled, e.g. *regret, regrettable*. Secondly, if the verb to which the ending is added, ends in an *e* letter, this is dropped before adding the suffix, e.g. *advise, advisable*. Thirdly, since the letters *c* and *g* before *e, i,* and *y* are usually pronounced "soft," i.e. /s, dʒ/, an *e* needs to be retained before the ending in order to avoid implications of a "hard" *c* or *g*, e.g. *notice, noticeable* (not *noticable*); *manage, manageable* (not *managable*). Fourthly, for verbs ending in a consonant letter followed by *y*, the *y* changes to *i* before adding the *-able* suffix, e.g. *rely, reliable*.

So, why is there this difference between *-able* and *-ible*? The answer, as is often the case in English, is to do with etymology. The *-able* suffix (e.g. *measurable*) came into English from French (*measurable*) and ultimately from Latin (*mensurabilis*). Most *-ible* words (e.g. *audible*), on the other hand, came into English directly from Latin (*audibilis*). Needless to say, this observation is of little use to the average English language learner, who will not know where words came from.

In deciding whether a word has -*able* or -*ible*, the following rules may be helpful. As with many other language rules, they are guidelines, with some exceptions.

- Numerically, the -*able* suffix is much more common than the -*ible*. Oxford Dictionaries (2012) reports that "our online dictionary of current English has around 180 adjectives ending in -*ible*, compared with over 1,000 that end in -*able*." So, if in doubt, plump for -*able*.
- If the stem (the part of the word to the left of the blank in the previous exercise) is a word in itself, then the ending is usually -*able*, e.g. *depend, dependable*. If it is not a word in itself, the ending is more likely to be -*ible*, e.g. *compatible, invincible* (*compat, invince* are not words).
- The -*able* suffix is productive, in that it (and not -*ible*) is added to make new words, e.g. *blog, bloggable* (not *bloggible*).
- Some -*able* adjectives are formed from verbs ending in unstressed -*ate*, by dropping the -*ate*, e.g. *communicate, communicable; educate, educable*.

As was forewarned above, all these rules are probabilistic, and have exceptions. There are -*able* words where the stem is not a complete word, e.g. *capable, durable*. Vice versa, some -*ible* words have complete stems, e.g. *reverse, reversible; suggest, suggestible*. There are -*able* words where the unstressed -*ate* of the stem has not been dropped, e.g. *palatable*. There are stems ending in *e* where it is not dropped before adding the suffix (or at best this is an alternative), e.g. *saleable, sizeable*. There are some words where both -*able* and -*ible* are possible, e.g. *collectable/collectible; contractable/contractible*.

All in all, as with many spelling rules about English, the rule is complex, probably too complex for most learners to learn, and there are exceptions.

Before leaving the topic of -*able* and -*ible*, it should be pointed out that there are a handful of comparable words that end in -*uble*, e.g. *soluble* (and related forms *dissoluble, resoluble*) and *voluble*. These come from Latin verbs *solvere* and *volvere*, which had related forms with *u* (*solubilis, volubilis*).

-ance *vs* -ence

The rules for predicting the spelling of nouns ending in -*ance* (e.g. *appliance, clearance, variance*) and -*ence* (e.g. *competence, experience, influence*) are similar to those above for -*able* versus -*ible*. The rules also apply to the related -*ant* versus -*ent*, and -*ancy* versus -*ency* endings.

- If the stem ends in -*y*, -*ure*, or -*ear*, then it is -*ance*, e.g. *vary, variance; assure, assurance; appear, appearance*.
- If the noun comes from a verb which ends in -*ate*, then the ending is -*ance*, e.g. *dominate, dominance*.

- If the ending is preceded by a "hard" *c* or *g* (/k, g/), then the ending must be *-ance*, e.g. *significance; elegance*.
- If the ending is preceded by a "soft" *c* or *g* (/s, dʒ/), then the ending must be *-ence*, e.g. *innocence, intelligence*.
- If the verb ends in *-er* or *-ere*, then the ending is *-ence*, e.g. *prefer, preference; interfere, interference*.
- If the ending is preceded by *-cid-, -fid-, -sid-*, or *-vid-*, the ending is *-ence*, e.g. *coincidence, confidence, residence, evidence*.

Again, there are exceptions, e.g. *vengeance* (not *vengence*), and pairs that are difficult to explain, e.g. *clearance, Clarence*.

The reason for this situation is again historical, and related to the fact that English has not consistently regularized borrowings.

> As Old French evolved from Latin, [*-ance* and *-ence*] were leveled to *-ance*, but later French borrowings from Latin (some of them subsequently passed to English) used the appropriate Latin form of the ending, as did words borrowed by English directly from Latin (*diligence, absence*).
> (Online Etymological Dictionary, n.d.)

Since these rules are not intuitive, quite complex, and not without counterexamples, it is not surprising that misspellings are produced. That is, words like *confidence* may be misspelled *confidance*. One common example of this, with both native and non-native speakers, is the word *dependent*. As an adjective, it is always *dependent*, with *-ent*, as in *a dependent clause*. However, as a noun, referring to people like your children, it is spelled *dependant* in BrE, and either *dependant* or *dependent* in AmE, for no good reason. Even worse, the negative of this, *independent*, is spelled this way in both varieties regardless of whether it is a noun or adjective: *an independent school; he stood as an independent*. This means that, for those speakers who spell the noun *dependant*, they must remember that the opposite is not spelled the same way. However, as Oxford Dictionaries note:

> the Oxford English Corpus shows that *independent* is misspelled as *independant* 737 times. Although this only represents 0.3% of the total occurrences of the word, what is significant is that this error appears in many newspapers (such as *The Guardian*) and specialist journals (e.g. *American Zoologist*), which have been edited and proofread.
> (Oxford Dictionaries, 2018)

Conclusion

The different spellings of unstressed vowels often follow no hard-and-fast rules. The motivation for the rules in Modern English is not clear, apart from a desire to preserve the historical origins of the word, often dating back as far as Latin. Unstressed vowels are a common source of misspellings.

Some of these can be resolved by looking at morphologically-related words where the vowel in question is not unstressed; for instance, someone hesitating between *confidance* and *confidence* need only think of the adjective *confidential*, where the vowel in the third syllable is stressed, and clearly spelled with *e* (see Chapter 22).

Answers

-able	*-ible*
acceptable	*audible*
available	*edible*
breakable	*feasible*
comfortable	*gullible*
measurable	*horrible*
navigable	*negligible*
practicable	*permissible*
	plausible

Summary

- Stress is an integral part of the English pronunciation system.
- Unstressed syllables weaken, typically by changing their vowels to schwa.
- There is no regular spelling for schwa and, as a result, misspellings occur.

Exercise

We have seen that the regular way of forming an adjective meaning "that can be [verb]ed" is to add *-able/-ible* to the verb, sometimes with slight changes to the spelling of the verb stem. One way linguists test this is to create new adjectives. The blanks in the following sentences can be filled with *-able/-ible* adjectives. However, you may not find them in any particular dictionary because (i) they are formed by regular processes, (ii) they are technical (often new, computer terms), and (iii) they are rarely, if ever, used. Give the spelling of the missing adjectives.

1   *A computer system that has poor security and can be easily hacked is h...........*
2   *A surface that can be painted is p...........*
3   *A DVD that can be burned is b...........*
4   *An aircraft that is fit to be flown is f...........*
5   *A computer program that can be debugged is d...........*

6 *A piece of information that can be found on the internet by googling is g*............
7 *Someone who can be easily enticed is e*............
8 *A vehicle that is small enough to fit into a garage is g*............
9 *An object that can be moved is m*............
10 *Someone who can be easily convinced is c*............

References

Brown, A. (2014). *Pronunciation and phonetics: A practical guide for English language teachers.* New York, NY: Routledge.

Dickerson, W. B. (1978). English orthography: A guide to word stress and vowel quality. *International Review of Applied Linguistics in Language Teaching, 16,* 127–147.

Dickerson, W. B. (1987). Orthography as a pronunciation resource. *World Englishes, 6,* 11–20. Also in A. Brown (Ed., 1991). *Teaching English pronunciation: A book of readings* (pp. 159–172). London, UK: Routledge.

Dickerson, W. B. (1989). *Stress in the speech stream: The rhythm of spoken English.* Urbana, IL: University of Illinois Press.

Dickerson, W. B. (2013). Prediction in pronunciation teaching. In C. A. Chapelle (Ed.), *The encyclopedia of applied linguistics.* (pp. 4638–4645). Hoboken, NJ: Wiley-Blackwell.

Online Etymological Dictionary (n.d.). Retrieved from www.etymonline.com/word/-ance

Oxford Dictionaries (2012). *Do you know your -ibles from your -ables?* Retrieved from blog.oxforddictionaries.com/2012/10/23/ibles-and-ables

Oxford Dictionaries (2017a). *Words ending in -er, -or, and -ar.* Retrieved from en.oxforddictionaries.com/spelling/nouns-ending-in-er-or-and-ar

Oxford Dictionaries (2017b). *Words ending in -ary, -ory, and –ery.* Retrieved from en.oxforddictionaries.com/spelling/words-ending-in-ary-ory-and-ery

Oxford Dictionaries (2018). *Is it -ance or -ence?* Retrieved from blog.oxforddictionaries.com/2013/05/03/ance-ence-suffixes

Roach, P. (2009). *English phonetics and phonology: A practical course* (4th edition). Cambridge, UK: Cambridge University Press.

15 Variation

Learning Objectives

At the end of this chapter, readers will be able to:

- list the main historical events in the development of American English, and of dictionaries
- list major differences between British (BrE) and American (AmE) spelling
- decide whether their own English spelling is influenced more by British or American spelling.

Introduction

Variation in language (pronunciation, grammar, vocabulary, etc., as well as spelling) is a core concept in sociolinguistics, the branch of language study that considers differences caused by social factors. Thus, speakers of a language may use it differently depending on gender (males and females differ in the words and constructions they use), occupation (different occupations use different sets of jargon and other technical vocabulary and expressions), formality (speaking in an interview is different from speaking in a café), in addition to idiosyncratic factors (even siblings do not use the language identically). Also, languages change through time; not only do younger users use modern expressions that older users do not, but over centuries rather than generations, languages change greatly.

In terms of spelling, factors such as gender, occupation, and formality play little part in the variation of spellings. The final factor in the last paragraph (change through time) plays a part; we saw in Chapter 5 that English was spelled differently in Shakespeare's time. However, the greatest influence on variation in Modern English spelling is geographical factors, and only these will be considered in the rest of this chapter.

In Chapter 4, it was shown that English started in England, and gradually spread over the rest of the U.K. As a result of colonialism, it was taken as a native language to the U.S.A. (current population 324 million; Central Intelligence Agency, n.d.), Canada (35 million), Australia (23 million) and New Zealand (4 million), and as a second or foreign language to other countries. It is therefore not surprising that two standards have emerged for English spelling worldwide: British, as the country of origin, and American, as by far the largest country it was exported to. The differences are, however, not great.

History

As has been stated before, English spelling was variable until the 18th century. This variation has led to problems in the modern analysis of old texts. For example, Demmen (2016) describes the problems in using computerized corpus linguistics to analyze the language of Shakespeare, while handling the variation in spelling. The algorithm used:

- drops word-final *e*, e.g. *home* is treated as *hom*
- converts -*ie* word-endings to -*y*, e.g. *hypocrisie* is treated as *hypocrisy*
- swaps *u* for *v* (*knaue* is treated as *knave* and, vice versa, *v* for *u* (*vp* is treated as *up*)
- converts word-initial *i* to *j* (*iustice* is treated as *justice*).

Even then, many words have to be analyzed manually; for instance *deere* could be a variant spelling of *deer* or *dear*.

Most people, when faced with a word they are unsure how to spell, would "look it up in the dictionary." So, the story of the standardization of English spelling is inextricably connected with the story of English dictionaries. Two in particular have contributed to the differences between British and American spelling.

Dr. Samuel Johnson

In 1755 Dr. Samuel Johnson published *A dictionary of the English language*. Although dictionary-like works had been published previously, it is considered the first major dictionary of English and was very influential at the time. It contained over 42,000 entries. Unlike modern dictionaries, Johnson allowed himself some whimsical personal commentaries. For instance:

Lexicographer:	"a writer of dictionaries, a harmless drudge, that busies himself in tracing the original, and detailing the signification of words."
Monsieur:	"a term of reproach for a Frenchman."
Oats:	"a grain which in England is generally given to horses, but in Scotland supports the people."

Naturally, Johnson had to decide on the spelling of the entries, and eliminated most of the variation that had occurred before then. However, his choosing between variants seems to have been one largely of personal taste. Bell (2012) notes three particularly unhelpful decisions:

1   He exempted most Latinate words from English consonant doubling (e.g. *poppy – copy*) thereby ruining the English method for showing short and long vowels (e.g. *copper – cope*). He damaged this even further by using doubling to show the Latin history of some English words, e.g. *apply* instead of *aply*, because it once had the prefix *ad* (*adplicare*).
2   He made many endings and prefixes less regular by changing them to Latin or French patterns (e.g. *importence* → *importance; inclose* → *enclose*).
3   He standardized the use of different spellings for different meanings (e.g. *but/butt*) for 335 words which earlier had just one spelling, or were spelled differently, willy-nilly.

He also saw fit to distinguish between variant spellings.

"Unfortunately he also thought that it would be a shame to lose all the spelling variety which still existed in his day, and so he decided to link several hundred alternative spellings to differences in meaning (*there/ their*), as was already beginning to happen with a few of them."

(Bell, 2012)

Johnson's spellings have been treated as standard in Britain ever since. Many of them were standard at the time. Others, however, seem to have been a matter of personal choice, as he had compiled the dictionary single-handed.

Noah Webster

Seven decades later, in 1828, Noah Webster published his *American dictionary of the English language*. This followed other similar books by Webster, including books on spelling, one of which bore the title *The American spelling book* (1786). Webster's purpose was to produce a work on American English, distinct from British. He was a spelling reformer (see Chapter 29), and preferred spellings that better matched pronunciations and were generally simpler. It is to Webster that Americans owe spellings such as *defense, color, traveler,* and *center*. While these caught on and became standard American spellings, other spellings did not. He proposed replacing the spelling *tongue* with *tung*, and *women* with *wimmen* (a spelling dating to Old English). Many of his proposed spellings were not original, but his choice from among variants current at the time.

Webster's dictionary was not embraced wholeheartedly at first, and it was the acquisition of the copyright to it by George and Charles Merriam in 1843 on Webster's death that led to its popularization. This is the origin of the present-day Merriam-Webster range of dictionaries and reference books.

COBUILD

COBUILD stands for Collins Birmingham University International Language Database, and it is the database part of it that is significant. The COBUILD project was started in 1980 at Birmingham University, U.K., by John Sinclair (see Sinclair, 1987). With the increasing availability of cost-effective computing at that time, a database (corpus) of observed language use was collected. In order to be balanced, it included both spoken and written data, of various genres, in British and American English. Computer programs called concordances then allowed the researchers to observe the patterns in the data.

The major difference between COBUILD and its resulting dictionary (first edition 1987) on the one hand, and previous dictionaries including Johnson's and Webster's on the other, was that the entries in the COBUILD dictionary and the definitions given were based on empirical evidence about the way English speakers used the words. In a nutshell, the COBUILD dictionary was descriptive, describing the way English speakers use the language, whereas previous dictionaries had been largely prescriptive, telling readers how words should be used, based often on little more than the lexicographer's preferences.

One conclusion arising from this corpus linguistics approach was the realization that words are not islands, but often occur in the presence of certain other words. The importance of such collocations had been expressed before, for instance in the writing of J. R. Firth, whose famous saying was "You shall know a word by the company it keeps!" (1957, p. 11). However, computerization allowed collocations to be observed more clearly, and led to the approach to language teaching known as the Lexical Approach (e.g. Lewis, 1993).

The relevance of COBUILD to spelling is that the spellings given in the dictionary were based on those observed in the written part of the corpus. And many of the spellings had variants of various kinds. Some are examples of BrE versus AmE variation, as in *pyjamas* and *pajamas*. Others are not geographically determined, e.g. both *artefact* and *artifact* are given as variant spellings in both AmE and BrE. Sometimes the difference is in word division; COBUILD gives both *eye shadow* (two words) and *eye-shadow* (hyphenated), and *eyeshadow* (one word) is found in other modern dictionaries. Nowadays all dictionaries are based on analysis of a sizeable corpus.

BrE vs AmE Spelling Differences

The differences in spelling between British and American English are not large, and fall into a small number of categories (Table 15.1).

In addition to these productive patterns, there are many individual spelling differences: *annexe/annex; axe/ax; (bank) cheque/check; grey/gray; (road) kerb/curb; mould/mold; plough/plow; (house) storey/story; (car) tyre/tire.* Fuller lists can be found online.

Table 15.1 BrE and AmE spelling differences

Category	British English spelling	American English spelling
Final -re/-er	*calibre, fibre, theatre*	*caliber, fiber, theater*
Final -our/-or	*colour, honour, favour*	*color, honor, favor*
Final -ce/-se	*defence, offence, pretence*	*defense, offense, pretense*
Final -ise/-ize	*organise, realise, recognise*	*organize, realize, recognize*
Final -yse/-yze	*analyse, catalyse, paralyse*	*analyze, catalyze, paralyze*
Final -ogue/-og	*analogue, catalogue, dialogue*	*analog, catalog, dialog*
-ae-/-e-	*anaemia, encyclopaedia, gynaecology*	*anemia, encyclopedia, gynecology*
-oe-/-e-	*diarrhoea, foetus, oesophagus*	*diarrhea, fetus, esophagus*
doubled/single *l* in unstressed syllables	*counsellor, labelled, traveller*	*counselor, labeled, traveler*
single/doubled *l* in stressed syllables	*fulfil, enrol, instalment*	*fulfill, enroll, installment*

While many people think that AmE uses *z* in words like *realize*, and that BrE writers use *s* (*realise*), British dictionaries such as Cobuild, Longman, Oxford, Cambridge, etc. usually give the *z* spelling as the first version. So the situation is not clear-cut. The fact that AmE always uses *z* rather than *s* means that the letter *z* is much more common in AmE, not just in spelling/ typing, but also in games such as *Scrabble* and *Wheel of Fortune*.

Learners often ask whether they should use British or American spellings. There are several possible answers to this question. At the outset, it is worth pointing out that the differences are not great. Also, nowadays the distinction is far less clear-cut than it was. Users of BrE are aware of AmE spellings, and may use some of them, perhaps because of the pervasive nature of American TV, film, and other media. Vice versa, Americans are aware of most British spellings. The context in which the teaching takes place may determine the reference model. In some countries of Asia, AmE is the model, while in others it is BrE.

There is one clear advantage to using American spellings. American spellings are the result of spelling reform, mostly by Noah Webster (as previously mentioned). These reforms were intended to make spelling more regular and, as a result, anyone using American spellings is less likely to make spelling mistakes. For instance, Americans write *defense*, while Brits write *defence*. Neither is right nor wrong; both are standard within their realms of influence. However, both Americans and Brits write *defensive*. Brits do not write *defencive*, and thus have to remember to change the *c* to *s* before adding the ending, something Americans do not need to remember to do. Likewise, Americans write *humor, odor*, while Brits write *humour, odour*. However, both write *humorous, deodorant*, Brits having to remember to drop the (silent and, to Americans, seemingly superfluous) *u* before adding the ending. British misspellings like *humourous, deodourant* result.

(Relatively) Free Variation

It is unusual in English for variant spellings to be almost interchangeable. What normally happens is that over time the two spellings come to represent different senses of the word.

One word where there seems to be nearly free variation is *disc* versus *disk*. This difference is discussed at length in many books, websites etc., but usually with no consensus. Even style guides differ in their verdicts. The etymology does not help, as they are both from Latin *discus* meaning a round, flat object. This is also the origin of both the English word *discus*, the athletic equipment, and *dish*.

Most commentators seem to agree that:

- *Disk* is more common in AmE, while *disc* is more common in BrE
- *Disk* is more common in its computer sense, as in *hard disk*, first produced and spelled with a *k* by IBM. When the word *diskette* was produced, it always had a *k*.
- *Disk* is more commonly used for magnetic media, such as a *floppy disk*, while *disc* is more common for optical media such as a *compact disc* (CD) first produced by Phillips.
- *Disc* is more commonly used for vinyl music records, as in an artist's *discography*.
- *Disc* is more common in medical terminology, e.g. *slipped disc*.

Whether the overlap in use between the two spellings continues, or whether the AmE *disk* supplants *disc*, remains to be seen.

Spelling in Other Dialects

As explained, the two main variants of English spelling worldwide are British and American. There are of course other countries where English is a native language, and the spelling of three of these will be briefly examined here: Australia, New Zealand, and Canada. In particular, the question of whether these varieties follow British or American spelling, or a mixture of the two, will be investigated.

Table 15.2 shows the typical spelling of these three countries, compared with America on the left and Britain on the right. Once again, it needs to be emphasized that these are the trends in those countries, or the predominant variant used. Few of these are 100% hard-and-fast spellings. In particular, the influence of American culture and media leads to American spellings being found in otherwise British environments.

In short, both Australian and New Zealand English overwhelmingly follow British spelling. A curious exception to this pattern is the spelling of the Australian Labor Party. The party was founded in 1901, and its name was spelled *Labour*. However, this was changed in 1921 to *Labor* under the influence of the U.S. labor movement, and a relative popularity of American spellings at that time. The word *labour*, like *colour* etc., is nowadays spelled the British way with *u*.

Table 15.2 Canadian, Australian, and New Zealand spelling

American	Canadian	Australian	New Zealand	British
center	centre	centre	centre	centre
color	colour	colour	colour	colour
defense	defence	defence	defence	defence
realize	realize	realise	realise	realise
analyze	analyze	analyse	analyse	analyse
catalog	catalogue	catalogue	catalogue	catalogue
anemia	anemia	anaemia	anaemia	anaemia
fetus	fetus	foetus	foetus	foetus
traveler	traveller	traveller	traveller	traveller
fulfill	fulfil	fulfil	fulfil	fulfil

Canada, on the other hand, is a mixture of British and American spelling. As Wright (2012) explains.

> As a member of the Commonwealth of Nations (formerly known as the British Commonwealth), Canada owes its 'spelling allegiance' to the British. It's the same in Australia and the English-speaking Caribbean islands. In reality, though, Canadians tend to straddle the fence and use what's convenient.

Naturally, the fact that Canada is a neighbor of the U.S.A. has led to the adoption of some American spelling patterns. This proximity may lead to awkward situations when Americans and Canadians mix.

> Nowhere was it more evident than at a job fair in Toronto several months ago hosted by two healthcare entities from the USA. A client, who is a nurse, heard of the job fair on short notice, and presented her resume formatted for the Canadian market. After reviewing her resume and cover letter, the recruiter told her that her resume had "several spelling errors." Of course, she was taken aback. Some of the "errors" were *centre, cheque, honour, judgement* and *practised*.
>
> (Wright, 2012)

The history of Canada, and in particular its trade relations with other countries, accounts for some of this variation between British and American spelling.

> . . . the British spelling of the word *cheque* probably relates to Canada's once-important ties to British financial institutions. Canada's automobile industry, on the other hand, has been dominated by American firms from its inception, explaining why Canadians use the American spelling of *tire* [BrE *tyre*] . . .
>
> (Wikipedia, n.d.)

In all three countries, a good rule of thumb is to use whatever spellings are recommended by reference books published in the country. In Australia, this includes the *Macquarie dictionary* (2017; n.d.) and the *Style manual: For authors, editors and printers* (Australian Government Department of Finance, 2002); in New Zealand, *The New Zealand Oxford dictionary* (Deverson & Kennedy, Eds., 2005); in Canada, the *Canadian Oxford dictionary* (Barber, Ed., 2005) and Tasko (2006).

A comparison of the spelling of other words in these dialects is given in Wikipedia (n.d.).

Summary

- Languages change through time, including their spelling systems.
- Reference books, such as dictionaries and style guides, have played a part in standardizing spellings.
- The two main spelling systems for English worldwide are British and American. However, the differences between them are small, and do not lead to loss of intelligibility.
- While Australian and New Zealand spelling follows British conventions, Canadian spelling is a mixture of British and American spellings.

Exercises

1 By searching online, discover whether the following English-speaking countries use (predominantly) British or American spelling.
   Barbados, India, Jamaica, South Africa, The Philippines
2 Ask your learners which model of English (British or American) is used for English language teaching in their country, and which spelling is (predominantly) used.
3 Open a book in English. How far do you have to read before you come across a word that shows that the book is in British or American English spelling?

Further Reading

On Johnson and his dictionary, see Johnson (1755, 2009), Boswell, (1791). On Webster and his dictionary, see Webster (1828), Noah Webster House and West Hartford Historical Society (n.d.), Kendall, (2011). On the COBUILD dictionary, see COBUILD (1987), Sinclair (1987). A detailed history of spelling in Canada is given by Dollinger (2010).

References

Australian Government Department of Finance (2002). *Style manual: For authors, editors and printers*. Milton, Queensland, Australia: John Wiley & Sons, Australia.
Barber, K. (Ed., 2005). *Canadian Oxford dictionary* (2nd edition). Don Mills, Ontario: Oxford University Press.

Bell, M. (2012). *History of English spelling.* Retrieved from englishspellingproblems. blogspot.co.nz/2012/12/history-of-english-spelling.html

Boswell, J. (1791). *The life of Samuel Johnson.* (Reprint edited by D. Womersley, 2008). London, UK: Penguin Classics. Original available at www.gutenberg. org/files/1564/1564-h/1564-h.htm

Central Intelligence Agency (n.d.). *The world factbook.* Retrieved from www.cia. gov/library/publications/the-world-factbook

COBUILD (1987). *Collins COBUILD English language dictionary* (1st edition). New York, NY: HarperCollins.

Demmen, J. (2016). *Smoothing out spelling variation.* Retrieved from wp.lancs.ac.uk/ shakespearelang/2016/10/22/smoothing-out-spelling-variation

Deverson T., & Kennedy, G. (Eds., 2005). *The New Zealand Oxford dictionary.* South Melbourne, Australia: Oxford University Press.

Dollinger, S. (2010). New data for an English usage puzzle: The long history of spelling variation in Canadian English and its linguistic implications. 16th International Conference on English Historical Linguistics. Retrieved from www.academia.edu/23083415/_Handout_with_data_New_data_for_an_ English_usage_puzzle_the_long_history_of_spelling_variation_in_Canadian_ English_and_its_linguistic_implications_2010_

Firth, J. R. (1957). *Papers in linguistics 1934–1951.* London, UK: Oxford University Press.

Johnson, S. (1755). *A dictionary of the English language.* Retrieved from johnsons dictionaryonline.com

Johnson, S. (2009). *Samuel Johnson: The major works* (Ed. D. Greene) Oxford, UK: Oxford University Press.

Kendall, J. (2011). *The forgotten founding father: Noah Webster's obsession and the creation of an American culture.* New York, NY: G. P. Putnam's Sons.

Lewis, M. (1993) *The lexical approach.* Hove, UK: Language Teaching Publications.

Macquarie dictionary (2017) (7th edition). Sydney, Australia: Macquarie Dictionary Publishers.

Macquarie dictionary (n.d.). Retrieved from www.macquariedictionary.com.au

Noah Webster House and West Hartford Historical Society (n.d.) *Noah Webster history.* Retrieved from www.noahwebsterhouse.org/discover/noah-webster-history.htm

Sinclair, J. (1987). *Looking up: An account of the COBUILD project in lexical computing.* New York, NY: HarperCollins.

Tasko, P. (Ed., 2006). *The Canadian Press stylebook: A guide for writing and editing* (14th edition). Toronto, Canada: The Canadian Press.

Wikipedia (n.d.). *English spelling comparison chart.* Retrieved from en.wikipedia.org/ wiki/Wikipedia:Manual_of_Style/Spelling#English_spelling_comparison_chart

Wright, D. (2012). *How to differentiate between Canadian and American spelling.* Retrieved from www.daisywright.com/2012/08/07/how-to-differentiate-between-canadian-american-spelling

16 Loanwords

Learning Objectives

At the end of this chapter, readers will be able to:

- recount the main stages in the development of the English language where there have been substantial influences from other languages
- explain how English has been haphazard in the assimilation/regularization of loanwords according to English spelling patterns
- clarify why (i) spelling bees are found in English-speaking countries, but not in others, and (ii) spelling bees contain many loanwords.

Terminology and Definition

When a language takes a word from another language and uses it, it is said to have borrowed the word from the source language. The word is now a loanword. As many writers have pointed out, this is a rather different use of the words *borrowing* and *lending*, from everyday use. If you borrow a screwdriver from your neighbor, they lend it to you, you use it, and then return it, so that you no longer have the screwdriver. However, when a language borrows a word from a lending language, there is no intention of returning it; instead, the loanword becomes part of the borrowing language.

Before discussing the status of loanwords, we need to remind ourselves of the main events in the history of English (see Chapter 4). English is deemed to have begun with Anglo-Saxon Germanic tribes migrating to England from northern Europe around the year 450. Four centuries later, the Vikings invaded from Scandinavia bringing their language called Old Norse. Following the Norman Conquest of 1066, French became the language of the upper echelons of society for the next three centuries. Four centuries after that, the Renaissance brought Latin and Greek words to English. All of this happened more than four centuries ago. So the question we have to ask is, What is the length of time a word has to have been in the language for it no longer to be considered a loanword, but simply a word of the language?

The *Oxford English dictionary* (OED) (n.d.) is the major reference work for finding out when words came into English. Research work on the dictionary started in 1857, and interim parts of the work were published, involving several editors and researchers. However, it was not until 1928 that the first full edition of the dictionary was published in ten volumes. It has been regularly updated ever since (Gilliver, 2016). From the start, it was conceived as an etymological dictionary tracing the historical development of English. Thus, unlike desktop printed ELT dictionaries, or online dictionaries, it states the date of the first recorded use of the word in English and, for words no longer in use, the last date it is recorded as having been used. Of relevance to the present book, the OED also gives spellings that have been used through the centuries, that are different from the modern spelling.

So, can we really call words "loanwords" that were introduced centuries, if not a millennium, ago from German, Norse, French, Latin, Greek, etc., and have been in use in the language for centuries?

What precisely is the definition of "an English word"? A word like *precise* (borrowed into English from French *précis* in the mid-15th century) is thought of by modern-day native speakers as a word of English, whereas *ayatollah* (used in English in the 1970s especially in connection with Ayatollah Khomeini of Iran) seems much more like a foreign word used in English.

The spelling may be an indication of how recently the word was borrowed and how modern speakers of the language view it. Words that have been in the language for a longer time tend to be regularized by having their spelling and/or pronunciation changed in order to conform with native English patterns. An example is the word *snorkel*. This was borrowed in the 1940s from the German *Schnorchel* /ʃnɔrxəl/. This word has been anglicized relatively quickly, and various processes have taken place:

- All German nouns have an initial capital letter. In English, this becomes lowercase.
- In German, *schn-* is a regular initial spelling of the cluster /ʃn/, e.g. *Wiener Schnitzel, Schnaps*. However, this cluster is impermissible in English pronunciation and as a result the spelling *schn-* is also impermissible. So, it is regularized as /sn-/, spelled *sn-*.
- The *ch* represents the German sound /x/, as in *Bach* (the composer's surname; also "stream"). Again, this is not a native English sound, so the nearest native sound is substituted: /k/. Perhaps because a *ch* representing /k/ might give the impression that this is a Greek word (see Chapter 23), the spelling changed to *k*.

An example at the other end of the spectrum – that is, a word that was borrowed a long time ago but has still not been anglicized – is *genre* /ʒɑ:nrə/. This was borrowed in the 18th century from French (and is historically related to *gender*). However, it still strikes English speakers as French, for two reasons. Firstly, native English words do not begin with /ʒ/. Indeed, there are very few other French loanwords like this, e.g. *gendarme*. Secondly, final *-re* representing /rə/ only occurs in French loanwords like *timbre*. In fact, there are a number of words like this of French origin that are spelled with final *-re* in British English, but have been anglicized to *-er* in American English: *calibre, fibre, goitre, litre, louvre, lustre, meagre, metre, mitre, ochre, reconnoitre, sabre, sceptre, sepulchre, sombre, theatre*. *Genre* is one of a small number of words that have not undergone this process, for various reasons:

- In *acre, lucre, massacre, mediocre*, a final *-er* would imply that the *c* represented a /s/ sound ("soft *č*") (*acer, lucer, massacer, mediocer*).
- In *ogre*, a final *-er* would imply that the *g* represented a /dʒ/ sound ("soft *g*") (*oger*).
- In *genre*, a final *-er* would imply an example of magic *e* /dʒi:nə(r)/ (*gener*) like *serener* (see Chapter 13). It would also imply that the /r/ is not pronounced immediately after the /n/. A similar word is (BrE) *macabre*, with pronounced /r/, which can be spelled *macaber* in AmE, and pronounced without an /r/.

In short, whether or not the spelling of the (originally borrowed) word conforms with English spelling patterns is an indication of whether modern speakers consider the word to be foreign and thus a loanword. So expressions like the French *ménage à trois* (with accents on the vowel letters) and German *doppelgänger* (with an umlaut on the *a*) are shown by this not to be fully assimilated loanwords. Similarly, *hoi-polloi* comes from Greek. However, the *i* at the end of each element shows that it has foreign origins. In English, the letters *oi* can only represent /ɔɪ/ when they are followed by a consonant sound/letter, e.g. *coin, boil*. If there is no final consonant sound/letter, the spelling is *oy*, e.g. *coy, boy*. So, if it conformed to English spelling patterns, this would be spelled *hoy-polloy*.

The final point that needs to be made with regard to loanwords borrowed into English is that they often refer to animals, plants, fruit, cuisine, etc. indigenous to the country of the source language. Thus, for example, many food and beverage terms come from the language of the country from which the items come, e.g. Chinese *chop suey*, French *bouillabaisse*, German *pumpernickel*, Hindi *kedgeree*, Italian *macaroni*, Japanese *sushi*, Russian *vodka*, Scandinavian *smorgasbord*. All of these can be considered non-English spellings for one reason or another.

To sum up, English has borrowed many words from many languages over its history. Many of these have been regularized to the spelling system of English, while others have not. In general, English has regularized spellings less often than many other languages do (see the example of Malay in Chapter 30).

A final consideration, in this book on teaching English spelling to learners, is whether learners know much about the history of English and of other languages. The answer is that they probably know very little about this. Therefore, formulating spelling rules in terms of word origins, while historically accurate, may be of little use in the classroom. For instance, *ch* has three main pronunciations:

- /tʃ/ in Anglo-Saxon words, e.g. *church, chicken, teach*
- /ʃ/ in words of French origin, e.g. *chalet, charade, panache*
- /k/ in words of Greek origin, e.g. *chemist, chaos, monarch.*

However, unless learners can identify words with Anglo-Saxon, French, and Greek origins, this rule is useless (see Chapter 23).

Source Languages

According to studies by Finkenstaedt and Wolff (1973) and Williams (1986) cited in Wikipedia (n.d.), the main source languages for loanwords in English are as shown in Table 16.1.

This corroborates what was said earlier, that the bulk of English words came originally from four main sources: Germanic languages, French, Latin, and Greek (a total of 90%). However, the majority of these words were borrowed long ago, and their spellings have been changed to conform to English spelling patterns, such that they are no longer considered foreign loanwords. That leaves only 6% of words that are true loanwords. Finally, 4% of loanwords derive from proper names (of people, places, etc.), e.g. *wellington boots, lesbian.*

There are few major world languages from which English has not borrowed words. Table 16.2 is a small set of examples illustrating the spread of source languages around the world.

The word *bungalow* comes from Hindi/Urdu, where it means a Bengal-style house. It has been borrowed not only by English, but by other languages, often from English, e.g. Malay *bangalo*. The explanation contained in the old joke of a British builder saying, "We were going to build a

Table 16.1 Source languages for English loanwords

Source language	Percentage of modern English vocabulary
Latin	29%
French	29%
Germanic languages (Old/Middle English, Old Norse, Dutch)	26%
Greek	6%
Other languages / unknown	6%
Derived from proper names	4%

Table 16.2 Source languages for English loanwords

Afrikaans: *apartheid*	Australian aboriginal*: *budgerigar*
Arabic: *alcohol*	Bantu*: *chimpanzee*
Cantonese: *lychee*	Malay: *cockatoo*
Czech: *robot*	Mandarin: *gung-ho*
Dutch: *booze*	Norwegian: *ski*
Hawaiian: *ukulele*	Persian: *bazaar*
Hebrew: *jubilee*	Portuguese: *cashew*
Hindi/Urdu: *bungalow*	Russian: *mammoth*
Hokkien: *ketchup*	Serbo-Croatian: *cravat*
Hungarian: *coach*	Spanish: *ranch*
Inuit: *anorak*	Swedish: *ombudsman*
Irish/Scots Gaelic: *galore*	Tagalog (Philippines): *boondocks*
Italian: *diva*	Tamil: *mulligatawny*
Japanese: *emoji*	Turkish: *turquoise*
Korean: *taekwondo*	Welsh: *corgi*

* There are many Australian aboriginal and Bantu languages, and it is often not clear which loanwords come from which of those languages.

two-storey house, but I think one storey's enough. So, just bung a low roof on it." (*bung* is British slang for "throw carelessly") is indicative of the folk etymology that sometimes occurs with words; that is, speakers, who often have little knowledge of history and foreign languages, attribute origins to words, some of them plausible, many of them implausible.

It is not always possible, even for the OED with its facilities for extensive research, to discover the historical origin of many English words, and it often has to resort to labelling them of "uncertain" origin.

A Borrower or a Lender?

While English has borrowed many words from many languages because of contact through trade, colonialization, etc., the present-day situation is perhaps one of lending rather than borrowing.

> Although English is now borrowing from other languages with a world-wide range, the number of new borrowed words finding their way into the shared international vocabulary is on a long downward trend. One big reason for this is the success of English as an international language of science, scholarship, business, and many other fields.
>
> (Durkin, 2014)

That is, many languages are nowadays borrowing words from English, often changing the spelling to conform to the system of the borrowing language.

Postscript: The Scripps National Spelling Bee and Loanwords

The Scripps National Spelling Bee is a competition held annually since 1925 (except during some of World War II) and organized by the E. W. Scripps Company, an American broadcaster. Participants must be 14-years-old or younger, and winners cannot enter subsequent years' competitions. While predominantly an American competition, it has in recent years admitted contestants from overseas countries. Since 1994, ESPN has televised the final rounds.

Two points are relevant here. Firstly, the existence of a spelling bee is testimony to the fact that the English spelling system is far from regular. Contestants spend hours learning the spelling of words, employing a combination of the strategies described in later chapters of this book. While being able to spell is an important skill, it is worth remembering that the entrants are all 14-years-old or younger. Hours spent memorizing the spelling of words seems like a very stressful and unnecessary way to occupy your childhood.

Secondly, while being able to spell is an important skill, it is revealing to look at the words that the children are learning. In the early days of the competition, the final words spelled correctly by the winners seem easy and everyday enough: *gladiolus* (1925), *luxuriance* (1927), *knack* (1932), *torsion* (1933), *intelligible* (1935), *therapy* (1940), *initials* (1941). However, the spelling bee has become far more competitive, and the words that competitors have to master have become far more complex and far less everyday. Nowadays there is an online study booklet (Merriam-Webster, n.d.) containing some 1,150 words. While many of these are established English words with complex spellings, many of them are relatively recent loanwords. The study booklet divides them according to their language of origin, including Arabic, Asian languages, Slavic languages, Japanese, Italian, and Spanish.

To illustrate how difficult, and how peripherally English, some of the winning words are, try the following exercise.

Exercise

Here are some winning words from recent Scripps champions. Give:

- the meaning of the word
- the language that it was borrowed from
- the last time you used the word
- an honest estimation of whether you would have been able to spell it correctly.

(If you have never heard the word before – despite quite possibly being a teacher of English – ignore these questions!)

koinonia (2018)

marocain (2017)

gesellschaft (2016)

nunatak (2015)

scherenschnitte (2014)

stichomythia (2014)

feuilleton (2013)

knaidel (2013)

guetapens (2012)

cymotrichous (2011)

stromuhr (2010)

appoggiatura (2005)

autochthonous (2004)

succedaneum (2001)

These are all difficult words because they are loanwords, and their spelling has not been changed from the original language, apart from changing them to Roman alphabet, where the original language (e.g. Greek) does not use it.

To conclude with the main point, languages other than English do not have spelling bees, because their spelling systems are more regular, and contestants would seldom or never make spelling mistakes.

Summary

- It is often difficult to state the difference between words originally borrowed into a language but nowadays considered proper words of the language, and loanwords.
- One criterion is spelling. If the word conforms to English spelling patterns, it is more likely to be considered a proper word of the language.
- Words that were borrowed from Germanic languages, French, Latin, and Greek over 400 years ago can hardly still be considered loanwords in Modern English.
- English no longer borrows so many words from other languages. The trend is in the opposite direction, with other languages borrowing from English.

Exercises

1   The spelling *ca-* is a regular English way of beginning words; *ka-* is not. Words starting *ka-* are therefore shown by this to be of foreign origin. Thus *cat, cage,* and *career* are regular English spellings, while *kat, kage,* and *kareer* look foreign. The following are all the words beginning *ka-* in dictionaries. For each one, make an educated guess at the language (or other source) from which they came into English. (In fact, one of them is not a loanword, but has been in English since Old English times. Can you guess which one?)

Word	Meaning
kabob	an American spelling of *kebab*: small pieces of meat and vegetables cooked on a stick
kaffeeklatch	(AmE) an informal social situation where people drink coffee and talk
kaffir	(South African English) an offensive word for a black African, used only by white people
kaftan	another spelling of *caftan*: a long loose piece of clothing worn in the Middle East
kagoul	another spelling of *kagoule, cagoule*: windbreaker
Kalashnikov	a type of rifle that can fire very quickly
kale	a dark green cabbage
kaleidoscope	a pattern that is always changing
kamikaze	a pilot who deliberately crashes his plane on enemy camps, ships, etc., knowing he will be killed
kanga	a woman's dress from Africa
kangaroo	an Australian animal
kaolin	a type of white clay used for making cups, etc.
kapok	a very light material like cotton
kaput	broken
karaoke	the activity of singing to recorded music for entertainment
karat	an American spelling of *carat*: a measurement that shows how pure gold is
karate	a style of fighting from the Far East, in which you kick and hit with your hands
karma	the force that is produced by the things you do in your life and that will influence you in the future, according to the Hindu and Buddhist religions
katydid	(AmE) a type of large grasshopper that makes a noise like the sound of the words *Katy did*
kayak	a type of light canoe
kazoo	a simple musical instrument that you play by holding it to your lips and making sounds into it

2   Similarly, native English words do not end in *-i*. We have already encountered counterexamples: *corgi, emoji, hoi-polloi, macaroni, ski, sushi.* So, words ending in *-i* are marked as being original loanwords. For the following *-i* words, make an educated guess at the language (or other source) from which they came into English.

Word	Meaning
alibi	defense of being somewhere else at the time of a crime
basmati	long-grain rice
bikini	a female two-piece bathing suit
borzoi	a breed of dog
broccoli	a type of vegetable
chai	tea
chilli	a spicy capsicum
deli	a shop, especially one selling unusual or imported foods
envoi	a postscript
hajji	a Muslim who has gone on a pilgrimage to Mecca
jacuzzi	a whirlpool bath
khaki	a dull yellowish brown
kiwi	a flightless bird
koi	an ornamental carp
lei	a wreath of flowers
mini	small
muesli	a breakfast cereal
Nazi	a person showing racism, brutality
okapi	a giraffe-like animal
pi	the ratio of the circumference of a circle to its diameter
rabbi	a Jewish religious leader
roti	a type of Indian bread
salami	a type of sausage
taxi	a car for hire with driver
wadi	a seasonal watercourse
wasabi	a pungent condiment
yeti	the Abominable Snowman

Further Reading

The *Oxford English dictionary* (n.d.) is the main source of knowledge about the etymology of English words. Free online etymological dictionaries are also available (e.g. *Online etymology dictionary*, n.d.; Oxford University Press, n.d.). A comprehensive list of English loanwords is given by Wikipedia (n.d.).

References

Durkin, P. (3 February 2014). *Does English still borrow words from other languages?* BBC News. Retrieved from www.bbc.com/news/magazine-26014925

Finkenstaedt, T., & Wolff, D. (1973). *Ordered profusion; Studies in dictionaries and the English lexicon.* Heidelberg, Germany: C. Winter.

Gilliver, P. (2016). *The making of the Oxford English dictionary.* Oxford, UK: Oxford University Press.

Merriam-Webster (n.d.). *Spell it!* Retrieved from www.myspellit.com

Online etymology dictionary (n.d.). Retrieved from etymonline.com

Oxford English dictionary (n.d.). Retrieved from www.oed.com

Oxford University Press (n.d.). *Oxford living dictionaries: English.* Retrieved from en.oxforddictionaries.com/?utm_source=od-panel&utm_campaign=en

Wikipedia (n.d.). *Lists of English words by country or language of origin.* Retrieved from en.wikipedia.org/wiki/Lists_of_English_words_by_country_or_language_of_origin

Williams, J. M. (1986). *Origins of the English language: A social and linguistic history* (2nd edition). New York, NY: Free Press.

17 Names of Letters

Learning Objectives

At the end of this chapter, readers will be able to:

- teach the inconsistent naming of English letters, and the difference between names and typical sounds
- explain misspellings that are caused by reliance on letter names.

Introduction

As a competent speaker (reader) of English, the names of the letters of the Roman alphabet, as used for English, will be familiar to you. However, there are several quirky features of these names that may not be so obvious, and which may pose problems for learners.

Let us start with the most basic feature, that is, the names that are given to the 26 letters of the alphabet (/eɪ, biː, siː/ etc.). These are taught to native children at kindergarten, and are one of the first things taught to foreign learners. There are many video versions of The ABC Song on YouTube.

The Pronunciation of Roman Alphabet Letter Names

It may not be apparent just how irregular the English names of the letters are. In some other languages, the names are very regular. For instance, all the letters of the Thai alphabet are referred to as the sound of that letter in syllable-initial position followed by the /ɔː/ vowel. Thus, the /s/ letter is known as /sɔː/. (The situation is in fact more complex than this, as there is more than one /s/ letter, with different tonal implications in this tone language.) In contrast, the letters of the Roman alphabet are referred to in English in various ways. The vowel letters are referred to by vowel sounds, but not necessarily the commonest vowel sound for that letter (see Chapter 13 for further discussion of this phenomenon). Some consonant letters are referred to by the consonant sound followed by the /iː/ sound (b, c, d, g, p, *t, v,* and, for Americans, *z*). Other consonant letters are referred to by the consonant sound(s) preceded by the /e/ vowel (*f, l, m, n, s,* and *x*). The letters *j* and *k* have the consonant sound followed by the /eɪ/ vowel. That leaves a mixed bag of *h, q, r, w, y,* and, for British speakers, *z*.

H has two possible pronunciations, with or without an initial /h/ sound. The pronunciation with /h/ is Irish in origin, but has traveled further afield. The *Longman pronunciation dictionary* (Wells, 2008, p. 360) shows that the pronunciation with /h/ is becoming more common in England (24% of people born after 1982).

W is the most interesting of the remaining letters. A question posed by many learners is "Why is it not called double *v*?," because that is the shape of the modern letter. The answer is historical. When the Roman alphabet was first used to write English (in the 6th century; see Chapter 5), scribes had no letter to represent the /w/ sound of Old English. The Roman alphabet of the time had *u* and *v* letters, but each had its own sound. So they resorted to writing two *u* letters together, that is, *uu,* literally "double *u*." In the following century, this was superseded by the runic letter *wynn.* However, the convention of using double *u* spread to German and some French words, and reappeared in English writing following the Norman Conquest. Double *u* came to be regarded as a letter of the alphabet and *wynn* died out around 1300. Many early printers of English originated from Europe, and used continental printing conventions, often using *vv* for *w*. However, the name "double *u*" had become established in English.

W is the only letter (along with the aitch pronunciation of *H*) the pronunciation of whose name does not contain a sound that the letter can represent. *W* is the only name with more than one syllable, in fact three syllables. This makes it strange as an abbreviation in initials. For example, the prefix *www* is used in many internet addresses. It stands for the World Wide Web (three syllables). However, the name of the abbreviation (double *u,* double *u,* double *u*) is nine syllables long, so hardly an abbreviation. For this reason, the name of *w* is often abbreviated to simply *dub,* thus *dub-dub-dub* (three syllables again). The Volkswagen car brand is often abbreviated to *V-Dub*.

Roman Alphabet Letter Names in Other Languages

English learners from other languages that use the Roman alphabet are at an advantage in that they already use the letters and are used to forming them in handwriting, etc. However, they do not necessarily use the same names for them.

For instance, the first nine letters of the alphabet are pronounced in English as /eɪ, biː, siː, diː, iː, ef, dʒiː, (h)eɪtʃ, aɪ/, but in French as /ɑ, be, se, de, ə, ɛf, ʒe, aʃ, i/. While several are the same or similar, others differ. Three are of special interest. In French, *W* is called /dublə ve/, that is, "double *v*"; this reflects the historical picture just described. *Y* is known as /i gʁɛk/, that is, "Greek *i*"; this dates back to what it was called in Latin, which used this non-native letter in foreign words. Not surprisingly, since France is across the British Channel from England, the French name for *z* follows the British form.

The same pronunciation may represent different letters in different languages. Thus, the pronunciation /i(:)/ represents *E* in English, but *I* in French. This difference between the English and French names for the same letters is part of the plot of the 1951 film *The Lavender Hill mob*. The main characters (played by Alec Guinness and Stanley Holloway) melt the gold stolen in a robbery, and smuggle it to Paris in the form of miniature Eiffel Towers. They instruct the lady running the souvenir kiosk in Paris to hold back the batch marked /ɑː/ for "R(eserve)." However, for the French lady, /ɑː/ is the letter *A*, and she blithely sells the solid gold souvenirs to a tour group of British schoolgirls.

The Spelling of Roman Alphabet Letter Names

All the discussion so far has concerned the pronunciation of Roman letter names. How are those names spelled? The normal answer is that the names are not spelled as such, but written as (often uppercase) letters, e.g. *How many Ls are there in "parallel"?*, *I heard it on the BBC*. Once again, it should be remembered that the distinction between capital and lowercase letters is a feature of the Roman alphabet used for English, but not of all other alphabets (Chapter 11). There is no standard universally accepted spelling for the pronunciation of the letter names. There are some individual examples. For instance, a *T-shirt* can also be spelled *tee-shirt*, a *DJ* (disc jockey) *deejay*, and an *MC* (master of ceremonies) *emcee*. However, those are isolated examples.

A set of spellings for the English names of Roman alphabet letters has been proposed by Grammarist (n.d.). A further question is then "How are the plurals of those letters spelled?", as in *How many Ls are there in "parallel"?* Spellings proposed by Grammarist (n.d.) include *pee, pees* (for *P*, *P*s), *cue, cues* (*Q*, *Q*s), *ar, ars* (*R*, *R*s), and *ess, esses* (*S*, *S*s). Some suggested plurals look strange; for example, *ues* looks possible (cf. *dues*) but awkward, but is at least better than *us*. It remains to be seen whether these suggested spellings catch on.

Letter Names in Teaching

The names of the 26 letters of the Roman alphabet are among the first things that are taught in early education of native-speaking children. They are the basis of *The ABC Song* ("Now I know my ABC, won't you sing along with me?"). They are a prominent and recurrent feature of *Sesame Street* ("Today's program was brought to you by the letter . . .").

Again, it must be emphasized that children whose language uses the Roman alphabet have to learn both capital and lowercase letters, and thus have twice the task of children from countries that use some other non-Roman alphabets, where there are no capitals.

While the names of the letters may be a frequent feature of teaching the alphabet in the U.S.A., greater emphasis is given in the U.K. to the sounds that the letters typically represent. This difference is shown by the following quotations from teachers (Ellefson, Treiman, & Kessler, 2009).

> I believe kindergartners are developmentally ready to learn both letter names and letter sounds. Younger children should be exposed to letter names but not necessarily sounds. Older children should focus more on sounds.
>
> (American teacher)

> I think that letter sounds for Foundation Stage children [those from reception year, year 1, and year 2], when used at all times, make the learning of reading, spelling and writing as simple as possible and shows rapid results . . . As children develop confidence with their "sounding out" words and learn other blends (about age 6–7) introduction of letter names and the alphabet would hopefully come quite easily.
>
> (British teacher)

Letter Names and Letter Sounds

Many young native-speaking children confuse the names of the 26 letters on the one hand, with the sounds that letters typically represent on the other. This is less likely to happen with letters where the name of the letter starts with the typical sound of the letter (acrophonic), e.g. the name of *b* (/bi:/) starts with the /b/ sound, which is the commonest sound of that letter. Confusion is much more likely to happen with letters where the typical sound is not the first sound of the name (e.g. *x*), or where the name of the letter does not contain a typical sound (e.g. *h, q, r, w, y*). Children in the U.S.A. sometimes suggest that the sound of *m* is /e/ and of *w* is /d/. When given pseudo-words, U.S. children often rely on the first sound of the letter name, e.g. since the name of the letter *y* starts with /w/, they spell *work, warm,* and *word* as *yrk, yrm,* and *yd* (Treiman, 2006).

The confusion of letter names and letter sounds exists in English because the names do not correspond in any regular fashion to the sounds. In a language like Thai, where the names of the letters are regular, this confusion does not occur; the sound of any Thai letter is its name minus the dummy /ɔ:/ vowel.

This confusion may lead to misspellings, where the child has resorted to the name of the letter rather than the typical sound of the letter. For instance, the misspelling *cr* (for *car*) may at first glance look like the omission of the letter *a*; however, the child's reasoning is that *c* represents /k/ and the name of the letter *r* is pronounced /ɑ:(r)/. Similarly, in the misspelling *fl* (for *fell*), *f* represents /f/ and the name of the letter *l* is pronounced /el/.

Such confusion is also common for instances of magic *e* (see Chapter 13). Magic *e* makes the vowel say its name; that is, for example, the effect of adding a final *e* to the word *sham* (/ʃæm/) is to change the vowel to /eɪ/ (*shame*), which corresponds to the name of the letter *a*. Examples of misspellings by children include *tam* (for *tame*) on the reasoning that *t* = /t/, the name of the letter *a* is pronounced /eɪ/, and *m* = /m/.

In informal English, plays on words sometimes rely on the pronunciation of the name of the letter, rather than the typical pronunciation of the letter. For example, people often briefly write *IOU $20* for "I owe you $20." The letter *Q* is often used for the word *queue*, e.g. *Please Q here.* Company and product names sometimes exploit this, e.g. *Toys R Us.* New Zealand's largest internet service provider is *Xtra*.

The Acquisition of Letter Names and Sounds

Several facts are known about the acquisition of letter names and sounds by children (Evans, Bell, Shaw, Moretti, & Page, 2006; Phillips, Piasta, Anthony, Lonigan, & Francis, 2012; Treiman, 2006):

- Knowledge of letter sounds is better for vowel letters than for consonant letters. (There are, of course, far fewer.)
- Knowledge of letter names for consonants with consonant-vowel names (e.g. *b* /bi:/) is better than for those with vowel-consonant names (e.g. *f* /ef/) or names having little correspondence to sounds (e.g. *y*).
- Knowledge of capital letters precedes that of lowercase letters.
- Letters where the lowercase version is simply a small version of the capital (e.g. *c* and *C*) are learned before those where there is a difference of shape (e.g. *d* and *D*).
- Children are more likely to know letters from the beginning of the alphabet (*a, b, c*) than those at the end (*x, y, z*).
- Children seem to be "prewired to attend to initial sounds more closely" (McBride-Chang, 1999, p. 303). In light of this, it is helpful that alphabet books teach letters in initial position in a word, e.g. "*p* as in *pat*" rather than "*p* as in *tap*." The odd letter out in this respect is *x*, which starts very few words in English, and is pronounced /z/ in those words (e.g. *xylophone*). A final example such as "*x* as in *box*" is unavoidable here.
- Children are 1.5 times more likely to know the letters of their own name, especially their first name and especially in initial position (11 times more likely; Justice, Pence, Bowles, & Wiggins, 2006). Thus a child named *Lucy* is likely to be very familiar with *L* and also *u, c*, and *y* to a lesser extent. Parents often put children's names on their bedroom doors, and teachers often put students' names in ECE classrooms. It would seem that the variety of names and initial letters in a class of children is a valuable resource for teaching letters and their names.

Summary

- There is an important difference between the names of the 26 letters of the alphabet and the sounds that they typically represent.
- The names of the letters *h, q, r, w, y* cause the most problems, because they do not relate well to their typical sounds.
- Some misspellings by young children are the result of relying on letter names rather than letter sounds.

Exercises

1   The 26 letters of the Roman alphabet are in a particular, alphabetical order (*a, b, c, d*, etc.). This order is used in dictionaries, indexes, etc. If you know a language that uses a non-Roman alphabet, what is the alphabetical order of its letters?

2   Malay (Chapter 30) and Indonesian are sister languages and both use the Roman alphabet. Online, find out how the letters of the alphabet are pronounced (differently) in these two languages, and explain the difference.

3   Explain the probable cause of the following misspellings.

apresheat (appreciate)	*pa (pay)*
hape (happy)	*pn (pen)*
indd (indeed)	*qt (cute)*
lbo (elbow)	*ski (sky)*
nd (end)	*tm (team)*

Further Reading

The distinction between letter names and letter sounds underlies much of the research of Rebecca Treiman (n.d.).

References

Ellefson, M. R., Treiman, R., & Kessler, B. (2009). Learning to label letters by sounds or names: A comparison of England and the United States. *Journal of Experimental Child Psychology, 102*(3), 323–341. doi: 10.1016/j.jecp.2008.05.008

Evans, M. A., Bell, M., Shaw, D., Moretti S., & Page, J. (2006). Letter names, letter sounds and phonological awareness: an examination of kindergarten children across letters and of letters across children. *Reading and Writing, 19*, 959–989. doi 10.1007/s11145-006-9026-x

Grammarist (n.d.). *Letter names*. Retrieved from grammarist.com/spelling/letter-names

Justice, L. M., Pence, K., Bowles, R. B., & Wiggins, A. (2006). An investigation of four hypotheses concerning the order by which 4-year-old children learn the alphabet letters. *Early Childhood Research Quarterly, 21*, 374–389. doi: 10.1016/j.ecresq.2006.07.010

McBride-Chang, C. (1999). The ABCs of the ABCs: The development of letter-name and letter-sound knowledge. *Merrill-Palmer Quarterly, 45,* 285–308.

Phillips, B. M., Piasta, S. B., Anthony, J. L., Lonigan, C. J., & Francis, D. J. (2012). IRTs of the ABCs: Children's letter name acquisition. *Journal of School Psychology, 50*(4), 461–481. doi: 10.1016/j.jsp.2012.05.002

Treiman, R. (2006). Knowledge about letters as a foundation for reading and spelling. In R. M. Joshi & P. G. Aaron (Eds.), *Handbook of orthography and literacy* (pp. 581–599). Mahwah, NJ: Erlbaum.

Treiman, R. (n.d.). Retrieved from pages.wustl.edu/treiman/publications-0

Wells, J. C. (1990). *Longman pronunciation dictionary* (1st edition; 2nd edition 2000; 3rd edition 2008). Harlow, UK: Pearson Education Ltd.

18 Spelling Pronunciation

Learning Objectives

At the end of this chapter, readers will be able to:

- define spelling pronunciations
- list some historical examples of spelling pronunciations
- list some English words commonly mispronounced by learners because of their irregular spelling.

Introduction

The topic of this chapter is spelling pronunciations; that is, pronunciations that deviate from established standard pronunciations, this deviation being caused by features of the spelling of words. For example, *debt* has no /b/ sound in standard pronunciation, but it has a *b* letter in the spelling. If someone pronounces the word with a /b/ sound, clearly under the influence of the spelling, this is a spelling pronunciation.

As has been emphasized with features of spelling examined previously in this book, it must be stated that spelling pronunciations exist in English because of the lack of a close correspondence between spellings and sounds. Such spelling pronunciations therefore do not exist in languages with more regular spelling systems.

In terms of the dual-path hypothesis of reading (Chapter 3), when readers encounter an unknown word, they naturally resort to the phonological processing path, matching spellings with (probable) sounds. In many cases, they will arrive at the correct pronunciation. In others, they will not, and the resultant pronunciation is a spelling pronunciation. So, a reader unfamiliar with *debt* will make the correct associations *d* = /d/, *e* = /e/, *b* = /b/, and *t* = /t/, and arrive at the incorrect pronunciation /debt/.

Silent Letters Introduced by 16th Century Scholars

We have already seen (Chapter 5) that historical processes are responsible for a number of modern-day spelling features, and they are a major cause of spelling pronunciations. In particular, many words were borrowed into English from French following the Norman Conquest of 1066. For many of them, their spellings were altered around the 16th century by scholars who felt that the spelling of English words should reflect their original etymology, especially the classical languages of Latin and Greek.

The example of *throne* illustrates Greek etymology being represented in spelling. While the word was borrowed into English from Old French *trone*, French having no /θ/ sound, it came into French via Latin from Greek *thronos* 'elevated seat' (Greek has a /θ/ sound). The pronunciation of the word has thus come full circle. In Greek, it had a /θ/ sound. When it was borrowed into French via Latin, it was pronounced with an initial /t/ spelled *t*, because French has no /θ/; its present-day French spelling is *trône*. When it was borrowed into English from French, it was still at first pronounced with an initial /t/. In the 16th century, scholars changed the spelling of the word to *th* to reflect its original Greek etymology. Then, English speakers started pronouncing it with a /θ/ because it was spelled with *th*.

A Latin example is the introduction of syllable-final *l*, sometimes in clusters. For instance, the word *falcon* came into English from French *faucon* with no *l*, which is still the modern French spelling. However, the *l* was added in the spelling in the 15th century because the word originally came into French from Latin *falx, falc-* meaning "sickle," because of the falcon's sickle-shaped wings. When the *l* was introduced in the spelling, English speakers started pronouncing it with an /l/ sound. The same is true of the words in Table 18.1.

A similar spelling pronunciation involving /l/ is *realm*. This came from Old French *reaume*, but the introduced *l* in the spelling was influenced by Old French *reiel* "royal."

These examples show the competing authority given to standard spelling versus standard pronunciation. Commentators on early Modern English, including H. C. Wyld (author of *The universal dictionary of the English language*, 1936) and E. J. Dobson (author of *English pronunciation 1500–1700*, 1957), note that as early as the 17th century there was a trend among intellectuals in England to pronounce as you spell, and this continued among teachers into the 20th century, as reported by H. W. Fowler (author of *A dictionary of modern English usage*, 1926; and, with his brother F. G. Fowler, *The King's English*, 1906).

Table 18.1 English spelling pronunciations involving *l*

Modern English spelling	Old French spelling	Latin spelling
assault	*asaut (noun), assauter (verb)*	*ad-* "to" + *saltare* "to leap"
cauldron	*caudron*	*calidarium* "cooking-pot"
fault	*faute*	*fallita* "shortcoming"
vault	*vaute*	*volta* "bowed, arched"

Anglicization of Borrowed Words

The examples given have all involved words borrowed into English, whose original spelling in English was later altered in order to reflect etymology. Some loanwords are borrowed complete with silent letters.

For example, many words starting with the letter *h* have been borrowed into English from French. In French, they are spelled with an *h*, because they come from Latin, where they were spelled with an *h* letter pronounced as /h/. However, there is no /h/ sound in French. Some of these French loanwords are still pronounced in English without an initial /h/ sound, but with *h* in the spelling: *heir, honest, honor, hour*. For others, the *h* letter is pronounced as an /h/ sound, i.e. a spelling pronunciation, historically speaking: *habit, history, hospital*. For the word *herb*, there is geographical variation; Americans do not pronounce the /h/, British speakers do.

This has implications for the occurrence of *a* or *an* as the indefinite article before the word. Everyone says *an hour* and *a hospital*. Americans say *an herb*, while British speakers say *a herb*. For some words like *hotel, historic*, where the stress falls on the second syllable, some people do not pronounce an /h/ sound (thus *an hotel, an historic moment*), although this is felt by many to be pedantic or old-fashioned.

Spelling Pronunciation of Morphological Examples

In Chapter 12, it was explained that some commentators feel that it is reasonable for the spelling of words to contain silent, unpronounced letters, if those letters are pronounced in morphologically-related words, e.g. *sign* has no /g/, but *signature* does. If someone were to pronounce a /g/ in *sign*, this would be considered a spelling pronunciation. This is unlikely, as a final /gn/ cluster violates English syllable-structure rules, and would thus be difficult for most people to pronounce.

An example where such a situation does arise is the word *southern*. This is clearly the adjective from the noun *south*. However, the *ou* in the spelling represents different pronunciations in the two words. In *south*, it is /aʊ/ as in *shout*, whereas in *southern* it is /ʌ/ as in *shut*. Neither of these correspondences is particularly irregular, as *ou* regularly represents /aʊ/ (e.g. *housing*) but may also represent /ʌ/ (e.g. *cousin*). Many learners and non-native speakers, influenced by the same *ou* spelling, pronounce the adjective with /aʊ/. This is an argument against the morphological view of spelling; while identical spelling may reflect identical morphemes, they may not reflect identical pronunciations, and thus lead to spelling pronunciations.

Proper Names

Some English placenames and surnames are notorious because of their spelling.

Names of well-known places that regularly trap foreigners include *Leicester, Gloucester, Tottenham,* and *Worcester.* These are two-syllable words, but are often pronounced as three syllables by foreigners, as spelling pronunciations. Vice versa, *Isleworth* looks as though it should be a two-syllable word (with the first syllable pronounced like *isle*), but is in fact three-syllable: /aɪzəlwɜː(r)θ/. Similarly, *Islington* /ɪzlɪŋtən/. Moreover, there are many names of less well-known places that trap native and non-native speakers alike. For example, *Alnwick* is /ænɪk/ and *Cholmondeley* is /tʃʌmli/.

An example of a difficult surname is *Mainwaring.* This is of Norman French origin, and is associated with Ireland and Cheshire. It is the name of a now lost place, *Masnil Warin,* "the domain of Warin." It is pronounced /mænərɪŋ/. The most famous example from popular culture is Captain Mainwaring of the BBC sitcom *Dad's Army,* in which his name is often deliberately mispronounced /meɪnweərɪŋ/, as a spelling pronunciation, by some subordinates.

Spelling Pronunciation as Explanation

In similar fashion to /meɪnweərɪŋ/, an incorrect pronunciation may be used in order to explain spelling. That is, a pronunciation that is not the standard one may be used in order to indicate the spelling of a word, whose actual pronunciation is unexpected from the spelling. For instance, for the place-name *Worcester,* an explanation would be that "it is spelled /wɔː(r)sestə(r)/, but pronounced /wʊstə(r)/." In this case, /wɔː(r)sestə(r)/ would be a spelling pronunciation.

Regularized Spelling of Spelling Pronunciation Examples

While many irregularly spelled placenames and surnames may trap language users, several of them have alternative, more regular spellings that are therefore not a problem in this respect. For instance, the surname *Mainwaring* has been respelled in many, more regular ways, including the now common *Mannering.* Nevertheless, the older *Mainwaring* spelling persists.

Similarly, while the pronunciation of *Worcester* may baffle some, the respelled *Wooster* does not. The most famous example from popular culture is Bertie Wooster, of P. G. Wodehouse's Wooster and Jeeves stories.

Likewise, while *Leicester* may stump some speakers, its regularized respelling *Lester* does not. *Lester* is a not uncommon surname and first name.

Informal Pronunciations

Connected speech processes (e.g. Brown, 2014, Chapters 15–17) are changes that affect words and stretches of speech when spoken at a normal, conversational speed. Examples of spelling pronunciations (and pronunciation spellings; see the next chapter) often involve compound words; that is, words made up of two existing words.

An example of this is the compound *waistcoat*; that is, *waist* + *coat*. Compounds are normally stressed on the first syllable/element (*waist*). As a result, the second syllable/element (*coat*) is unstressed and may be weakened. With *waistcoat*, the second syllable was reduced from /oʊ/ to /ɪ/ and consequently the word began to be spelled *weskit* in the 19th century to reflect this. However, the standard modern pronunciation (a spelling pronunciation) has reverted to what one would expect from the full spelling: /weɪstkoʊt/.

Similarly, the compound *forehead* originally had /h/ in the middle. However, as a result of weakening, this was dropped. In this respect, it is similar to the history of the word *shepherd* (with no /h/ in modern pronunciation), from *sheep* + *herd*. As a surname, it has been respelled *Sheppard* to reflect this. Also, the second syllable of *forehead* was weakened to /ɪ/, as in *waistcoat*. As a result, its pronunciation came to rhyme with *horrid*, as in the famous verse by Henry Wadsworth Longfellow:

> There was a little girl,
>
> And she had a little curl
>
> Right in the middle of her forehead.
>
> When she was good
>
> She was very, very good,
>
> And when she was bad she was horrid.

However, the pronunciation since then has reverted to what one would expect from the full spelling (/fɔː(r)hed/), a spelling pronunciation. Wells's *Longman pronunciation dictionary* (1990 and subsequent editions) gives the result of research into the present-day occurrence of both pronunciations. It reports 1988 research showing 65% of British speakers and 1993 research showing 88% of American speakers pronounce /h/ in the word. Moreover, the /h/ pronunciation is more common with younger speakers than with older. This is known as apparent time, using the difference between younger and older speakers at one time (synchronically) to discern the trend of language change through time (diachronically).

A similar application of connected speech processes relates to the letter *t* in the middle of words with the spelling pattern *-ften*, *-sten*, or *-stle*. This may be dropped (elided) in pronunciation in normal, fast speech (see Brown, 2014, Chapter 16). In many cases, retention of the letter *t* in the spelling may be justified by pointing out that the word is composed of a stem that ends in *-t*, with the *-en* ending; thus, *christen, fasten, hasten, moisten*, and *soften* are clearly the stems *Christ, fast* ("secure"), *haste, moist*, and *soft* (all of which are pronounced with a final /t/) followed by *-en*. Similarly, the silent *l* letter in *epistle* may be justified by the related adjective *epistolic*, which has a /t/. Also perhaps the *t* in *castle*, from *Castilian; nestle* from *nest*; and *listen* from the archaic or poetic *list* ("hark").

However, morphology does not help with single-morpheme words like *glisten, pestle,* and *whistle.*

The interesting example here is the word *often*, which may or may not be pronounced with /t/. In the 15th century, this was pronounced with /t/, and it is of course related to the old-fashioned word *oft*, of which it is an extended form. In the 17th century, the /t/ began to be pronounced again, as a spelling pronunciation. However, the pronunciation with /t/ did not catch on; Wells's *Longman pronunciation dictionary* reports 1988 research showing 73% of British speakers, and 1993 research showing 78% of American speakers do not pronounce /t/ in *often*.

Spelling Pronunciation in Non-native Speech

The typical sequence of acquisition of speech and writing differs between native and non-native speakers. Native children learn to speak at a young age, having mastered virtually all the sounds (plus grammar and a sizeable vocabulary) by the time they start primary school at age five or so. At primary school, they typically learn to read and write. For native speaker children, it is thus a matter of discovering, "So that is how that word is spelled." For non-native speakers, on the other hand, English is typically learned at primary or secondary school, or later, although they may have acquired some English via films, television, etc. School classes are often very book-based, such that words are learned in their written form along with an explanation of how the written forms are pronounced. The sequence is thus often more one of "So that is how that word is pronounced." Deterding and Nur Raihan (2017) warn that "Mesthrie (2005: 127) urges caution in making this assumption, but he acknowledges that instances of spelling pronunciation inevitably occur in Black South African English, particularly in unfamiliar proper nouns."

In an investigation of spelling pronunciations in Brunei English, Nur Raihan (2015) gives various examples that are commonly found in other non-native varieties:

- *often*, with a pronounced /t/ (see the previous section)
- *company*, with the vowel of the first syllable /ɒ/ (cf. *competent*) rather than /ʌ/
- *doubt*, with a pronounced /b/ (*debt* is a similar example)
- *comfortable*, with four syllables, having a vowel between the /f/ and /t/
- *vegetables*, similarly four syllables, with a vowel between the /dʒ/ and /t/
- *honest*, with an initial /h/ (see above).

The word showing the greatest amount of spelling pronunciation in Nur Raihan (2015) is *salmon*, which is a curious example. Like *assault*, etc., listed earlier, it was borrowed into English from French *saumoun*, with no *l* in the spelling or /l/ in the pronunciation. Like *assault*, etc., an *l* was added in the spelling by 16th century scholars who knew that it came originally from Latin *salmo*, with the same meaning. But unlike *assault*, etc., the written *l* did not come to be pronounced as /l/, for no obvious reason. Many non-native speakers of English, however, pronounce the word with an /l/ sound, as a spelling pronunciation. As Deterding and Nur Raihan (2017) conclude, "Perhaps one day we will all be saying *salmon* with an [l] in it."

You may wonder why we still have the /l/ sound in *salmonella*. The answer is that it is not related to the *salmon* fish (which has no /l/) but is named after its discoverer, U.S. veterinary surgeon Daniel E. Salmon (1850–1914), whose name was pronounced with an /l/ sound.

Cross-linguistic Spelling Pronunciation

A curious example of cross-linguistic spelling pronunciation concerns the written sequence *ung*. In English, this can only represent the pronunciation /ʌŋ/ as in *hung*. However, in words from other languages, including transliterations (rewriting from another alphabet into Roman alphabet), the letter *u* is often used to represent a vowel of the /uː, ʊ/ variety. This causes a problem for English speakers because /ʊ/ cannot occur before /ŋ/ in English words (see Brown, 2014, Chapter 11). So, English speakers tend to pronounce the word as if it were an English word, with /ʌŋ/ rather than /ʊŋ/.

An example of this is the name of the martial art *kung fu*. In Chinese, this is /kʊŋ fuː/. However, English speakers tend to pronounce this /kʌŋ fuː/. Similarly, a suburb of Auckland is named *Onehunga*. In Māori, this is /ɔnehʊŋa/, while English speakers tend to pronounce it /ɔnehʌŋə/. A slightly different example is the name of the Korean electronics company *Samsung*. While English speakers tend to pronounce it /sæmsʌŋ/, its Korean pronunciation is /samsɒŋ/; the vowel is /ɒ/ rather than /ʊ/, but nevertheless English speakers are influenced by the transliteration spelling to pronounce it as /ʌ/.

Similarly, the *i* at the beginning of *iPhone, iris, isolate*, etc. is pronounced /aɪ/. Some speakers have by extension pronounced the names of the countries *Iraq* and *Iran* (and also the island *Ibiza*, the car company *Isuzu*, and the furniture company *IKEA*) with /aɪ/. Some commentators have been quick to call this uneducated and a mispronunciation (Wells, 2009). It can still be considered a spelling pronunciation. In Arabic, Farsi, Spanish, and Japanese respectively, these all begin with /iː, ɪ/, as does the English pronunciation of the country names *India, Indonesia, Italy*. For *IKEA*, see Chapter 25.

Summary

- Spelling pronunciations are pronunciations that deviate from established standard pronunciations, this deviation being caused by features of the spelling of words.

- Many spelling pronunciations are caused by silent letters, especially those introduced around the 16th century.
- Loanwords, placenames, and surnames are often ripe for spelling pronunciations.

Exercises

1　The pronunciation of the following British placenames is not obvious from their spelling. Firstly, find out the pronunciation by searching online or in a pronunciation dictionary. Then, suggest a pronunciation that would convey the spelling of the word. Finally, suggest a more regular spelling for the placename.

Beaulieu	*Burpham*	*Leominster*	*Ruislip*
Belvoir	*Frome*	*Lewes*	*Slough*
Brough	*Gotham*	*Mousehole*	*Welwyn*

2　The following placenames are pronounced differently. Find out the pronunciation by searching online or in a pronunciation dictionary.

Birmingham, England	*Birmingham*, Alabama
Cairo, Egypt	*Cairo*, Indiana/Georgia
Milan, Italy	*Milan*, Indiana/Ohio
Peru, South America	*Peru*, Indiana
Versailles, France	*Versailles*, Indiana

3　If you have learned a language with poor spelling-sound correspondences, e.g. French, German, have you found yourself making spelling pronunciations?

4　If you are a teacher, listen to the mispronunciations by your learners. Can many of them be explained as spelling pronunciations?

Further Reading

Spelling pronunciations are discussed in Carney (1994), Deterding & Nur Raihan (2017), and Upward & Davidson (2011).

References

Brown, A. (2014). *Pronunciation and phonetics: A practical guide for English language teachers*. New York, NY: Routledge.

Carney, E. (1994). *A survey of English spelling*. London, UK: Routledge.

Deterding, D., & Nur Raihan Mohamad (2017). Spelling pronunciation in English. *ELT Journal, 71*, 87–91.

Dobson, E. J. (1957). *English pronunciation 1500–1700*. Oxford, UK: Oxford University Press.

Fowler, H. W. (1926) *A dictionary of modern English usage*. Oxford, UK: Clarendon Press.

Fowler, H. W., & Fowler, F. G. (1906). *The King's English*. Oxford, UK: Clarendon Press.

Mesthrie, R. (2005). Putting back the horse before the cart: The "spelling form" fallacy in second language acquisition studies, with special reference to the treatment of unstressed vowels in Black South African English. *English World-Wide*, *26*(2): 127–151.

Nur Raihan, M. (2015). Spelling pronunciation: A new norm in Brunei English? *Southeast Asia: A Multidisciplinary Journal*, *15*, 36–42. Retrieved from www.researchgate.net/publication/290315514_Spelling_Pronunciation_A_New_Norm_in_Brunei_English

Upward, C., & Davidson, G. (2011). *The history of English spelling*. Chichester & Malden, UK: Wiley-Blackwell.

Wells, J. C. (1990). *Longman pronunciation dictionary* (1st edition; 2nd edition 2000; 3rd edition 2008). Harlow, UK: Pearson Education Ltd.

Wells, J. C. (2009). *Eye-rack and Eye-ran*. Retrieved from phonetic-blog.blogspot.co.nz/2009/09/eye-rack-and-eye-ran.html

Wyld, H. C. (1936). *The universal dictionary of the English language*. London, UK: Herbert Johnson.

19 Pronunciation Spelling

Learning Objectives

At the end of this chapter, readers will be able to:

- explain why some misspellings by native speakers are caused by pronunciation features
- explain why some misspellings by their learners are caused by pronunciation features
- diagnose possible pronunciation problems from spelling problems.

Introduction

In the previous chapter, we discussed pronunciations that differ from the standard pronunciation, under the influence of features of the spelling of words. In this chapter, we discuss the opposite; namely spellings that differ from the standard spelling, under the influence of features of the pronunciation of words. These are of three types. Firstly, informal spellings may reflect the informal pronunciation of words. Secondly, the spellings of foreign speakers may reflect their pronunciation, and thus be a clue to the phonological representation of words in their brains. A brief third section discusses pronunciation respellings, as found in some dictionaries and non-technical writing about language.

Informal Pronunciation Spelling

In spelling, words in English are typically defined as stretches of letters separated by spaces (see Chapter 10). In pronunciation, words can be spoken by themselves, in isolation. However in normal speech, words are run together. There are no small silences between them, and the sounds affect surrounding sounds in various ways. These are known as connected speech processes (e.g. Brown, 2014, Chapters 15–17). As a result of these processes of running words together, speech may sound very different from what might be expected from the spelled version of the passage.

Table 19.1 Pronunciation spellings

Pronunciation spelling	Slow formal spelling	Example context
doncha	don't you	Doncha know?
dunno	don't know	I dunno why.
gonna	going to	He's gonna be angry.
gotcha	got you(r)	You gotcha keys?
gotta	got to	I gotta go.
helluva	hell of a	They made a helluva mess.
ja, dja, didja	do you, did you	When dja get here?
kinda	kind of	He's kinda cute.
nope, nah	no	
o'	of	a cup o' tea
praps	perhaps	
samwidge	sandwich	
spose	suppose	I spose so.
wanna	want to	I wanna go home.
whatcha, whaddaya	what do you	Whatcha call this?
wheredja	where do you	Wheredja want this put?
wontcha	won't you	Wontcha let me help?
yeah, yep, yup	yes	

Nonce spellings of certain words and phrases have been used to reflect informal pronunciations. Examples of such pronunciation spellings are given in Table 19.1. Note that they need to be spoken at a fairly fast colloquial speed.

Spellings of Foreign Speakers

While the spellings in Table 19.1 are informal, reflecting informal pronunciation, many of them have become standardized in informal writing, e.g. *dunno, gonna, wanna, yeah*. In contrast, the pronunciation spellings of foreign speakers are not standardized, but rather are influenced by aspects of their non-standard pronunciation. Since they are not standardized, and would not be spelled this way by native speakers, they are often referred to as mistakes and misspellings. Native speakers also misspell words, but their misspellings are caused by incomplete mastery of English spelling (sound-to-spelling correspondences, etc.), rather than by incomplete mastery of English pronunciation.

Corpora of misspellings by foreign speakers have been compiled (see Al-Jarf, 2010; Flor, Futagi, Lopez, & Mulholland, 2013). The following examples come from Singaporean English (Brown, 1988, 2006).

Like many others, Singaporeans do not typically distinguish the /θ/ consonant sound as in *thick* from the /t/ sound as in *tick*, pronouncing both as /t/.

How do they remember which words begin with *th* and which with *t*? For those speakers who do distinguish the two sounds, this is simple: /θ/ is *th*, and /t/ is *t*. However, since Singaporeans conflate the two, misspellings occur, e.g. *toms* (for the intended *thorns*), *photosyntesis* (*photosynthesis*), *strenghtening* (*strengthening*) and *Baltazar* (*Balthazar*). Similarly, as a vowel example, the vowels /e/ and /æ/ are often conflated, leading to misspellings like *massy* (*messy*), *dack* (*deck*), *contect* (*contact*), *frengipani* (*frangipani*), *chrysenthemum* (*chrysanthemum*), *extand* (*extent*), *expansive* (*expensive*).

Misspellings may thus be a window into the phonological system of speakers.

Spellings of Native Speakers

There are occasional examples where words are spelled differently from the conventional spelling, because speakers do not pronounce the word in the conventional way. One such example is *orangutan*. This comes from the Malay *orang* ("person") and *hutan* ("forest, jungle") (an /h/ sound, and therefore the *h* letter, is often omitted in such a context in English, cf. *Sheppard*). However, many English speakers pronounce this with /ŋ/ at the end, perhaps because the first element (*orang*) ends that way. As a result, these speakers are likely to spell the word *orangutang*.

Pronunciation Respelling

A final word needs to be said about the ways in which some dictionaries avoid phonemic transcription and instead attempt to convey pronunciation by respelling the word using the 26 letters of the Roman alphabet, perhaps with diacritics (accents, macrons, etc.). It is sometimes known as the "newspaper system." Thus, for instance, the two pronunciations of *putting* ((i) placing, (ii) in golf) can be represented by *pŏoting* versus *pŭtĭng*.

It can be seen that such a system (and there are many of them) is confusing. The more reliable system used by dictionaries is phonemic transcription. While this takes a little learning, once learned, it is regular and reliable.

The use of phonemic transcription in English dictionaries is necessitated by the lack of a regular correspondence between sounds and spellings in English writing.

Summary

- A few informal English spellings reflect informal pronunciations.
- The misspellings of speakers may indicate features of their pronunciation.
- Phonemic transcription is the most reliable method of indicating pronunciation.

Exercises

1   The next time you are marking essays, make a note of misspellings. Do they fall into patterns? Are these patterns related to the writers' pronunciation?

2   If you know another language than English, how do dictionaries in that language show the pronunciation of words?

Further Reading

Pronunciation exercises containing pronunciation spellings are in Vaughan-Rees (2002, 2010).

References

Al-Jarf, R. (2010). Spelling error corpora in EFL. *Sino-US English Teaching*, 7(1), 6–15. Retrieved from www.finchpark.com/KNUFLE/book-1/unit06/Spelling-error-corpora-EFL.pdf

Brown, A. (1988). A Singaporean corpus of misspellings: Analysis and implications. *Journal of the Simplified Spelling Society, 1988*(3), 4–10.

Brown, A. (2006). Misspellings as indicators of writers' phonological systems: Analysis of a corpus by Singaporean secondary students. In Azirah Hashim & Norizah Hassan (Eds.), *Varieties of English in SouthEast Asia and beyond* (pp. 119–132). Kuala Lumpur, Malaysia: University of Malaya Press.

Brown, A. (2014). *Pronunciation and phonetics: A practical guide for English language teachers*. New York, NY: Routledge.

Flor, M., Futagi, Y., Lopez, M., & Mulholland, M. (2013). Patterns of misspellings in L2 and L1 English: A view from the ETS Spelling Corpus. *Bergen Language and Linguistic Studies (BeLLS)*, 6, 107–132. Retrieved from www.academia.edu/12725054/Patterns_of_misspellings_in_L2_and_L1_English_a_view_from_the_ETS_Spelling_Corpus

Vaughan-Rees. M. (2002). *Test your pronunciation*. Harlow, UK: Pearson Education (Penguin).

Vaughan-Rees. M. (2010). *Rhymes and rhythm* (2nd edition). Reading, UK: Garnet.

20 Homophones and Homographs

Learning Objectives

At the end of this chapter, readers will be able to:

- define *homophone, homograph, homonym,* and *polyseme*
- explain why homophones and homographs exist in English, but not (or far less) in other languages
- list some strategies for helping learners remember the spelling of homophones.

Introduction

We have already explained in Chapter 2 that the alphabetic principle states that letters represent sounds (vowel and consonant phonemes), and that sounds are represented by letters. We have also noted that some languages have correspondences that are 100% or close to it: Spanish, Finnish, Malay. Equally, we have pointed out that the sound-spelling correspondences in English are far from 100%, but instead are one-to-many and many-to-one. For instance, the /s/ sound is found in words like *sit, dress,* and *cent.* Vice versa, the letter *c* is found in words like *cent* and *academy.* This situation is shown diagrammatically in Figure 20.1.

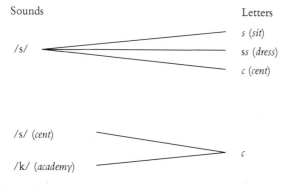

Figure 20.1 One-to-many and many-to-one correspondences

The existence of one-to-many and many-to-one correspondences in a language gives rise to the possibility of homophones and homographs.

Homophones

Homophones represent the first situation in the opening paragraph to this chapter (*sit, dress, cent*), where one sound is represented by more than one letter or letter combination. Homophones are thus words in a language that are pronounced the same, but spelled differently (Figure 20.2). The word *cent* sounds the same as *sent* and *scent*; the three words are homophones in English. The term *homophone* comes from the Greek *homo-* "same" and *phone* "sound." By focusing on the spelling rather than the pronunciation, homophones have also been called *heterographs* (Greek *hetero-* "different," *graph* "writing").

The largest set of homophones in English is /eə/ (BrE), /er/ (AmE): *air, heir, ere* (a poetic word meaning 'before'), *e'er (a* poetic version of *ever), Aire* (name of river in England and Australia), *Ayr* (placename in Scotland), *Eyre* (as in *Jane Eyre* by Charlotte Brontë). Most English homophone sets, however, involve only two possible spellings, e.g. *beach, beech.*

Homographs

Homographs are the opposite of homophones; namely, words that have the same spelling but are pronounced differently (Figure 20.3). This different pronunciation is not a matter of variation in the pronunciation of one word because of geographical or other variation ("You say tom/eɪ/to, and I say tom/ɑ:/to"), but two separate words with distinct meanings. An example would be *wind*: 1 /wɪnd/ "breeze", 2 /waɪnd/ "turn."

As for the term *homophone*, similarly homographs ("same spelling") can also be called *heterophones* ("different sound").

While English homophones can extend up to seven distinct spellings, homographs only seem to have a maximum of two possible pronunciations, as in *wind*.

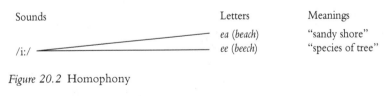

Sounds		Letters	Meanings
		ea (*beach*)	"sandy shore"
/i:/		ee (*beech*)	"species of tree"

Figure 20.2 Homophony

Meanings	Sounds		Letters
"breeze"	/ɪ/ (/wɪnd/)		
"turn"	/aɪ/ (/waɪnd/)		i (*wind*)

Figure 20.3 Homography

Homonyms

In order to complete the picture, two other phenomena need to be explained: homonyms and polysemes.

Homonyms are words that have the same spelling and the same pronunciation. However, they are distinct words, with different meanings and different etymologies (historical origins). An English example is *bark*. This can mean "the noise made by a dog" or "the outer covering of a tree." In both meanings, the word is spelled *bark* and pronounced /bɑː(r)k/. However, they are different words with unrelated meanings (despite the fact that some people might hold fanciful ideas about them being connected). In dictionaries, the two are given separate entries. Historically speaking, they have different origins: in the "noise made by a dog" sense, the word comes from Old English *beorcan*, while for "outer covering of a tree," it is from Old Norse *bǫrkr*. Through historical change over the centuries, the two have come to be spelled and pronounced the same.

Note in Figure 20.4, there is no fork either way between the sound and the spelling, and thus there is no problem here caused by the spelling system. The sound and spelling represent two different words of English.

Homophones and homonyms commonly appear in plays-on-words.

A deer, a skunk and a duck went for a meal in a restaurant and started arguing who was going to pay. Not the deer: she didn't have a buck. Not the skunk: he didn't have a /sent/. So they put it on the duck's bill.

During Donald Trump's presidential campaign, graffiti appeared mocking his slogan, "Ban pre-shredded cheese. Make America grate again."

Homographs are rare in jokes, probably because most jokes rely on spoken forms. An example is, "We don't need to get married. We get on fine the way we are. Why altar it?" However, they are more common in shop signs. Cook (2004, p. 68) gives examples like *Whichcraft* (design), *The Old Wearhouse* (clothing), *And Sew On* (fabrics), *Board Stupid* (surf- and skateboards), and *Scent with Love* (flowers).

Polysemes

The final phenomenon similarly does not represent any fork between the sound and the spelling, or any problem in terms of spelling. The difference

Sounds	Letters	Meanings
/ bɑː(r)k / ——————————	*bark* ⟨	"noise made by a dog" / "outer covering of a tree"

Figure 20.4 Homonymy

Sounds	Letters	Meanings
/hed/ ———	*head*	1 "top part of the body," 2 "manager of a department"

Figure 20.5 Polysemy

is that the two different meanings are connected. Usually one of them is the original, more basic, literal meaning, and the other a metaphorical extension of that original meaning.

An English example is *head*. The basic meaning of this is the top part of your body, containing the brain which controls the rest of your body. However, in *head of department*, the meaning has been extended to the boss (the top person in an organization chart, for instance) who manages the members of the department. There is a clear connection in meaning between the two senses (Figure 20.5).

As for homonyms, since there is no fork between the sound and the spelling, there is no problem here caused by the spelling system.

Unusual Polysemes

Very surprisingly, there are some words of English that have the same historical origin, and in Modern English have the same pronunciation but different spellings.

One such example is *flour* and *flower*. The origin is the Latin word *floris* meaning "flower." This survives in Modern English words such as *floral* and *florist*. This came into Middle English from French with various spellings including *flure, floure, flowre,* and *flower*. From the 13th century, the word came to be used also to mean "the finest part of something," as in (perhaps slightly dated) Modern English *The flower of the nation's youth were killed in the war*. In terms of food, it came to refer to the finest part or quality of ground wheat. The French expression for this was *fleur de farine* ("flower of wheat"). According to *The Oxford guide to etymology* (Durkin, 2011), Cruden's 1738 Bible concordance used the modern spellings of the words (*flower* and *flour*). However, Johnson's 1755 dictionary used *flower* for both meanings, and listed them under the same entry. It was not until around 1830 that the modern spellings were standardized. In short, historically speaking, *flower* and *flour* are polysemes, in that they have the same origin. However, most modern speakers of English are likely to be influenced by the different spelling, and therefore call them homophones. Many learners are influenced by the spelling of English words, and thus many claim that they pronounce these two words differently, despite the fact that they are given the same transcription in dictionaries.

Another example is *metal* and *mettle*. The origin is Greek *métallon* "mine, quarry, metal" via Latin *metallum* to Old French *metal* and Middle English *metal*. In addition to the literal meaning of *metal*, by the 1500s the word had come to be used for the strength of your character, how tough you are. Around 1700, the spelling *mettle*, originally just a variant of *metal*, came to be used for this latter meaning.

Similarly, *lightening* and *lightning*. The original word is *lightening*, being the *-ing* form of the verb *lighten*. In the late 14th century, the flash of electricity in the sky came to be spelled *light'ning* and then the modern *lightning*. The two words *lightening* and *lightning* may or may not be pronounced the same; *lightening* may be reduced to two syllables in faster speech.

Teaching

From the point of view of spelling and pronunciation, there is no problem teaching homonyms and polysemes, because there is one spelling and one pronunciation. The difference is to do with the meanings and whether they are related.

Homographs may not be too much of a problem because often one of the pronunciations represents a regular spelling-sound correspondence (with plenty of similar words) and the other is the exceptional one. For instance, *wind* with the pronunciation /waɪnd/ "turn," patterns with *bind, blind, find, grind, hind, kind, mind*, and *rind*. However, with the pronunciation /wɪnd/ "breeze," it does not pattern with any other word except *rescind*. The second is therefore the exceptional one, and the one that needs to be taught explicitly.

Similarly, *wound* can be pronounced /waʊnd/ "past tense of *wind*" or /wuːnd/ "injury." As /waʊnd/, it patterns like *bound, found, ground, hound, mound, pound, round*, and *sound*. As /wuːnd/, it is the only word in English ending in /uː/ and *-nd*, and patterns like other words where it is followed by *-p*, e.g. *coupon, group*, and *soup*.

Live may be the verb /lɪv/ or the adjective /laɪv/. The adjective patterns like *chive, dive, drive, five, hive, jive*, and *thrive*. In Chapter 13, we referred to this as "magic *e*." In contrast, the only (monomorphemic, i.e. not using *-ive* as an ending) words that pattern like the verb /lɪv/ are *give* and *olive*.

Homophones are the real problem. Given the pronunciation, there is no way of knowing which spelling represents which meaning, apart from learning them by heart. Rote learning like this puts a strain on the memory, and mistakes naturally occur.

Some writers propose (sometimes ingenious) mnemonics to help remember which spelling represents which meaning. For example, *stationery* ("letters, envelopes, etc.") and *stationary* ("not moving") are pronounced identically. How does anyone (foreign learner, native child, or native adult) remember which one has *e* and which *a*? One method is to look at related words; a person who sells *stationery* is a *stationer* (admittedly a rather old-fashioned word nowadays), not a *stationar*. The spelling *stationery* is for things like *paper*. *Stationary* is for something that isn't moving, like a *parked car*. Analytical and mnemonic devices like this are examined in Chapters 22 and 26.

(Incidentally, *stationary* and *stationery* have the same historical origin: Latin *stationarius* "tradesman (at a fixed location)." Itinerant peddlers were more common in the Middle Ages, while sellers with a fixed location were often bookshops licensed by universities. The *stationery* spelling became established around 1700.)

Summary

- The existence of homophones and homographs in English is caused by the lack of a one-to-one correspondence between sounds and spellings. Homophones and homographs are thus impossible (or far less common) in more regular languages.
- Homophones are words with the same pronunciation but different spelling. Homographs are words with the same spelling but different pronunciation.
- Homophones are the main problem for language learning, and often have to be learned by heart using mnemonics.

Exercises

1   Find a homophone (that is, another word that has the same pronunciation but a different spelling) for each of the following.

alter	*piece*
ascent	*plane*
baron	*profit*
brood	*roll*
ceiling	*serial*
choose	*shoot*
cygnet	*steel*
hole	*straight*
lesson	*sword*
minor	*tighten*
moose	*waste*
naval	*wrecks*

For the following list, you need to find two extra words (homophones). The use of capital letters (*bill*, *Bill*) is counted as a new word, and proper names are therefore also allowed.

beetle	*praise*
cord	*rain*
heel	*road*
knows	*vain*
main	*wise*
meat	*your*

The following are of four-way homophones, so you need to find three more words.

cue	*seize*
mark	*tease*
peas	*you*

2   The following spellings represent two words with different pronunciations and meanings (homographs). Explain them.

bass	*moped*
bow	*putting*
entrance	*read*
invalid	*row*
lead	*sow*
minute	*tear*

3   The meanings of many parts of the body, like *head*, can be extended as polysemes, e.g. *leg* (of a table). Find polysemes for the following body parts: *arm, back, brow, chest, finger, foot, hand, heart, limb, mouth, neck, nose, rib, shoulder, spine, teeth, tongue.*

4   There are two ways of looking at homonymy (two different words that happen to be spelled and pronounced the same) and polysemy (one word with an original and an extended meaning). Firstly, we can look the word up in an etymological dictionary; if the two senses have different historical origins, the words are homonyms and if not they are polysemes. Secondly, we could ask Modern English speakers for their intuitions; if they feel the two words are connected, they are polysemes and if not, they are homonyms.

So, what are your intuitions about the following words with two meanings? Are the two meanings related (and the words are thus polysemes) or not (homonyms)?

1 *earth* ("world, soil")
2 *eye* ("of the face, of a needle")
3 *pupil* ("of the eye, student")
4 *ear* ("of the face, of corn")
5 *corn* (grain, on the foot)
6 *meal* (flour (oatmeal), feast)
7 *sole* (of the shoe, fish)
8 *fork* (in a road, for eating)
9 *steer* (to guide, young bull)
10 *bank* (of a river, for money)

Further Reading

A comprehensive list of homophones and homographs in (British) English is given by Higgins (2016); almost all are homophones and homographs in American English too. The examples given in this chapter have all related to vowel and consonant patterns; Higgins lists many examples that relate to stress and other phenomena, e.g. *object* (noun, verb), *advocate* (noun, verb), *supplement* (noun, verb), *remark* ("comment, mark again").

References

Cook, V. (2004). *Accomodating brocolli in the cemetary*. London, UK: Profile Books.
Durkin, P. (2011). *The Oxford guide to etymology*. Oxford, UK: Oxford University Press.
Higgins, J. (2016). *Lists by John Higgins*. Retrieved from https://minimal-pairs. 000webhostapp.com
Johnson, S. (1755). *A dictionary of the English language*. Retrieved from johnsons dictionaryonline.com

21 Other Consequences of English Spelling

Learning Objectives

At the end of this chapter, readers will be able to:

- explain the need for phonemic transcription (or similar re-spelling) in English
- explain why spelling bees do not exist in non-English-speaking countries
- describe how many learners bypass the alphabetic principle and learn spelling by rote
- sympathize with the amount of time spent on spelling in classes teaching English compared with other languages
- explain how the English spelling system affects literacy.

Introduction

In previous chapters, we have discussed various consequences of features of the English spelling system: the existence of silent letters, spelling pronunciations, homophones and homographs, etc. In this chapter, we look at other consequences, all of which stem from the lack of a sound-spelling correspondence that is close to 100%.

In the first chapter, we asked what the purpose of a spelling system is. While there were many facts that follow on from the existence of a spelling system, it was suggested that the main purpose for devising a spelling system in the first place is to enable literacy. The final, and major, consequence examined in this chapter is therefore the poor literacy of native English-speaking societies.

Phonemic Transcription

As teachers of English, we are probably all familiar with the phonemic symbols contained in English dictionaries and books on English pronunciation, etc. We have all probably had learners from languages with more regular spelling systems who express irritation at having to learn a completely new set of symbols, in addition perhaps to the novelty of the Roman alphabet, and to the spelling patterns using the Roman alphabet in English.

It may therefore come as a surprise to learn that dictionaries for other languages do not always have phonemic transcriptions. The spelling is in effect a phonemic transcription. This depends, of course, on the spelling system having a good spelling-sound correspondence.

Spelling Bees

The topic of spelling bees was introduced in Chapter 16, because most of the words given to the last-standing contestants nowadays are clearly recent loanwords. Spelling bees make some sense, given the current lack of correspondence between sounds and spellings in English, and the fact that English tends not to regularize the spelling of loanwords. However, in many languages, spelling bees would not make sense, namely those languages with regular systems of sound-spelling correspondences. In those languages, if a word is pronounced as X, it is spelled as Y and, vice versa, if it is spelled as Y, it is pronounced as X. Once children and foreign learners have mastered the system, there is no uncertainty over the spelling of words.

Bypassing the Alphabetic Principle

The alphabetic principle – namely that letters represent sounds – underlies the current English spelling system. The problem is that the correspondence in English is poor, and several strategies other than a purely alphabetic one (the phonological strategy; Chapter 24) come into play. These are covered in Chapters 22, 23, 25, and 26: morphological, etymological, analogical, and visual.

The situation with many learners is that they find the many strategies too much, and resort to learning the spelling of all words by rote. For example, many learners spell *occasion* as *occassion*. However, spelling rules of English show that this cannot be correct. We have already seen (Chapter 13) that doubled consonant letters typically indicate a preceding short vowel (e.g. *passion*, with /æ/), whereas the vowel in *occasion* is long (/eɪ/). By analogy, there are several other words in English ending in *-asion*, all with long /eɪ/, including *abrasion, dissuasion, evasion, invasion, persuasion*.

A result of bypassing the alphabetic principle and relying on rote memory is that learners are then ill-equipped to deal with new vocabulary encountered in spelling, or with uncertainty over spelling. Learners often ask, "How do you spell . . . ?" Good teachers will reply, "How do you think it is spelled?" because it is often the case that there is only one possible way that it could be spelled in English, according to alphabetic phonological patterns.

Length of Texts

We have already seen (Chapter 12) that English spelling contains many silent letters; that is, letters that do not represent anything in the pronunciation and, in many cases, could be omitted without loss. One result of this is that texts in English spelling are around 10% longer than they need be. Proposed reformed spelling systems for English (Chapter 29) typically omit silent letters, and texts are correspondingly more concise in terms of the number of letters.

Teaching Time

English teachers typically spend a fair amount of time, even at more advanced levels, teaching and correcting spelling. Many teachers resent having to spend this time, as there are many other aspects of language (grammar, vocabulary, the four skills, etc.) on which this time could be more profitably spent.

Edward Rondthaler relates the equivalent process in Spanish, in order to highlight the difference in class time spent.

> An American professor, Edward Rondthaler, related that his grandson who lived in Mexico had just started to learn Spanish. Since the professor was interested in spelling, he asked the boy what Spanish spelling lessons were like. The boy didn't seem to understand the question. "Well, how did you learn to spell Spanish?" Rondthaler asked. "In the first lesson," his grandson replied, "the teacher wrote up the letters of the alphabet and told us what sound they each represented. Then we got on with learning the language."
>
> (Brown, 1996, p. 23)

Many teachers wish that English spelling were as easy as that.

Literacy

A 1992 study by the U.K. Adult Literacy and Basic Skills Unit (now part of the U.K. Learning and Work Institute) involved 1,000 native speakers over the age of 16 (reported in The Simplified Spelling Society, 1993). They were simply asked to spell the following six words: *height, business, sincerely, necessary, separate, and accommodation*. The results are shown in Figures 21.1 and 21.2.

Nine percent of the respondents spelled all six words incorrectly, and over half the respondents got at least two wrong. The most problematical word was *accommodation*, with only a quarter of respondents knowing its spelling. It is worth pointing out the six words were everyday words of English (unlike those used in spelling bees; see Chapter 16) and that the respondents were native-speaking adults with no learning difficulties.

A similar survey in 1995 by the Basic Skills Agency tested 980 people aged 16–60 on various words, and yielded similar results, summarized in Figure 21.3.

Among the findings were that women are better spellers than men; respondents in the 16–24 age range had the worst spelling; more people who are out of work have more difficulty than those in work; more good spellers come from higher socio-economic groups; and there is a strong correlation between educational qualifications and ability to spell. The Basic

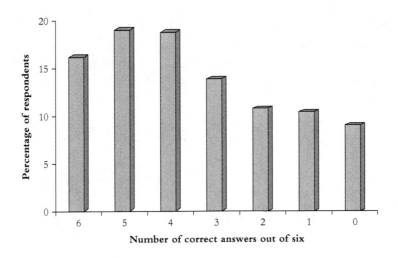

Figure 21.1 Correct answers to the spelling of six words (1992 survey)

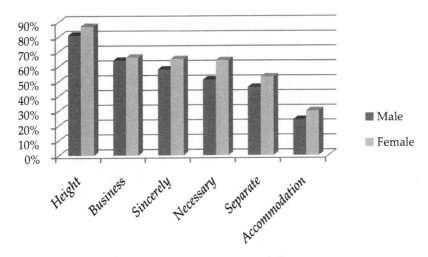

Figure 21.2 Percentage of correct answers per word (1992 survey)

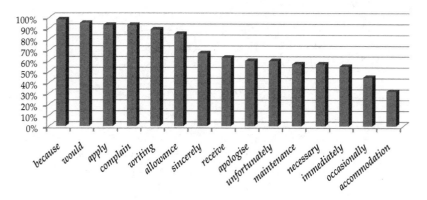

Figure 21.3 Percentage of correct answers per word (1995 survey)

Skills Agency (1995) concludes, "many people have a level of competence [in spelling, punctuation, and ability to fill in a form] far from good enough to cope with the changing demands of daily life and the world of work."

An interesting question is, "If most native speakers misspell the word *accommodation* (presumably by using the wrong number of *c*s and *m*s), in what way can *accommodation*, with two *c*s and two *m*s, be called the correct spelling?" Appealing to the word's etymology does not answer the question. The verb *accommodate* came into English in the 16th century from Latin (the Renaissance; see Chapter 4). The Latin word *accomodatus* meant "suitable," and came from the Latin verb *accommodare* meaning "to make fit," itself formed by adding the prefix *ad-* "to" to *commodare* "make fit." The word similarly came into other Romance (Latin-based) languages, but they saw no reason to retain the double consonant letters: Spanish *acomodar*, Romanian *acomodare*, Catalan *acomodar*, Italian *accomodante* ("accommodating").

Another indication of the poor spelling skills of native speakers of English was given by Upward (1992), who analyzed the spelling mistakes in English and in German of 33 university undergraduates writing essays on similar topics. The students were all British native speakers of English, with German as a foreign language learned at school. The results showed that the students made far more spelling mistakes in English, their native language, than they did in German, a foreign language.

Conclusion

Among languages of the world, there are relatively few that bring with them the consequences outlined in this chapter for English. In particular, it is difficult to think of other languages where literacy is so poor in native-speaking countries, and where native speakers make fewer spelling mistakes in languages that are foreign to them.

Summary

- There are several ramifications of the fact that English has a poor sound-spelling correspondence.
- The main one of these is poor literacy rates.

Exercises

1 Think of foreign languages that you know. Do dictionaries in those languages contain phonemic transcriptions of words?
2 As an English teacher, when was the last time you corrected written work, without having to correct any spelling?

Further Reading

The everyday impact and economic cost of poor literacy (often researched in connection with poor numeracy) are summarized in readable language in Cardoza (2013) for the U.S.A., and Full Fact (n.d.) for the U.K. The research data on which such summaries are based include Reder (2010) for the U.S.A., and the Department for Business, Innovation and Skills (2012) for the U.K.

References

Brown, A. (1996). The trouble with spelling. *Speak Out! (Newsletter of the IATEFL Pronunciation Special Interest Group)* 17, 23–31.

Cardoza, K. (4 November 2013). *Adding up the cost of low literacy among adults.* National Public Radio. Retrieved from www.npr.org/2013/10/30/241910094/adding-up-the-cost-of-low-literacy-among-adults

Department for Business, Innovation and Skills (2012). *The 2011 skills for life survey: A survey of literacy, numeracy, and ICT levels in England.* London, UK: Department for Business, Innovation and Skills Research paper 81. Retrieved from www.gov.uk/government/uploads/system/uploads/attachment_data/file/36000/12-p168-2011-skills-for-life-survey.pdf

Full Fact (n.d.). *Counting the cost of poor literacy and numeracy skills.* Retrieved from fullfact.org/economy/counting-cost-poor-literacy-and-numeracy-skills

Reder, S. (2010). *Adult literacy development and economic growth.* Washington, DC: National Institute for Literacy. Retrieved from lincs.ed.gov/publications/pdf/AdultLiteracyDevEcoGrowth.pdf

The Basic Skills Agency (1995). *Writing skills: A survey of how well people can spell and punctuate.* London, UK: The Basic Skills Agency.

The Simplified Spelling Society (1993). *Newsletter January 1993.* Retrieved from spellingsociety.org/uploaded_newsletters/n5-newsletter-1422725316.pdf

Upward, C. (1992). Is traditionl english speling mor dificlt than jerman? *Journal of Research in Reading, 15*(2), 82–94.

Strategies for Teaching and Testing English Spelling

22 Morphological Strategy

Learning Objectives

At the end of this chapter, readers will be able to:

- better appreciate the morphological relationships of words
- use morphological relationships to explain spellings, including silent letters
- devise techniques for teaching the spelling of such related words in class.

Introduction

In Chapter 12, when discussing why there is a *g* letter in the word *sign*, we saw that many words are composed of more than one unit of meaning (morpheme), and that some commentators argue that it is acceptable, for example, to have a (silent) *g* letter in *sign* because it is related to *signal, signature, signatory, signet, significance, resignation*, etc. These words all come from the Latin *signum*, although most of them came into English via French, in which the *g* is not pronounced.

The English spelling system, while being basically alphabetic, also contains elements where letters do not unambiguously represent sounds. Morphology therefore has to be considered, a fact acknowledged many years ago. Hockett (1958, p. 542) explains that, "The complexities of English spelling cannot be accounted for completely on the assumption that the system is phonemic with irregularities . . . It is necessary to assume that the system is partly phonemic and partly morphemic."

The relationship between morphology, etymology, and modern spelling in English was discussed by Chomsky and Halle (1968) (C&H). They proposed two features of an optimal spelling system. Firstly, it should have only one representation (spelling) for each entry (morpheme). Secondly, phonetic variation should not be explicitly indicated where it is predictable by a general rule. They conclude with the often-quoted statement that Modern English spelling is "a near optimal system for the lexical representation of English words" (p. 49).

C&H's contention is based on their view of phonology. They suggest that there are two levels of analysis. The pronunciation that people use when speaking is the overt phonological representation (OPR). However, there is an underlying phonological representation (UPR) that is related to the OPR by phonological rules, and that shows the morphological relatedness of words and often corresponds to the etymology. For example, the UPR of *night* is /nixt/, which corresponds to its pronunciation in Middle English. This is converted into the modern OPR /naɪt/ by rule. They argue that it is the relatedness of words that is shown in spelling; that is why *night* is still spelled that way, despite the fact that the /x/ sound no longer exists in English. For instance, *courageous* is the adjective from the noun *courage*; the spelling of *courageous* contains the spelling of the noun *courage*, even though the two words are pronounced in different ways, largely as a result of different stress placement (*COUrage* /kʌrɪdʒ/, *couRAGEous* /kəreɪdʒəs/).

This led to a distinction between spelling systems that are (more) morphemic, showing the underlying constituent morphemes in a consistent way, and those that are (more) phonemic, showing the surface pronunciation in a consistent way. Knowles (1988) applies this dichotomy to Slavonic languages of Eastern Europe. "[O]ne cannot read Russian by a purely sequential, phonic method: it requires a combination of the phonic and 'look-and-say' methods. This is the case with almost all the Slavonic orthographies." Russian has morphemic implications and is thus at the opposite end from a phonemic system. At the other extreme, Serbo-Croat uses the Cyrillic alphabet and the Roman alphabet, with a near-100% phonemic integrity. However, this is the work of Vuk Karadžić (1787–1864), a Serbian linguist who regularized sound-spelling correspondences. Between Russian and Serbo-Croat on this continuum is Byelorussian which, like Russian, is largely morphemic, but with some phonemic changes, as a result of which, Knowles reports, "it is claimed that this particular spelling system has helped to improve literacy in Byelorussia."

Underlying C&H's claim is the assumption that a spelling system should be at least partly morphemic; that is, the spelling of a morpheme should not change regardless of affixes added to it. An example often quoted for English is *electric, electricity, electrician*. The argument is made that it is beneficial that the spelling of the stem *electric* does not change, despite the fact that its pronunciation changes, with differences in stress placement and thus the occurrence of strong and weak vowels, especially schwa, and with different final consonants: /k/ in *electric*, /s/ in *electricity*, and /ʃ/ in *electrician*. This, it is claimed, helps the reader see the relatedness. The argument seems to hold water for English, until we look at the corresponding words in other, related languages. In French these words are *électrique, électricité*, and *électricien*, with two different final letter patterns (and pronunciations). In German, they are *elektrisch, Elektrizität*, and *Elektriker*, where all three words have different final spelling patterns (and pronunciations). The imperative for the spelling to unambiguously represent the pronunciation is the overriding factor in these languages.

Is English spelling, as C&H claim, an optimal, morphemic system or, like Byelorussian, is it somewhere in the middle of this continuum? The following sections discuss examples from English where spelling reflects morphology (i.e. is morphemic) and where spelling does not reflect morphology (i.e. is not morphemic).

Spelling Reflecting Morphology

In this section, we give some examples of where English spelling reflects the morphemes of the meaning rather than the phonemes of the pronunciation. That is, the spelling does not change, even though it represents different pronunciations.

Invariant Endings

A commonly quoted example is the endings *-(e)s* and *-(e)d*.

The *-(e)s* may represent four different morphemes. Firstly, it may be the 3rd person singular present tense form of verbs, e.g. *I go, he goes*. Secondly, it may be the plural form of nouns, e.g. *one hedge, two hedges*. Thirdly, it may be the possessive form of nouns; these may be singular nouns or plural nouns, depending on the placement of the apostrophe (see Chapter 9), e.g. *one teacher, one teacher's class; two teachers, two teachers' classes*. And finally, it may be the written form of the abbreviated form of *is* or *has*, e.g. *He's rich, He's got lots of money*.

From the pronunciation point of view, there are three different ways in which this ending is pronounced (see Brown, 2014, Chapter 14). After /s, z, ʃ, ʒ, tʃ, dʒ/, it is /ɪz/, e.g. *horses*. After other voiceless final consonants, it is /s/, e.g. *cats*. After other voiced final consonants, it is /z/, e.g. *dogs*.

From the spelling point of view, the spelling does not change (apart from the placement of the apostrophe, which is a different matter), e.g. *He pats the dog, three pats of butter, This is Pat's car, Pat's gone home*. In each case, an *s* letter is added. An *e* letter is also added in two contexts. Firstly, where the ending creates a new syllable in the pronunciation. This happens when the stem ends in the sounds /s, z, ʃ, ʒ, tʃ, dʒ/, e.g. *buses, quizzes, bushes, garages, witches, hedges*. In terms of spelling, this means when the stem ends in *-s -ss*, or *-x; -z* or *-zz; -sh; -ch* (where it represents /tʃ/) or *-tch*. Other examples, like *garage* and *hedge* already end in *-e*. There are some other nouns that take *-es*, where there is a change in the stem, e.g. *wolf, wolves*.

The second context is when the stem ends in *-o*, but here the ending is variable. The *Oxford dictionary* (Oxford Living Dictionaries, n.d.) gives the possibilities shown in Table 22.1.

Table 22.1 Spelling possibilities for nouns ending in *-o*

Singular noun	Plural noun with –s	Plural noun with –es
avocado	avocados	
banjo	banjos	banjoes
buffalo		buffaloes
cargo	cargos	cargoes
domino		dominoes
echo		echoes
embargo		embargoes
embryo	embryos	
flamingo	flamingos	flamingoes
fresco	frescos	frescoes
ghetto	ghettos	ghettoes
halo	halos	haloes
hero		heroes
mango	mangos	mangoes
memento	mementos	mementoes
mosquito		mosquitoes
motto	mottos	mottoes
potato		potatoes
solo	solos	
studio	studios	
tomato		tomatoes
tornado	tornados	tornadoes
torpedo		torpedoes
tuxedo	tuxedos	tuxedoes
veto		vetoes
volcano	volcanos	volcanoes
zero	zeros	
zoo	zoos	

It is difficult to formulate any rules here. Nouns that end in two vowel letters take *-s*, e.g. *radios, videos*. Nouns ending in double *o* take *-s*, e.g. *cockatoos, shampoos*. However, apart from this, there seems to be no system, for no good reason. Sound advice is therefore to check in a dictionary or use your computer's spell-checker.

In a similar fashion, the past tense or participle ending is spelled *-(e)d*, although it can represent three pronunciations. After /t, d/, it is /ɪd/, e.g. *wanted*. After other voiceless final consonants, it is /t/, e.g. *missed*. After other voiced final consonants, it is /d/, e.g. *banned*.

The spelling of this ending is always *-ed*, apart from two situations. The first is where the verb already ends in a single or double *-e*, e.g. *baked, named, guaranteed*. The second is a small set of verbs that can form their past tense in

BrE by adding *-t* in the spelling and /t/ in the pronunciation (contradicting this rule): *burnt, dreamt, dwelt, knelt, leant, leapt, learnt, smelt, spelt, spilt, spoilt.* In AmE, these are generally regular verbs adding *-ed* (*burned, dreamed*, etc.). Changes that may be made to the stem, for both *-(e)s* and *-(e)d* endings, are that a final *-y* changes to *-i* before adding the ending (*fry, fries, fried; marry, marries, married*) unless the *-y* is preceded by a vowel letter (*employ, employs, employed; stay, stays, stayed*). In Chapter 13, we saw that final consonant letters are doubled in certain circumstances (*regret, regretted*).

Historical Morphemes

A knowledge of the classical languages of Latin and Greek is helpful in understanding the meanings, origins, and spellings of some words. An overseas-based Greek Cultural Society advertised a *Meditteranean Cuisine Evening*. The word *Mediterranean* was misspelled; surprising given that Greece is on the Mediterranean Sea. The overseas-based expats may never have been to Greece, but surely a society devoted to Greek culture should get the spelling right.

It is easy to remember the spelling if you know that the Latin word *terra* meant "land, earth." It occurs in the middle of *Mediterranean*, so-called because for the Romans the Sea was the middle (*medi*) of their world (*terr*). The *terr* element is quite productive in English, occurring in the words shown in Table 22.2.

While *inter* may look like an exception, it is not, because (i) English words do not regularly end in *-rr*, and (ii) in inflected forms, the *r* letter is doubled, e.g. *interred*.

There are some other expressions that are used in Modern English but are of clear foreign origin (Table 22.3).

Table 22.2 The *terr* element in English words

Word	Explanation, literal meaning, origin
terrace	"Platform built on or supported by a mound of earth."
terrain	
terrestrial	
territory	"Land around a town."
terrarium	"Pen for small land animals, or glass container for growing plants or keeping worms." The *-arium* element comes from *aquarium*.
subterranean	*Sub* means "under."
inter	With stress on the second element (*inTER*). "Bury," i.e. put in the ground.
terrier	So-called because they were bred to pursue foxes, badgers, etc. into their burrows in the ground.

Table 22.3 The *terr* element in English loanwords

Word	Explanation, literal meaning, origin
terrazzo	From Italian "terrace, balcony."
terra-cotta	From Italian "cooked earth," i.e. fired clay.
terra firma	From Latin "solid ground."

Spelling Not Reflecting Morphology

Chomsky and Halle's argument that English spelling is a near-optimal, morphemic system has been criticized ever since it was made. In an early rebuttal, Steinberg (1971) listed the three assumptions underlying the claim:

1   Readers need read only for meaning and not for sound.
2   A spelling system based on C&H's UPRs would not be exceptionally difficult to learn.
3   There is no direct link between the phonetic aspect of a word and its meaning.

He concludes that:

1   A C&H spelling system would require as much abstracting as an OPR-based one. While *night* and *kite*, and *sign* and *divine* rhyme, this cannot be accounted for with a purely morphemic or orthographic account.
2   The spelling of words would be more difficult (if not impossible) to learn (and teach). *Time, team,* and *tame* are different words, in both spelling and pronunciation, in Modern English. However, their UPRs are /tiːm/ (which corresponds to modern *team*), /teːm/ (like modern *tame*), and /tæːm/ respectively, a very confusing situation for modern learners.
3   An OPR-based spelling would allow for virtually direct identification of both sound and meaning. A basic feature of human language is the arbitrariness of the signal; that is, there is no connection between the (written or spoken) form, and the meaning.

It is not difficult to find words in English that are clearly related (in meaning, and historically), but whose spellings are different (e.g. Yule, 1978).

Table 22.4 Related words with differences in spelling

Word 1	Word 2	If Word 2 were morphemically regular, it might be spelled . . .
absorb	absorption	absorbtion
awe	awful	aweful
brief	abbreviate	abbrieviate
comparative	comparison	comparason
explain	explanation	explaination
fly	flight	flyt
for	therefore	therefor
gelatine	jelly, jello	gelly, gello
high	height	hight
joke	jocular	jokular
marriage	marital	marrital
message	messenger	messanger
mouse	mice	mise
practice	practitioner	practicioner
prey	predator	preyator
proceed	precede	preceed
reign	regime	
Shaw	Shavian	Shawian
space, spacious	spatial	spacial
speak	speech	speach
strategy	stratagem	strategem
suspect	suspicion	suspection

There is a good reason why some words like this could not change in order to have constant morphemes. It is that the resultant spelling would not be a plausible spelling for the pronunciation of the word. For instance, the noun *example* gives us the adjective *exemplary*. In order to maintain the spelling consistency of the underlying morpheme, the adjective could be spelled *examplary*. However, that would then not be a plausible spelling, given the /e/ vowel in the pronunciation of *exemplary*. Similarly, there is a pronounced /d/ in *predator*; if this were spelled *preyator*, it is difficult to show how this represents the pronunciation. Likewise, the verb *obey* gives the noun *obedience* with a pronounced /d/ that should be represented in the spelling; the more technical legal term *obeyance* is more regular in this respect. In short, the pronunciation over-rules C&H's suggested requirement for consistency in spelling of the morpheme. Similar examples include *broad, breadth; doubt, dubious; peace, pacific; people, popular; restaurant, restaurateur.*

A productive example of the spelling of morphemes not remaining constant is words ending in -*er*, e.g. *anger, hunger, disaster, monster*. When these take certain suffixes, the *e* is lost: *angry* (not *angery*), *hungry, disastrous, monstrous*.

Yule (1978) concludes, "Clearly it seems pure luck whether Chomsky's principle applies or not – and it applies rarely, amid such morphological and orthographic inconsistencies as are found in the English language."

Another example, well-known to English teachers, is the noun *pronunciation*. The vowel in the second syllable is /ʌ/, and its spelling is a regular *u* letter. However, it comes from the verb *pronounce*, and many learners assume it should be a more regular *pronounciation* with *ou* in the spelling, and /aʊ/ in the pronunciation. Similarly, some learners do not pronounce *maintenance* with the shift in stress from the verb *maintain* (*main*TAIN, MAIN*tenance*). The vowel spelling in the second syllable changes from *ai* to *e* to reflect this. For these learners, however, the vowel spelling remains the same, because the pronunciation remains the same for them; thus *maintainance* or *maintainence*. Notice that the learners are, with some justification, regularizing the pronunciation and the spelling; it is the standard form that is out of step with C&H's theory of invariantly spelled morphemes.

Is English Spelling Optimal?

Yule (1978) quotes the point made by Francis (1970) "that if conventional English orthography was a near optimal system for representing the spoken language, then why do people have so much trouble reading and writing it?"

Researchers have tried to quantify the regularity of English spelling, and to compare the benefits of morphemic systems with phonemic systems. Little (2001) analyzed 100 bases (morphemes and their related words) in standard spelling and in a reformed and more phonemic spelling called Sound-spel, by means of an optimality percentage, finding that while standard spelling was 95% optimal, this rose to 97% with the Sound-spel system.

A recent investigation (Nicolai & Kondrak, 2015) measured phonemic transparency by averaging two elements: phonemic perplexity (sound-to-letter correspondences) and graphemic perplexity (letter-to-sound correspondences). They used a computer algorithm to generate English spellings, and find the best compromise between these two perplexities. They conclude that, "traditional orthography is closer to the level of a phonemic transcription than to that of a morphemic concatenation" and that they have "provided a constructive proof that it is possible to create a spelling system for English that is substantially closer to theoretical optimality than the traditional orthography" (p. 544).

In short, contrary to C&H's claim, standard English spelling is not near optimal.

Using Morphemes in Teaching Spelling

Many English-users – and not just learners – misspell *definite* as *definate*. From a pronunciation point of view, there is some justification for this, as the vowel is schwa, which can be spelled with any of the vowel letters. From the morphological point of view, on the other hand, there is no justification for this. The word is related to *finite* and *definition*, both of which are clearly spelled with the vowel *i* rather than *a* (they cannot be *finate*, *defination*). Historically speaking, all these words derive ultimately from the Latin verb *finire* "limit, finish."

Morphological connections like this may not be immediately obvious to speakers, but they are a good way of teaching them to remember the spelling. A telling example is the verb meaning "register," spelled *enroll* in AmE, but *enrol* in BrE. It may not be obvious to BrE speakers that this word is related to the word *roll* meaning "register, namelist," as in *on the roll*. In this respect, it is analogous to the verb *enlist*.

Another feature of morphology that is helpful in spelling, is elements put before or after the stem of multi-morphemic words. English prefixes include *cyber-, dis-, multi-, over-, pre-, un-*. Suffixes include *-ful, -ish, -ity, -less, -er*. These prefixes and suffixes seldom change their spelling. One counterexample is *in-*, expressing an opposite, as in *distinct, indistinct*. When this occurs before stems beginning with the sound /r/ (the letter *r*), this changes to *r: relevant, irrelevant*. When the stem begins with /l/ (*l*), it is *l: logical, illogical*. When the stem begins with /p, b, m/ (*p, b, m*), it is *im-: pure, impure*.

Some commentators have suggested that it is useful to have homophones in English, in order to distinguish in writing words that are the same in pronunciation, e.g. *pair, pear*. This is a spurious argument; by the same argument, if it is good, for the sake of clarity, to distinguish the words in spelling, it would also be good to distinguish them in pronunciation, and that does not happen. In a similar fashion, it has been suggested that it is useful for affixes that are pronounced the same to be distinguished in spelling. For instance, in terms of pronunciation, the final syllable of *definition* and *physician* are the same. They have the same sounds (/ʃən/) and they have same implications for stress (stress falls on the syllable before this suffix). This is true of other possible spellings of such a final syllable, as in *conversion, cushion, passion, ocean*. Some would argue that it is good that *-tion* and *-cian* are spelled differently, in order to show that those words ending in *-tion* are abstract nouns, usually derived from verbs (*attraction, construction, pollution, relation, translation*, etc.), while those ending in *-cian* describe professions, usually derived from adjectives (*electrician, magician, mathematician, optician, politician*, etc.). Some would argue further that another benefit from the different spelling of the suffix is that it shows the spelling of the stem. Thus the *t* at the beginning of the ending in *attraction* shows that its stem has a final *t* (*attract*), omitted by many learners because of the final cluster in the pronunciation. However, there are counterexamples to this; while *exert* gives us *exertion, convert* gives *conversion*. More reliable is the fact that *-cian* words have stems ending in *-c* (*magic, magician*). It works for most examples, but not for *beautician* (there is no stem *beautic*). While there is an adjective *dietic*, giving us BrE *dietician*, it is a very rare word, which is probably why in AmE this is *dietitian*.

The exercises at the end of this chapter give more examples where morphology may help in remembering spelling.

Summary

- English spelling is basically phonological (that is, alphabetic, with letters representing sounds) rather than morphemic (with stretches of letters representing morphemes).
- Nevertheless, morphology can be used in teaching and remembering the spellings of certain words.
- Standard English spelling is not optimal.

Exercises

1 The following Latin roots are quite productive, in the same way as *terr*, described in this chapter. For each one, find five more English words that contain this root.

Root	Latin form	Meaning	Sample English word
cent	centum	"hundred"	percent
corp	corpus	"body"	corpse
loc	locus	"place"	locate
mari_	maris	"sea"	maritime
nav	navis	"ship"	navy
port	portare	"carry"	porter
sanct	sanctus	"holy"	sanctity
scrib / scrip	scribere / scriptum	"write / written"	scripture
uni	unus	"one"	unity

2 Explain how you would use morphological information to help a learner make the following spelling decisions.

just deserts or *just desserts?*   *memento* or *momento?*
grammar or *grammer?*   *neccesary* or *necessary?*
helth or *health?*   *sacreligious* or *sacrilegious?*
integrate or *intergrate?*   *writing* or *writting?*

Further Reading

The contribution of morphemes to English spelling, and their use in teaching spelling, are discussed in Bryant & Nunes (2004), and the writings of

Kristian Berg, e.g. Aronoff, Berg, & Heyer (2016), Berg, Buchmann, Dybiec, & Fuhrhop (2014).

References

Aronoff, M., Berg, K., & Heyer, V. (2016). Some implications of English spelling for morphological processing. *The Mental Lexicon, 11,* 164–185.

Berg, K., Buchmann, F., Dybiec, K., & Fuhrhop, N. (2014). Morphological spellings in English. *Written Language & Literacy, 17*(2), 282–307.

Brown, A. (2014). *Pronunciation and phonetics: A practical guide for English language teachers.* New York, NY: Routledge.

Bryant P., & Nunes, T. (2004). Morphology and spelling. In T. Nunes & P. Bryant (Eds)., *Handbook of children's literacy* (pp. 91–118). Dordrecht, Germany: Springer.

Chomsky, N., & Halle, M. (1968). *The sound pattern of English.* New York, NY: Harper & Row.

Francis, W. N. (1970). Linguistics and reading: A commentary on chapters 1 to 3. In H. Levin & J. P. Williams (Eds)., *Basic studies on reading.* New York, NY: Basic Books.

Hockett, C. F. (1958) *A course in modern linguistics.* New York, NY: Macmillan.

Knowles, F. (1988). Morphology versus phonology in the spelling of Slavonic languages. *Journal of the Simplified Spelling Society, 8*(2), 11–16. Retrieved from spellingsociety.org/uploaded_journals/j8-journal.pdf

Little, J. R. (2001). The optimality of English spelling. *Journal of the Simplified Spelling Society, 29,* 4–13. Retrieved from spellingsociety.org/uploaded_journals/j29-journal.pdf

Nicolai, G., & Kondrak, G. (2015). English orthography is not "close to optimal." *Human Language Technologies: The 2015 Annual Conference of the North American Chapter of the ACL* (pp. 537–545). Denver, CO: Association for Computational Linguistics. Retrieved from aclweb.org/anthology/N/N15/N15-1056.pdf

Oxford Living Dictionaries (n.d.). *Plurals of nouns.* Retrieved from en.oxford dictionaries.com/spelling/plurals-of-nouns

Steinberg, D. D. (1971). Would an orthography based on Chomsky and Halle's underlying phonological representations be optimal? *Working Papers in Linguistics* (University of Hawaii, Honolulu), *3*(3), 1–18. Retrieved from archive.org/stream/ERIC_ED053596#page/n0/mode/2up

Yule, V. (1978). Is there evidence for Chomsky's interpretation of English spelling? *Spelling Progress Bulletin,* Winter *1978,* 10–12. Retrieved from spellingsociety. org/uploaded_bulletins/bt78winter-bulletin.pdf

23 Etymological Strategy

Learning Objectives

At the end of this chapter, readers will be able to:

- help learners spell loanwords by referring to the (plausible, guessed) historical origins of the words.

Introduction

This chapter deals with loanwords; that is, words that have been borrowed from other languages. English has a long history of this (see Chapter 16). Unlike some other languages, such as Malay (see Chapter 30), English does not typically change the original spelling of the word. If the lending language does not use the Roman alphabet, there may still be vestiges of its spelling.

The result of this is that, while English spelling may contain traces of the spelling in the original language, the English spelling may thereby be further from a regular spelling than otherwise, and as a result more difficult for learners.

Do English language learners know much about the historical origins (etymology) of words? They probably know very little. However, some discussion of etymology may help with spelling. This chapter gives a few examples, and hints.

Knowing the Etymology

In Chapter 25, we discuss the word *gout* ("joint disease"). We state there that, even if learners did not know the word (and it is quite uncommon), they can still work out the pronunciation on analogy with words like *about, scout, shout.*

However, they may have come across the expression *chacun a son gout*, used to mean "to each his/her own" or "there's no accounting for taste." Here, *gout* is not pronounced /gaʊt/, but /guː/. In this sense, we here have homographs; that is, two words with unrelated meanings that have the same spelling, but different pronunciation (see Chapter 20).

Knowing that the expression is of recent French origin, we can expect there is possibly a different pronunciation from *gout* ("joint disease"). If a learner knows some French, then they may be able to spell it (with *ou* representing /u:/ and its silent final *t*).

In fact, the borrowing of this expression from French is a bit more complex than this. The French expression is not *chacun a son gout*, but rather *à chacun son goût* (literally "to each one his/her taste"). Note that French *goût* has a circumflex accent on the *u*, which got lost in the borrowing process. A circumflex usually shows that an original *s* has been lost; *goût* comes from Old French *goust* (cf. the Modern English word *gustation*). The same has happened with *hotel* (French *hôtel*; cf. English *hostel*), *pate* (*pâté*; cf. English *paste*), *depot* (*dépôt*; cf. English *deposit*), *creme brulee* (French *crème brûlée*; Old French *brusler*). Also, it is a much more common expression in English than in French. The English expression is *chacun a son gout*, usually without any accents, which if translated directly into French could be either *chacun à son goût* ("each one to his taste") or *chacun a son goût* ("each one has his taste").

Gout meaning "joint disease" has a similar, but earlier origin. It is from Old French *gote*, and its modern French form is *goutte*. However, since it was borrowed into English around 1200, its pronunciation underwent the Great Vowel Shift (see Chapter 4), becoming /aʊ/. *Gout* meaning "taste" in *chacun a son gout* is much more recent.

Carney (1994) gives an example of an etymological strategy, coincidentally using a similar word of French origin: *ragout* (French *ragoût*, historically related to *gout*).

Suppose you are writing about life at sea and find that a favorite dish of working seamen was called /bɜ:'gu:/. If you think that this word is just nautical slang, you will spell it *burgoo*. But if you think, perhaps because of the final stress, that it may have something to do with French cooking, you will look for possible French elements and spell it *burgout*, presumably on analogy with *ragout*.

(Carney, 1994, p. 468)

The Case of *ch*

The digraph *ch* is often quoted as a good example of the etymological system at work. It may represent three different pronunciations. Firstly, it can be /tʃ/, usually in words of Anglo-Saxon origin.

beach, cheese, Chelsea, chicken, church, finch, much, rich, Richard, speech, such, which

It can be /k/, usually in words of Greek origin, where they are spelled with the Greek letter *chi*.

ache, chaos, character, Chloe, Christopher, echo, monarch, orchid, stomach, technical

It can be /ʃ/, usually in words of French origin. French has no /tʃ/ sound.

chalet, champagne, Charlotte, chassis, chef, machine, Michelle, niche, panache, parachute

How could learners possibly know which language such words come from? If the learners are French or Greek, they should know.

There are some other clues in the words. For instance, the French words contain other French spelling elements like -*otte*, -*agne*, -*elle*, the silent final -*s* in *chassis*, and the pronunciation of final -*et* as /eɪ/ (cf. *ballet, sachet*, etc.). In this way, the French word *buffet* ("self-service meal") with final /eɪ/ is distinct from the Anglo-Saxon word *buffet* ("strike, push") with a more regular final /ɪt/.

Similarly, any words that start *chr-* (*chrome, Christmas, chronicle, chrysalis, chromosome*, etc.) must be of Greek origin, and pronounced with /k/. The reason for this is that /kr-/ is a permissible initial consonant cluster in English (e.g. *crab*), whereas /tʃr-/ is not; and /ʃr-/ words, e.g. *shrimp*, are always spelled with *shr-*, not *chr-*. The same is true of *chl-* words, e.g. *chlorine, chloroform*.

This does not exhaust the possibilities for *ch*, although the remainder are rare: /dʒ/ as in *Norwich, sandwich*; /x/ or /k/ in *loch, MacLachlan*; and silent as in *Crichton, yacht*.

Applying the Etymology

It is all well and good to say that a word comes from French, or Greek, etc. However, that does not necessarily mean that this is helpful in knowing the pronunciation in French, or Greek, and thus in English. How many English speakers or learners already know French or Greek, including its spelling system and letter-sound correspondences, silent letters, etc? Probably very few.

An authentic, observed example of this is the statement "I always thought it was pronounced /tʃaʊks/ pastry." The native English speaker clearly did not know that the word *choux* comes from French, where it means "cabbages." A baker in the 18th century produced choux buns, which people thought looked like cabbages. Not knowing the French origin, the speaker applied regular English letter-sound correspondences: *ch* = /tʃ/, as in *church, ou* = /aʊ/, as in *about*, and *x* = /ks/, as in *fox*, together giving /tʃaʊks/.

So, the speaker did not know that the word was of French origin. However, even if she had known this, it does not mean that she would have pronounced it correctly in English, because she did not speak French. She would thus not have known that French *ch-* words begin with /ʃ/ (although she could have guessed it from English loanwords like *champagne*, etc.), that *ou* = /u:/ (cf. *souvenir*), and the final *x* is silent (cf. *grand prix*). The word *choux* is thus pronounced /ʃu:/, as a homophone with *shoe / shoo*.

For many learners, English, as arguably the world's most useful language, is the first foreign language they learn in school. Expecting them to use information about other foreign languages like French and Greek is hardly realistic, at least at lower proficiency levels.

Etymological Elements

Just as the pronunciation of *ch-* in *choux* shows that it is of French origin, so there are other elements in the English spelling of words that are indicators of their (probable) etymology. These may be individual letter-sound correspondences, or whole morphemes (prefixes and suffixes). Learners may use this information in order to predict the spelling. In spelling bees (see Chapter 16), contestants are allowed to ask the etymological origin of a word, in order to use this information to help them predict the spelling. Learners may also note that elements from one source language are unlikely to mix with elements from a different source language.

Stirling (2011; Chapter 4) gives a useful summary of some key elements, summarized below.

Old English

Old English (Anglo-Saxon) elements include the sequences:

- *wh-*, e.g. *whether, white, wheel*
- *kn-*, e.g. *know, knife, knight*
- *-gh*, e.g. *daughter, through, enough*
- *-igh*, e.g. *fight, high, eight*
- *aw*, e.g. *law, raw, drawer*
- *ow*, e.g. *below, cow, show.*

These are spelling patterns, and may represent different sounds; for instance, *cow* does not rhyme with *show*.

The following prefixes and suffixes are of Old English origin.

- *mid-*, e.g. *midstream*
- *over-*, e.g. *overcoat*
- *under-*, e.g. *undercurrent*
- *with-*, e.g. *withstand*
- *-dom*, e.g. *kingdom*
- *-ful*, e.g. *beautiful*
- *-ness*, e.g. *kindness*
- *-ward*, e.g. *eastward.*

This knowledge can be used, for example, to learn *gh* as an indivisible unit.

Latin

Features of Latin loanwords include:

- they do not usually contain the letters *k, w, th, sh,* or *gh*
- they may end with the suffix *-ion* (*-tion, -sion, -ssion, -cion*) or are related to words that do
- they may have the negative prefix *in-* or be related to a word that does. This includes the prefixes *im-* (*impossible*), *il-* (*illogical*), and *ir-* (*irresponsible*), which are motivated by pronunciation
- many scientific words, with plurals that are irregular in English, but regular in Latin, e.g. *cactus* (*cacti*), *formula* (*formulae*), *bacterium* (*bacteria*).

The following prefixes, suffixes, and roots are of Latin origin.

- *ab-,* e.g. *abstract*
- *carn-,* e.g. *carnivorous*
- *noct-,* e.g. *nocturnal*
- *prim-,* e.g. *primary*
- *-cide,* e.g. *fungicide*
- *-fix,* e.g. *suffix.*

This knowledge can be used, for example, to predict that words with Latin elements do not also have *k, w, th, sh,* or *gh.*

French

French elements include the sequences:

- *ch* pronounced /ʃ/, e.g. *chandelier*
- *-et* pronounced /eɪ/, e.g. *beret*
- *-ure,* e.g. *leisure*
- *-eur,* e.g. *chauffeur*
- *-eau,* e.g. *plateau*
- *-que,* e.g. *boutique.*

The following prefixes and suffixes are of French origin.

- *con-,* e.g. *conceive*
- *trans-,* e.g. *transport*
- *pre-,* e.g. *premonition*
- *-ance,* e.g. *admittance*
- *-ment,* e.g. *impediment.*

This knowledge can be used, for example, in learning *eau* as an indivisible sequence. Words containing French elements are unlikely to contain Old English elements like *-igh.*

Greek

Features of Greek loanwords include:

* *ch* pronounced /k/
* silent initial *p*, e.g. *pneumatic, psychology*
* *ph* pronounced /f/.

The following prefixes, suffixes and roots are of Greek origin.

* *ethn-*, e.g. *ethnic*
* *phon-*, e.g. *phonetics*
* *neur-*, e.g. *neurosurgeon*
* *tele-*, e.g. *television*
* *-graphy*, e.g. *geography*
* *-oid*, e.g. *humanoid*
* *-ology*, e.g. *biology*
* *-scope*, e.g. *stethoscope*

Other Languages

We have already seen (Chapter 16) that many words of Italian origin, especially cooking terms, end in *-i*, e.g. *macaroni*. Such patterns may also be found in other lending languages.

Summary

* Throughout its history since Old English, the language has absorbed influences from many other languages, principally French, Latin, and Greek.
* A knowledge of etymology may be useful, at higher levels of proficiency, for mastering the spelling and pronunciation of words.
* It may also be useful for affixes, because they do not usually change their spelling.

Exercise

You probably have never encountered the following words before. However, you will have encountered the morphemes that compose them, because they are regular and productive. They also usually do not change their spelling. Can you work out what the words mean?

bicompartmental

autothermic

quadrupedal

carditis

illimitability

ichthyoid

demigoddesshood

glossectomy

agrometeorology

hydrogeomorphology

Further Reading

The etymology of English words can be found in etymological dictionaries, both online (e.g. *Online etymology dictionary*, n.d.) or in book form (e.g. Hoad, Ed., 1996).

References

Carney, E. (1994). *A survey of English spelling*. London, UK: Routledge.

Hoad, T. F. (Ed., 1996). *The concise Oxford dictionary of English etymology*. Oxford, UK: Oxford University Press.

Online etymology dictionary (n.d.). Retrieved from www.etymonline.com

Stirling, J. (2011). *Teaching spelling to English language learners*. Raleigh, NC: Lulu.

24 Phonological Strategy

Learning Objectives

At the end of this chapter, readers will be able to:

- explain the alphabetic principle of English spelling
- enumerate the main features of phonological awareness
- use phonics techniques in class.

Introduction

The phonological strategy puts heavy emphasis on the alphabetic principle that underlies the spelling system of English, and most other languages. That is, the alphabetic principle states that the symbols (letters) in the spelling represent the sounds (phonemes) in the pronunciation. The phonological strategy (also known as *phonics*) merely makes explicit the sounds in the speakers' pronunciation, and relates them to their spellings.

There are two main problems with this. Firstly, as has been repeated several times in this book, English is a poor example of an alphabetic system, so that the correspondence between sounds and spellings is far from one-to-one, or 100%. In Chapter 2, we examined measures of this correspondence. In languages with spelling systems closer to 100%, the phonological strategy allows readers and writers to master spelling, and recourse to the strategies described in other chapters (morphological, etymological, analogical, and visual) is not necessary.

Secondly, it assumes that speakers are aware of the sounds they are pronouncing. While readers and writers are well aware of the letters used in spelling, because they are visible marks on paper, a screen, etc., the sounds that come out of our mouths when we speak are far more intangible and not at all obvious.

Nevertheless, an understanding of the sounds that we produce is an important first step in literacy, and comes under the umbrella term *phonological awareness*. The following sections describe various aspects of phonological awareness.

The term *phonics* must be distinguished from other similar-sounding terms, all containing *phon* (Greek for "voice, sound"), often used in teaching.

Phonics is the method of teaching spelling described here, in which learners' phonological awareness is increased, so that the correspondence between the sounds and their spellings can be taught. *Phonemes* are the distinctive sounds of a particular language; English has about 44 phonemes, depending on the accent. *Phonetics* is the study of how sounds are produced using the vocal organs (vocal cords, tongue, lips, etc.). *Phonology* describes the way sounds function in particular languages. And finally, *phonotactics* is a technical word for syllable structure.

Phonics

While the term *phonics* is used for a method of teaching spelling in which the relationship between the sounds and the letters is emphasized, there are in fact several terms using the word *phonics*; these describe methods that differ in terms of whether a bottom-up approach starting with sounds or a top-down approach starting with words in context in sentences is taken. The now-defunct U.S. National Reading Panel (2000) succinctly defined the differences.

> Synthetic phonics programs teach children to convert letters into sounds or phonemes and then blend the sounds to form recognizable words. Analytic phonics avoids having children pronounce sounds in isolation to figure out words. Rather children are taught to analyze letter-sound relations once the word is identified. Phonics-through-spelling programs teach children to transform sounds into letters to write words. Phonics in context approaches teach children to use sound-letter correspondences along with context cues to identify unfamiliar words they encounter in text. Analogy phonics programs teach children to use parts of written words they already know to identify new words. The distinctions between systematic phonics approaches are not absolute, however, and some phonics programs combine two or more of these types of instruction.
>
> (National Reading Panel, 2000, pp. 2–89)

A British literacy expert quoted in BBC News (2005) reports that "Most teachers do both synthetic and analytic phonics, and 90% of teachers probably don't know the difference between the two. It's something the academic world argues about." That is, in the classroom, teachers use phonics as and when it seems appropriate.

It is also worth remembering that the above report was from the U.S. National *Reading* Panel, and its report was entitled *Teaching children to read*. In other words, they see various types of phonics as potentially usable for the perceptual process of reading. However, many of these types of phonics cannot be used when we are dealing with the productive process of spelling (as part of writing). In a text, a learner may guess the word *goldfish* because the text is talking about pets and has used the simpler words *dog* and *cat*, and *goldfish* begins with *go-*. However, this is a very different process from asking a child, without any such context, to spell *goldfish*, with its /ld/ cluster and its *sh* digraph. In such a situation, only synthetic phonics is usable.

Synthetic phonics was introduced in U.K. schools in 2010 by requiring all first-year schoolchildren to take a screening check of phonics skills and adopting a systematic approach to phonics. The U.K. schools minister, Nick Gibb (2015), proudly reports that this has led to

> a fourth year of consecutive improvement. In 2012, 58 per cent of six-year-olds met the national standard for decoding simple words. This year, that figure has risen to 77 per cent, the equivalent of 120,000 more 6-year-old children on track to read effectively.

International league tables for reading literacy (in addition to science and mathematics ability) published by the OECD's Programme for International Student Assessment (PISA, n.d.) showed that, despite ten years of school, 17% of British 15-year-olds did not have a minimum level of reading proficiency.

There are many freely available websites and downloadable worksheets and books with phonics material and guidance on how to choose and use it, e.g. British Council (n.d.), Drabble (2013), Jolly Learning (n.d.), LiteracyPlanet (2016), Mumsnet (n.d.), PBS (n.d.), U.K. Department for Education and Skills (2007), U.K. Government (n.d.).

Accurate Pronunciation

In order to relate letters to sounds, speakers must first be able to pronounce the sounds accurately.

For native speaking children, the problem is one of physiological development. Not all sounds are learned at the same time. Some are learned early, while others take time to be mastered. In particular, the fricative sounds /s, z, ʃ, ʒ, θ, ð/, and the approximants /r, l/ are mastered late; as late as eight years (Kilminster & Laird, 1978; Schriberg, 1993). Mastery of the fricatives develops late because of a process called myelinization, whereby "myelin, a white fatty substance, forms an insulating sheath around the auditory nerve, thereby improving audition in the higher-frequency range" (Weisler & Milekic, 2000, p. 28). Clearly, if native children cannot hear or pronounce the distinction between /t/ and /θ/, they cannot learn the different spelling (*t* and *th*) by the phonological strategy (Brown, 2015a).

Similarly, for non-native users of English, /θ/ is not a sound commonly found in languages of the world, and thus may be a pronunciation problem. Many non-native users conflate /θ/ with /t/, /s/, or /f/. They thus have only one sound in their psychological representation, and cannot arrive at the correct spelling via the phonological strategy, and are likely to produce misspellings as a result.

Number of Syllables

Learners need to be able to say how many syllables there are in words of more than one syllable. For instance, *bait* is one syllable, *debate* two, and *debated* three. Several books (e.g. Gilbert, 2001, pp. 12–18) contain exercises aimed at helping learners decide how many syllables words contain. Since syllables are often thought of as beats, these exercises often involve tapping out the syllables.

For example, the word *department* has three beats, thus three syllables. When asked what the syllables are, learners usually have no problem responding /dɪ/, /pɑ:(r)t/, and /mənt/.

Separating the Onset and the Rhyme

Syllables are composed of two parts. The onset is the initial consonant sound(s), if any, before the vowel. Thus, *load* has /l/ in the onset, *glowed* has /gl/, and *owed* has no onset consonant. In *department*, the first syllable has /d/ in the onset, the second /p/, and the third /m/. Words that have the same onset are said to alliterate, e.g. the /l/ words in *He who laughs last, laughs longest*.

The rhyme (sometimes spelled *rime*) is the rest of the syllable apart from the onset; that is, it is the vowel plus any final consonant(s). In *load*, *glowed*, and *owed*, all three syllables have the same rhyme: /oʊd/. This is why they are said to rhyme, as at the ends of lines in poetry. There may be no final consonant; thus, *say*, *stay*, and *stray* all have /eɪ/ with no final consonant as the rhyme. Multisyllable words rhyme if everything from the vowel of the stressed syllable is the same, e.g. *made*, *displayed*, and *lemonade* all rhyme (/-eɪd/), as do *follicle* and *diabolical* (/-ɒlɪkəl/ (BrE), ɑ:lɪkəl (AmE)).

Note that alliteration and rhyme depend on the sounds. They are thus features of pronunciation, regardless of how the words are spelled.

Pronunciation activities (e.g. those in Vaughan-Rees, 2010) can be used to highlight onsets and rhymes. Questions related to onsets and rhymes can be asked:

"Which word has a different first sound: *cheap, cap, kind?*"

"Which word does not rhyme: *speak, trick, week?*"

"Which word does not rhyme: *teach, speech, meat?*"

The poems of Dr. Seuss (real name Theodor Seuss Geisel) are full of alliterations and rhymes. The titles of his books *Horton Hears a Who!*, *Hooper Humperdink . . . ? Not Him!*, and *The Butter Battle Book* exemplify alliteration, while *The Cat in the Hat, Hop on Pop, Fox in Socks, Mr. Brown Can Moo! Can You?, Hunches in Bunches,* and *Yertle the Turtle* illustrate rhyme. The spelling of the onset is largely independent of the spelling of the rhyme. Activities can be used that highlight this. For instance, learners can be asked to put the consonants /b, kl, d, g, h, dʒ, m, p, s, st, sl, θ/ before the rhyme /ʌmp/. Or, in spelling terms, the letters *b, cl, d, g, h, j, m, p, s, st, sl, th* before the unchanging rhyme *ump*. Most of the resulting words are relatively simple: *bump, clump, dump,* (Forrest) *Gump, hump, jump, mumps, pump, sump, stump, slump,* and *thump*.

Separating the Peak and Coda

The rhyme is the vowel in the syllable (known as the peak) followed by the final consonant(s), if any (the coda). Learners therefore need to be able to separate the two. However, it is a feature of English syllable structure that short vowels do not end a syllable, i.e. there is always a final consonant. So, long vowels need to be used for such exercises.

"Say *seed*. Now say it without the /d/ sound at the end."

"Say *brown*. Now say it without the /n/ sound at the end."

Being able to change the vowel while keeping everything else the same leads to an appreciation of the function of the vowel.

"Say *seed*. Now say it again, but instead of /iː/ say /æ/."

"Say *spoon*. Now say it again, but instead of /uː/ say /ɪ/."

Various other exercises can be used to distinguish the three parts of the syllable (onset, peak, coda).

"Say *shout*. Now say it again but don't say /ʃ/."

"Say *pray*. Now say it again but don't say /p/."

"Say *stink*. Now say it again but don't say /t/."

"Say *bend*. Now say it again but don't say /d/."

Table 24.1 (from Brown, 2015b) shows various possibilities for syllable structures in English. C stands for any consonant sound, V for any vowel sound, and O for an empty position, i.e. no consonant(s). It is important to remember that syllable structure refers to the combinations of sounds, regardless of how they are spelled.

Table 24.1 Syllable structure of various English words

Word	Onset	Peak	Coda	Formula
owe		oʊ		OVO
own		oʊ	n	OVC
toe/tow	t	oʊ		CVO
tone	t	oʊ	n	CVC
owns		oʊ	nz	OVCC
stow	st	oʊ		CCVO
stone	st	oʊ	n	CCVC
tones	t	oʊ	nz	CVCC
stones	st	oʊ	nz	CCVCC

Where there is more than one consonant in either onset or coda position, this is known as a cluster. So, the last five words in Table 24.1 contain clusters.

The term *cluster*, meaning two or more consonant sounds occurring both in onset or in coda position, must be distinguished from a *digraph*, meaning two letters representing one sound, e.g. the *sh* in *shout*. A cluster is a pronunciation phenomenon, while a digraph is a spelling phenomenon. In literacy circles, the term *blend* is sometimes used confusingly for either cluster or digraph, so it is not used here in this book. *Blending* is also sometimes used to mean the joining of individual sounds, e.g. putting together the regular correspondences *sh* (= /ʃ/), *r* (/r/), *i* (/ɪ/), *m* (/m/), and *p* (/p/) to give the full word *shrimp*.

Teaching Sequence

As in many aspects of teaching, simple features are introduced before more complex features. So, in what sequence should English letters and digraphs be introduced? Lloyd (1998) suggests the following.

"The first group *s, a, t, i, p, n* have been chosen because they make more simple three letter words than any other six letters" (p. 36). In terms of three-letter CVC words, these six letters generate the following 17 words.

nap

nip

nit

pan

pat

pin

pip

pit

sap

sat

sin

sip

sit

tan

tap

tin

tip

All of these are simple beginners' words, in addition to words like *tat* and *tit*, which are hardly likely to be known by beginners.

All these words have a CVC structure, and use the six letters in their pronunciation as /s, æ, t, ɪ, p, n/, as opposed to any other pronunciations they may represent.

When two-consonant clusters are introduced, they also produce initial cluster examples like *snap* and *spin*, and final cluster examples like *pant* and *pits*, and more complex examples like *pants*, etc. The word *pint* should not be used, because it does not use *i* in its /ɪ/ pronunciation.

Once these six have been learned, other groups are introduced, giving the following order:

1   *s, a, t, i, p, n*
2   *ck, e, h, r, m, d*
3   *g, o, u, l, f, b*
4   *ai, j, oa, ie, ee, or*
5   *z, w, ng, v*, "little *oo*" (representing /ʊ/), "long *oo*" (representing /u:/)
6   *y, x, ch, sh*, "voiced *th*" (representing /ð/), "unvoiced *th*" (representing /θ/)
7   *qu, ou, oi, ue, er, ar*

While we may dispute the number of groups and the precise sounds in each group, it is clear that there needs to be a progression from common sounds with simple correspondences, to less common sounds and those with more complex correspondences.

Conclusion

The phonological strategy, including phonological awareness and phonics, is based on the underlying alphabetic principle of English and most other languages, that letters represent sounds. In languages with transparent spelling systems, little more is needed than this, and children learn to spell quickly. Because of the opaque nature of English spelling, other strategies may also be needed and children learn more slowly.

Let us illustrate this with the word *department* /dɪpɑː(r)tmənt/ (the /r/ is pronounced in AmE, but not in BrE.). A phonics approach requires this to be split into its component syllables: /dɪ/, /pɑː(r)t/, and /mənt/. The syllables are then segmented into their onset and rhyme (thus /pɑː(r)t/ > /p − ɑː(r)t/), and the onset and rhyme into their constituent individual sounds (/p − ɑː − (r)t/).

These individual sounds can then be associated with their (probable) spellings. In the first syllable, /d/ is regularly spelled with *d*; in the second, the /p/ and /t/ sounds are regularly spelled with *p* and *t* letters (and /r/ with *r* for AmE speakers); and in the third, /m, n, t/ are regularly spelled *m, n, t*.

That leaves the vowel sounds, where other strategies come into play. However, notice that the vowel sounds comprise only three out of the nine (ten for AmE) sounds in the word.

The vowel letter in the first syllable could be *e* or *i*; however, *de-* (*decide, descend, detract*) is a much more common (historical) prefix than *di-* (*diphthong*), which usually conveys the meaning "two" (Chapter 22).

In the second syllable, for BrE speakers, /ɑː/ is often *ar* (60% of the time according to Carney, 1994). However, knowing that AmE speakers pronounce the /r/ here, clearly shows that it is spelled *ar*. The spelling of *part* may be related to the spelling of other words with the same rhyme (peak + coda), such as *cart, start*. The only common counterexample is *heart*. Carney (1994, p. 102) points out that an awareness of other accents of English may help in such decisions: "Anyone [BrE] who knows that an American would say *tomato* with their equivalent of /eɪ/ would not be tempted to spell *tomato* as **tomarto*."

The vowel in the final syllable could be *e* or *a* (as in *adamant*). Learners should be taught that -*ment* is a common and productive noun ending (*excitement, statement, treatment*, etc.), whereas -*mant* is a much less frequent ending (*claimant, dormant, format, informant*). Another morphological strategy is to think of the adjective from *department* (*departmental*), which has a full /e/ vowel sound that could not be spelled *a*.

Summary

- The English spelling system is alphabetic, meaning that the letters in the spelling reflect the sounds they typically make. The phonological strategy is based on this correspondence.
- Phonological awareness involves being able to decide the number of syllables in multisyllable words, separating the onset from the rhyme, and the peak from the coda, and assigning letters to the individual sounds.

Exercises

1 Alliteration refers to words that have the same consonant sounds in the onset. There are a number of common idioms that use alliteration. Supply the missing words in the following expressions.

- *The building had gone to rack and . . .*
- *My brother and I are like chalk and . . .*
- *Marking is part and . . . of being a teacher.*
- *She chooses her clothes so that she can mix and . . .*
- *My kids were so excited they jumped for . . .*
- *A new haircut works . . . for your confidence.*
- *She keeps her house spick and . . .*
- *His face was black and . . .*

2 In the chapter, *cart* and *start* were given as rhymes for *part*. They can therefore be used, as a phonological and analogical strategy, for helping students with the correct spelling of *part*.

- Give three more, common words that rhyme with *part*.
- Give three common words that rhyme with *worm*.
- Give three common words that rhyme with *dust*.
- Give three common words that rhyme with *fanatic*.
- Give three common words that rhyme with *fiction*.

3 Supply the missing rhyming words in the following limericks. They have been chosen because the missing words are spelled the same way as the given words.

A rocket inventor named Wright
Once traveled much faster than . . .
He departed one day
In a relative . . .
And returned on the previous . . .

There was a young lady of Kent
Whose nose was remarkably . . .
One day, they suppose,
She followed her . . .
For no one knows which way she . . .

There once was a fly on the wall
I wondered, "Why doesn't it . . .?
Are its feet stuck?
Or is it just . . .?
Or does gravity miss things so . . .?"

There once was a young boy named Sid
Who thought he knew more than he . . .
He thought that a shark
Would turn tail if you . . .
So he swam out to try it. Poor . . .!

A crossword compiler named Moss,
Who found himself quite at a . . . .,
When asked, "Why so blue?"
Said, "I haven't a . . . .
I'm 2 Down to put 1 . . . ."

Further Reading

Rhymes for almost any word can be found at Stands4 Network (n.d.). There are many limerick sites on the internet, e.g. Brownielocks and the Three Bears (n.d.), *Dave's big fat limerick site* (n.d.). For materials devoted to phonological awareness, see Layton, Deeny & Upton (1998), Munro (1998).

References

BBC News (2005). *Spelling out success in reading.* Retrieved from news.bbc.co.uk/2/ hi/uk_news/education/4419955.stm

British Council (n.d.) *LearnEnglish kids: Phonics stories.* Retrieved from learnenglishkids. britishcouncil.org/en/apps/learnenglish-kids-phonics-stories

Brown, A. (2015a). Barriers to learning the English *th* sounds. Part 1: Articulatory and acoustic considerations. *Speak Out! (Newsletter of the IATEFL Pronunciation Special Interest Group), 53,* 6–14.

Brown, A. (2015b). Syllable structure. In M. Reed & J. Levis (Eds.), *The handbook of English pronunciation.* Malden, MA: Wiley Blackwell.

Brownielocks and the Three Bears (n.d.). *Limericks.* Retrieved from www.browni-elocks.com/Limericks.html

Carney, E. (1994). *A survey of English spelling.* London, UK: Routledge.

Dave's big fat limerick site (n.d.). Retrieved from davesbigfatlimericksite.weebly. com/clean.html

Drabble, E. (2013). How to teach . . . phonics. *The Guardian.* Retrieved from www.theguardian.com/education/teacher-blog/2013/apr/01/phonics-teaching-resources-schools

Gibb, N. (24 September 2015). *Schools minister: Focus on phonics is working. The Telegraph.* Retrieved from www.telegraph.co.uk/education/education-news/11888603/Schools-minister-Focus-on-phonics-is-working.html

Gilbert, J. B. (2001). *Clear speech from the start: Basic pronunciation and listening comprehension in North American English.* Cambridge, UK: Cambridge University Press.

Jolly Learning (n.d.). *Teaching literacy with Jolly Phonics.* Retrieved from jollylearning. co.uk/overview-about-jolly-phonics/

Kilminster, M. G. E., & Laird, E. M. (1978). Articulation development in children aged three to nine years. *Australian Journal of Human Communication Disorders, 6*(1), 23–30.

Layton, L., Deeny, K., & Upton, G. (1998). *Sound practice: Phonological awareness in the classroom*. London, UK: David Fulton Publishers.

LiteracyPlanet (2016). *Phonics: Establishing a strong foundation for early reading*. Retrieved from www.literacyplanet.com/au/schools/skills/phonics

Lloyd, S. (1998). *The phonics handbook* (3rd edition). Chigwell, UK: Jolly Learning.

Mumsnet (n.d.). *Mumsnet by parents for parents*. Retrieved from www.mumsnet.com/learning

Munro, J. (1998). *Assessing and teaching phonological knowledge*. Melbourne, Australia: ACRE (Australian Council for Educational Research) Press.

National Reading Panel (2000). *Teaching children to read: An evidence-based assessment of the scientific research literature on reading and its implications for reading instruction*. Retrieved from www.dys-add.com/resources/SpecialEd/TeachingChildrenToRead.pdf

PBS (n.d.). *What is phonics?* Retrieved from www.pbs.org/parents/education/reading-language/reading-tips/what-is-phonics

PISA (n.d.). Retrieved from www.oecd.org/pisa

Schriberg, L. (1993). Four new speech and prosody-voice measures for genetics research and other studies in developmental phonological disorders. *Journal of Speech and Hearing Research, 36*, 105–140.

Stands4 Network (n.d.). *Rhymes*. Retrieved from www.rhymes.net

U.K. Department for Education and Skills (2007). *Letters and sounds: Principles and practice of high quality phonics*. Retrieved from www.gov.uk/government/uploads/system/uploads/attachment_data/file/190599/Letters_and_Sounds_-_DFES-00281-2007.pdf

U.K. Government (n.d.). *Teaching phonics: Information for schools*. Retrieved from www.gov.uk/government/collections/phonics

Vaughan-Rees. M. (2010). *Rhymes and rhythm* (2nd edition). Reading, UK: Garnet.

Weisler, S., & Milekic, S. (2000). *The theory of language*. Cambridge, MA: MIT Press.

25 Analogical Strategy

Learning Objectives

At the end of this chapter, readers will be able to:

- help learners relate unknown words to known words with similar spelling.

Introduction

The analogical strategy works on the principle of relating unknown words and their spelling patterns, with known words. As with many other aspects of spelling covered in this book, the analogical strategy is only necessary because English does not have a good sound-spelling correspondence. In other languages, with better correspondences, sounds can be related to spellings without having to decide, "If the word patterns like word A, then it is pronounced B, but if it patterns like word C, it is pronounced D."

If a learner meets the unfamiliar word *gout* ("joint disease"), spelling by analogy will allow them to relate it to known words such as *about, scout, shout*, and assume that *gout* is pronounced /gaʊt/. They thus arrive at the correct English pronunciation. However, see Chapter 23 for further discussion of *gout*.

Is this an example of a learner using analogy or, more simply, using sound-spelling correspondences? After all, *g* regularly represents /g/, *ou* represents /aʊ/, and *t* represents /t/. While learners may be encouraged to look for familiar analogical words (*about*, etc.), those words may contain the same (phonological strategy) correspondences: *ou* = /aʊ/, and *t* = /t/.

The *-ough* Words

We therefore perhaps need to look at examples where such regular correspondences do not exist. One commonly quoted example of this is the notorious *-ough* words of English. There are several correspondences for this sequence, although none of them can hardly be called patterns, since they occur in very few example words.

- /oʊ/ as in *though* (cf. *toe*)
- /uː/ as in *through* (cf. *true*)

- /ʌf/ as in *rough* (cf. *cuff*)
- /ɒf (BrE), ɑːf (AmE)/ as in *cough* (cf. *coffin*)
- /ɔː/ as in *thought* (cf. *taut*)
- /aʊ/ as in *bough* (cf. *how*)
- /ə/ as in *thorough, Peterborough* (/oʊ/ in AmE)

Unfamiliar words ending in *-ough* can only be tackled by either trying to use analogy or looking the word up in a dictionary. For example, the *chough* is a member of the crow bird family. It is impossible to guess with any certainty which of the above correspondences this word contains. In fact, it is a /tʃʌf/, thus patterning like *rough* and *enough*.

Brand Names

Some companies give their company or products names, perhaps deliberately, where it is not obvious from the spelling how it should be pronounced. Just such a dilemma occurs with the name of the budget clothing, cosmetics, and houseware store originally known as Penneys in the Republic of Ireland (incidentally, without an apostrophe; see Chapter 9). Success led to expansion to the U.K., and it opened its first store in Derby in 1973. It now has over 300 stores throughout Europe, and eight in the U.S.A. However, none of them are called Penneys because the U.S. department store JCPenney had already registered the name (note the camel case in their name; see Chapter 11). So it called itself Primark. The problem with that choice of name is that people are unsure how to pronounce the *i* letter – either as /aɪ/ or /iː/. Both are possible, from an analogical sound-spelling point of view. For instance, the noun *privacy* can be pronounced /praɪvəsi/ (like the adjective *private*) or /prɪvəsi/ (a vestige of the historical origin). The company itself says that it is /aɪ/ (BBC News, 2017); it seems that people feel this is an upmarket pronunciation (perhaps because of the association with *prime*?) thus disguising the fact that Primark is a budget store. However, at least in the U.K., the /iː/ pronunciation seems to be the commonest. A comment by a reader in BBC News (2017) writes, "Like literally every single person I know pronounces it 'Preemark' cause saying 'Prymark' makes it sounds like you think it's upmarket."

BBC News (2017) gives several other brand names that are mispronounced, according to the preferred pronunciation of the brand owners.

- The name of the Swedish furniture company *IKEA* was produced as an acronym of the initials of Ingvar Kamprad (the founder), Elmtaryd (the farm where he grew up), and Agunnaryd (his hometown in Småland, Sweden). As a Swedish word, it is therefore pronounced /ɪkeɪə/. However, a common pronunciation outside Sweden is /aɪkiːə/ (see Chapter 18).
- The *adidas* company (note the lower-case initial *a*; see Chapter 11) was founded in 1949 by German Adolf Dassler. Probably because the German name Adolf was stigmatized after World War II because of its association with Adolf Hitler, Dassler used the abbreviated nickname

Adi, with stress still on the first syllable. Taking the first three letters of his surname, his company was named *adidas*, with stress still on the first syllable. However, it is not uncommon for the name to be pronounced with stress on the second syllable, on analogy with words like *Candida*.

- When the U.S. sports good company *Nike* began under that name in 1971, it was not obvious to customers how to pronounce the name, given the spelling. Many, using analogy, thought it patterned after the word *like* (i.e. was an example of magic *e*; see Chapter 13), and pronounced it as a one-syllable /naɪk/. The company clarified that it was named after Nike, the Greek goddess of victory, with a two-syllable /naɪki/.

Personal Names

An episode that illustrated the analogical strategy at work was in the late 1990s when the first Harry Potter book was published. Harry has a schoolfriend named Hermione Granger. However, many young readers had never come across the (nowadays rather old-fashioned) name *Hermione* before, and they were encountering it in writing. They were therefore unsure how to pronounce it. Many resorted to the analogical strategy. Perhaps the name is a regular English word, and the final three letters are an example of magic *e* (see Chapter 13) as in *bone, cone, lone, phone, stone, tone, zone*; they therefore guessed it was pronounced /hɜː(r)mioʊn/. Or could it be a less regular English word patterning like *gone, scone, shone*, and therefore /hɜːmiɒn (BrE), hɜːrmiɑːn (AmE)/? Although the word *done* is very irregular in its sound-spelling correspondence, maybe *Hermione* resembled it, and was thus /hɜː(r)miʌn/. The final three letters of *Hermione*, as a word, are the number *one*, so it could be /hɜː(r)miwʌn/. Many users of English know little about the historical origins of words, so perhaps *Hermione* is of Italian origin, like *minestrone*, and thus /hɜː(r)mioʊni/.

In fact, the name is of Greek origin; it is related to the male name *Hermes*. It is also stressed on the second syllable, unlike all the above guesses. That syllable is pronounced as in *lion*, so it is actually /hɜː(r)maɪəni/.

As it is fashionable with some parents nowadays to give children unusual nonce names, the phenomenon of wrongly pronouncing names because of analogy is likely to increase.

While on the subject of Greek Hermes (pronounced /hɜː(r)miːz/ in English), the name of the French high fashion company *Hermès* is not related. The accented *è* might give that away. The company was named after its French-German founder, Thierry Hermès. Jeffries (2014) explains the pronunciation in lay language:

> Nightmare: another Greek deity turned global brand. Obvious, isn't it? You take *her*, add *me*, and put an *s* on the end. Put them together and what have you got? Her-mees. Mais non, non, non! In fact, one drops the *h*, and sounds the *e* as in *dress*. Plus you need to sound the *s* more like a *z*: *Ermez*.

Jeffries (2014) also explains the pronunciation of the name of the car company Audi:

> Remember American war hero and actor Audie Murphy? Me neither, but his first name was pronounced 'Or-dee', which – quite possibly – has led to confusion about the pronunciation of the uninteresting motor car company. It's not pronounced 'Or-dee', but 'Ow-dee' – imagine you're a cowboy who drops his aitches if that's any help.

Using Analogy in Teaching

As teachers, we often use analogy in teaching English. For example, regular English verbs (e.g. *like*) take *-(e)d* to make the past tense (*He liked it*), and also *-(e)d* to make the participle (*She is much liked*). Irregular verbs, by definition, do not. One irregular pattern is for a verb with an *i* vowel letter (e.g. *sing*) to change to *a* for the past tense (*sang*) and *u* for the participle (*sung*). Other irregular verbs, perhaps less common than *sing*, can then be described as patterning like *sing: begin, drink, ring, sink, spring, stink, swim*. Another set of similar-looking verbs (e.g. *stick*) pattern in a slightly different way, in that the past tense also takes *u*, not *a* (so *He stuck the stamp on the envelope*): *cling, dig, fling, sling, slink, sting, string, swing, wring*. So, teachers can point out that *sting* patterns like *stick*, not like *sing*. This picture is clouded by the fact that one or two verbs can go either way, as historical or geographical variation. For instance, some dictionaries give *span* as the past tense of *spin*, but label it archaic. The title of the 1989 film is *Honey, I Shrunk the Kids*, where British speakers would more commonly say *shrank*.

Similarly, in spelling, analogy can be used to help learners remember spelling patterns and examples. It is simple to point out that *grove* patterns like *stove* (this is magic *e*), while the less regular *glove* patterns like *love*, and the very irregular *prove* patterns like *move*.

Summary

- Spelling by analogy relates the spelling of unfamiliar words with the spelling of familiar words.
- It is a useful strategy in teaching.
- However, it may simply be a case of referring to regular sound-spelling correspondences.

Exercises

1   The following words all contain the *ough* sequence, but are rare words. It is therefore not obvious or predictable which of the *ough* patterns outlined in this chapter they belong to. Find out their pronunciation, if necessary by looking in a pronouncing dictionary (e.g. Wells, 1990).

brougham	"a one-horse carriage"
clough	"a valley or ravine"
doughty	"brave and capable"
hough	"a hind leg joint"
slough	(noun) "muddy ground"
	(verb) (e.g. of a snake) "to shed skin"
sough	"a murmuring sound, sigh"

2   Likewise, the following surnames and place names all contain the *ough* sequence, but are rare words. Find out their pronunciation, i.e. analogical pattern.

Bough	*Coughton*	*Loughborough*	*Stoughton*
Broughton	*Gough*	*Poughill*	*Troughton*

Further Reading

Further examples of brand names mispronounced because of false analogy are given by Jeffries (2014).

References

BBC News (14 August 2017). *Primark sets the record straight on pronunciation*. Retrieved from www.bbc.com/news/uk-40926473

Jeffries, S. (3 June 2014). *It's official: Nike rhymes with spiky – and you're saying all these wrong too*. The Guardian. Retrieved from www.theguardian.com/media/shortcuts/2014/jun/03/nike-how-to-pronounce-correctly-brand-names-audi-adidas-porsche-yvessaintlaurent

Wells, J. C. (1990). *Longman pronunciation dictionary* (1st edition; 2nd edition 2000; 3rd edition 2008). Harlow, UK: Pearson Education Ltd.

26 Visual Strategy

Learning Objectives

At the end of this chapter, readers will be able to:

- help learners cope with the spelling of words where none of the other strategies can be used.
- devise mnemonics, where appropriate.

Introduction

The visual strategy, at least in its strictest sense, is in effect a last resort. If all else fails, learn the spelling of certain words by rote, because their spelling is so irregular. Once again, it needs to be pointed out that this strategy is sometimes needed in English, because English contains many words whose spelling is very irregular. In languages with more regular sound-spelling correspondences, this strategy is needed less, if at all, as a last resort.

However, the spelling of no word is totally irregular. The alphabetic principle that underlies English spelling operates on the basis that letters represent sounds. As we saw in Chapter 2, some languages have alphabetic systems that are close to 100%, i.e. very regular. At the other extreme, the correspondence in English is well below 100%. But it is still well above 0%; otherwise, we could not claim it is an alphabetic system.

While some English words may seem to be spelled so irregularly that a visual rote strategy seems appropriate, that is not to say that the other strategies described in the preceding chapters (morphological, etymological, phonological, and analogical) do not play some part in helping to learn the spelling. An interesting example of this is the word *choir* /kwaɪə(r)/. It is clearly a strange spelling for the pronunciation.

By investigating its etymology, we could say that this spelling could be learned partly by morphological strategy (Chapter 22). The word comes from Latin *chorus* meaning "a dance in a circle, the persons singing and dancing, the chorus of a tragedy," and ultimately from Greek *khoros*, with the same meanings. It was borrowed into English around 1300 from a French word alternatively spelled *cuer* or *quer* meaning "a chorus of singers, especially in a theatrical sense." When borrowed into English, it was spelled *queor* and later *quyre*. This was respelled as the modern spelling *choir* in the mid-17th century (the Renaissance; Chapter 4) in order to resemble the Latin origin more closely. The Latin word *chorus* also gives us the English words *choral, chorale, chorister,* and of course *chorus,* all of which have much more regular spellings. Appealing to the morphological strategy may thus help.

Adopting a visual strategy would simply mean to tell learners to learn the spelling by heart, without any great reference to sound-letter correspondences. In this regard, it is interesting to note that *choir* has a homophone, *quire,* meaning "24 sheets of paper." In contrast to *choir,* the spelling of *quire* is quite regular by English spelling patterns. The initial *qu-* represents /kw/ in many other words, e.g. *quality, queen, quick, quote.* Similarly, the final *-ire* represents /aɪə(r)/ in many words, e.g. *fire, hire, spire, tire, wire.* It is an example of magic *e,* like *satire, satirical;* see Chapter 5. In regard to *choir,* on the other hand, *ch-* may represent /k/, especially in words of Greek origin (e.g. *chaos, chemist, character*), but there are no other words where *ch* represents /k/ where it is followed by /w/. The spelling *-oir* is common in words of French origin, and represents /wɑː(r)/ (e.g. *abattoir, memoir, reservoir*), never /aɪə(r)/.

A visual strategy is thus necessary for words that deviate greatly from a one-to-one sound-to-letter correspondence. A visual strategy is needed, for instance, for words with silent initial letters. Learners looking up the words *gnome, hour, knee, mnemonic, pneumonia, who,* and *write* in a dictionary would naturally try the *N, O, N, N, N, H,* and *R* sections first, rather than the *G, H, K, M, P, W,* and *W* sections where these words actually are to be found, because of silent initial letters. Likewise, who would look for the word *one* in the *O* section, rather than *W*? Or *eye* in the *E* section, rather than *I*? This illustrates the occasional dilemma of using an English dictionary: "How can I look up the spelling of a word in the dictionary, if I don't know (and can't guess) the spelling to be able to search in the right place?"

It is surprising and confusing that the logo of the popular BBC sci-fi series *Doctor Who* contains the letters *DW.*

Sight Words

It is an unfortunate fact about English that many of the commonest words are also words that are irregular in their spelling. This has led some writers to propose that many words should be learned as "sight words"; that is, words that should be learned by rote with little reference to the regular sound-letter correspondences that they may contain. This is known as the "whole word" approach, one of its earliest advocates being Edward William Dolch (1889–1961). By examining popular children's books of the time, in 1936 he produced lists of high-frequency words which he argued needed to be recognized by sight in order to facilitate literacy at various educational levels. These lists are still used in American schools, and can be found on many websites, with the instruction that they must be learned without trying to sound them out, i.e. bypassing the alphabetic principle that underlies English spelling and the phonics approach.

Similar word lists for sight words were produced by Edward B. Fry (1925–2010), containing what he claimed were the 1,000 commonest words divided by frequency into sets of 100.

It is informative to compare the two lists (Dolch's pre-kindergarten (40 words) and kindergarten words (52 words), with Fry's first 100 words). Words that the two lists have in common are the following, in alphabetical order:

a, all, and, are, at, be, but, can, come, did, do, down, find, for, get, go, have, he, I, in, into, is, it, like, look, make, my, no, not, now, on, one, out, said, see, she, so, that, the, there, they, this, to, two, up, was, we, what, who, will, with, you

Words that are not shared are the following, in alphabetical order:

Dolch

am, ate, away, big, black, blue, brown, came, eat, four, funny, good, help, here, jump, little, me, must, new, our, play, please, pretty, ran, red, ride, saw, say, soon, run, three, too, under, want, well, went, where, white, yellow, yes

Fry

about, an, are, as, been, by, called, could, day, each, first, from, had, has, her, him, his, how, if, long, made, many, may, more, number, of, oil, or, other, part, people, sit, some, than, their, them, then, they, time, use, water, way, were, when, which, words, would, write, your

In fairness, it should be pointed out that Dolch's list does not contain nouns, which comprise a separate 95-word list. However, very few of the extra Fry words are nouns. In short, there are substantial differences between the two lists; roughly half the lists differ.

Since the 1980s, the increasing availability of inexpensive computing power has enabled linguists, lexicographers, etc. to produce much more accurate, observation-based measures of the frequency of English words. This decade saw an explosion in corpus linguistics, using computers to store and analyze passages of language. According to the Oxford English Corpus, a 2.1 billion-word corpus of written English from various countries, the 100 commonest words are the following, in descending order of frequency:

the, be, to, of, and, a, in, that, have, I, it, for, not, on, with, he, as, you, do, at, this, but, his, by, from, they, we, say, her, she, or, an, will, my, one, all, would, there, their, what, so, up, out, if, about, who, get, which, go, me, when, make, can, like, time, no, just, him, know, take, people, into, year, your, good, some, could, them, see, other, than, then, now, look, only, come, its, over, think, also, back, after, use, two, how, our, work, first, well, way, even, new, want, because, any, these, give, day, most, us

Exercise

Take the first 20 words in the Oxford English Corpus (*the* to *at* in the above list). Which ones:

- are totally regular in their spelling?
- are regular but involve complexities of spelling such as digraphs (two letters representing one sound) or rare correspondences?
- contain irregularities?

The whole word approach is part of a literacy approach called whole language, which emphasizes meaning over form. That is, learners are encouraged to create their own interpretations of texts when reading and give free expression to ideas when writing. The role of spelling proficiency in both these processes is downgraded. The whole language approach has therefore received several criticisms.

Firstly, overlooking the spelling of words gives learners the impression that the spelling bears little correspondence to the pronunciation. In an alphabetic spelling such as is used for English, that is simply not the case. While English has a poor correspondence between letters and sounds, the underlying principle of English spelling is undoubtedly alphabetic, and the whole language approach denies this. Decades ago, this was criticized as being responsible for functional illiteracy in the U.S.A. (Flesch, 1955). "The new method [whole word] reduces English to the status of Chinese" (Mathews, 1966, p. 90). That is, ignoring the correspondences that do exist between letters and sounds in English treats the system as if it were logographic, like Chinese (see Chapter 2). And it clearly is not.

Secondly, "creating meaning" is impossible for learners at lower levels of proficiency. Learners cannot recognize English words if they have never encountered those words before; that is, if they have small but developing English vocabularies. Similarly, whole word learners cannot begin to attempt to spell new words.

The root problem in deciding the relevance of the whole language approach to literacy is in the word *literacy* itself. Whole language, including whole words, may be of relevance to literacy at higher learning levels, where the learners have good proficiency in grammar, vocabulary, etc, and are engaged in exploring the writer's intentions in producing the text, "reading between the lines," creating meaning, etc. However, this high-level literacy is far removed from the literacy, in its more traditional sense, of deciphering words from their spellings, and learning to spell words.

In summary, sight words and the whole word approach relate to the left-hand, lexical side of Figure 3.1 (see Chapter 3), while phonics relates to the right-hand, phonological side. Both types of processing are required for efficient reading and writing, but each with their own particular types of word, and at different levels of proficiency.

Mnemonics

Mnemonics may be useful tools for learning spellings with no reference to sound-letter correspondences. It is a moot point whether the mnemonics are themselves easier to learn than the words they are mnemonics for, and whether mnemonics improve spelling ability.

As we saw with the example of *stationery/stationary* in Chapter 20, mnemonics may be helpful when trying to remember the spelling of homophones; that is, words that are pronounced the same, but spelled differently. There are even websites with such mnemonics, e.g. Mnemonic Devices Memory Tools (n.d.).

Some mnemonics use sentences, the initial letters of whose words spell out a word. Some may be easy to remember because they relate to the meaning of the word, e.g. *Rhythm has your two hips moving (rhythm)*. Others do not, e.g. *Only cat's eyes are narrow (ocean)*. Some have alternative versions, so you can take your choice, e.g. *George eats old grey rats and paints houses yellow, George Eliot's old grandmother rode a pig home yesterday, General Eisenhower's oldest girl rode a pony home yesterday (geography)*. Likewise, *A rat in the house might eat the ice cream, A rat in Tom's house might eat Tom's ice cream, A red Indian thought he might eat tomatoes in church (arithmetic)*.

Some mnemonics relate to parts of words, e.g. *You take the bus to business, The principal is my pal*.

Some relate to the English problem of single versus double consonants:

- Two cots need two mattresses in any *accommodation*.
- A vicar has one collar and two socks. (*necessary*)
- *Desert* versus *dessert*. The sweet one has two sugars.
- One tea, two sugars. (*potassium*)

In many cases, people have invented mnemonics when simpler strategies seem appropriate. For example, *Big elephants can always understand small elephants* is a mnemonic for the spelling of *because*. However, English and writing teachers always cover the organizational device known as cause and effect. The fact that the last five letters of *because* spell *cause* is a clear indication of the spelling of *because* and that it introduces the cause side of the relationship.

Conclusion

In Chapter 3, the dual-route hypothesis was discussed. It posits that many words, and certainly words that are unfamiliar, are recognized or pronounced by phonological processing using letter-to-sound correspondences.

High-frequency familiar words, on the other hand, are unlikely to require this phonological processing, but are recognized as a whole. That is, for instance, while it is true that *a* = /æ/, *n* = /n/, and *d* = /d/, *and* is such a common word of English that lexical processing tells us that *and* as a whole represents /(ə)n(d)/, its precise pronunciation depending on how unstressed it is, and surrounding sounds. It is thus a sight word, identified by visual strategy.

Summary

- English is a poor example of an alphabetic spelling system and, as a result, there are a few words that are very irregular in terms of sound-letter correspondences.
- The best way to learn the spelling of these words is by rote.
- High-frequency words account for a large percentage of any text, and are also among the first words needing to be mastered by learners. It is an unfortunate fact that many of them have irregular spellings requiring the visual strategy.
- Mnemonics may help – and may not.

Exercise

What difficult spellings are the following mnemonics for?

Do In A Rush. Run Home, Or Expect Accident.

Never Eat Cress. Eat Salad Sandwiches And Remain Youthful!

Please Say You Can Hit Old Ladies, Or Get Yogurt.

A Rude Girl Undresses. My Eyes Need Taping!

Further Reading

A full list of Fry's sight words can be found at Sight Words (n.d., a), and Dolch's at Sight Words (n.d., b). The 100 commonest words in English, with more detailed statistical information, can be found in Oxford Living Dictionaries (n.d.).

References

Flesch, R. (1955). *Why Johnny can't read: And what you can do about it.* New York, NY: William Morrow Paperbacks.

Mathews, M. M. (Ed., 1966). *Teaching to read historically considered.* Chicago, IL: University of Chicago Press.

Mnemonic Devices Memory Tools (n.d.). Retrieved from www.mnemonic-device.com

Oxford Living Dictionaries (n.d.). *What can the Oxford English Corpus tell us about the English language?* Retrieved from en.oxforddictionaries.com/explore/what-can-corpus-tell-us-about-language

Sight Words (n.d., a). *Fry sight words list.* Retrieved from www.sightwords.com/sight-words/fry/#lists

Sight Words (n.d., b). *Dolch sight words list.* Retrieved from www.sightwords.com/sight-words/dolch/#lists

27 Teaching English Spelling

Learning Objectives

At the end of this chapter, readers will be able to:

- list a sequence for teaching the features of English spelling
- adapt exercises, especially vocabulary exercises, for spelling purposes
- create their own classroom spelling exercises.

Introduction

The preceding chapters have already given a lot of ideas about how to teach English spelling. Many of the exercises contained in those chapters can be used as classroom exercises, with adaptation for the age and level of the learners. Most of them can be integrated with classroom work on other aspects of language, especially vocabulary and pronunciation, but also grammar, the four skills, etc.

The title of Peters' seminal (1985) book was *Spelling, caught or taught?* That is, should spelling be caught (picked up on the fly while ostensibly studying some other aspect of English) or taught (learned through explicit instruction)? At beginner level, whether for native-speaker children or non-native learners, some explicit instruction in the features and patterns of English spelling is necessary; that is, whole parts of English classes can be devoted to spelling. However, at higher levels, spelling can be surreptitiously inserted into many kinds of classroom exercise.

This chapter starts, however, with discussion of the sequence of features of English spelling that should be applied with native-speaking children, and that could be judiciously applied to the teaching of non-native learners.

The latter half of the chapter discusses the kind of exercise that can be used in class with learners.

Sequence for Teaching

While the task for learners is eventually to learn all the features of the spelling system, clearly some features are more basic, easier to learn, and more useful than others. And some learners never completely master the system.

The following sequence is suggested for introducing features of the English spelling system to native-speaking children. It is based on various such lists given by writers including Moats (2000), Nicholson (2005), and Venezky (1999).

1 *Accurate pronunciation*. As was discussed in Chapter 24 on the phonological strategy, the task of assigning spellings to sounds is harder if the sounds are not pronounced accurately by learners; that is, if the phonemes of spoken English are not kept distinct from one another. Common problem sounds, not only for native-speaking children but also for foreign learners, are the *th* sounds (/θ, ð/). If they are not kept distinct from /s, t, f/, then assigning the spelling *th*, rather than *s, t,* or *f*, will be problematic.

2 *Phonemic awareness*. The child learns that letters represent sounds. They can count the number of syllables in words. They can also identify words that rhyme and alliterate, and can separate the vowel from any final consonants (see Chapter 24).

3 *Names of letters*. The child learns the names of the 26 letters of the alphabet, and can probably sing "The Alphabet Song." They can therefore use the names when giving the spelling of words.

4 *Individual letter-to-sound correspondences*. The most common sounds represented by letters are learned. These are in general the kind of correspondences found on alphabet wallcharts and books: A for *apple*, B for *book*, etc.

5 *CVC words*. Simple words that have a consonant + vowel + consonant structure (in terms both of letters and of sounds) are taught. Sample words include *cat, leg, bit, dog, cut*. These are all words that young children are likely to know, the sound-spelling correspondence is one-to-one, and there are no digraphs. In Chapter 24, it was shown that the letters *s, a* (= /æ/), *t, i* (= /ɪ/), *p, n*, as simple letters representing simple sounds, could be introduced first, and they generate a large number of relatively simple words. The second and third sets of letters in that list also comprise simple letters representing simple sounds, apart from *ck*.

   All the above features can be introduced and hopefully mastered by the end of the first year of school. They also account for a large number of the initial Dolch and Fry sight words (see Chapter 26).

6 *Simple words with consonant clusters*. Consonant clusters are easier to master than digraphs because clusters involve two letters representing two sounds; in short, they still follow the alphabetic principle. Usable words include *flat, drip, spin, stop* for word-initial position, and *dent, fits, hunt, left* for word-final position.

7 *Simple words with consonant digraphs*. Consonant digraphs are more complex because they break the alphabetic principle by having two letters for one sound. In word-initial position, these can include *ch* (/tʃ/), *sh* (/ʃ/), *th* (θ/), and *wh* (/w/) in words with one syllable and a CVC

sound structure such as *chop, shed, thin, when*. In word-final position, *ng* (/ŋ/) can be added, in total giving words like *fish, moth, ring*.

8 **Magic e.** Magic *e* is another, more complex, spelling phenomenon, in that the *e* has no inherent sound (is silent in this sense; see Chapter 13), but it does have the rather complex function of making the preceding vowel long. Again, it breaks the alphabetic principle. Example words, all one-syllable and using a CVC sound structure, include *lute, hope, life, mate*.

9 **Vowel letter + r.** The *r* letter is pronounced as /r/ in rhotic accents including AmE, while it is not pronounced in non-rhotic accents including BrE. For rhotic accents, words like *car* follow the alphabetic principle, in that *c* = /k/, *a* = /ɑ:/ (although this is not its simplest correspondence) and *r* = /r/. For non-rhotic accents, the correspondence is less alphabetic, in that *r* represents nothing in the pronunciation, but may affect the sound of the vowel (/kɑ:/). Other example words include *cart, firm, hurt, storm, term*.

The age at which learners master these features depends on individual differences, the regularity and way in which they are taught, etc. However, most of the preceding features can be mastered by the age of about seven.

10 **Vowel digraphs.** Vowel digraphs – that is, two letters (not necessarily both vowel letters) representing one vowel sound – are an added complexity. For instance the digraph *ew* representing /(j)u:/ can be introduced with simple CV words like *chew, dew, few, new*, and words involving clusters such as *crew, screw, stew*. Two further points can be highlighted. Firstly, one-syllable words with *ew* have no final consonant, except *n* in archaic or rare participles such as *hewn, strewn*. Secondly, a few past tense verbs end in *ew*: *drew, flew, grew, threw*.

Which is the more common digraph representation of /i:/: *ea* or *ee*? The answer is that both are fairly common, although *ee* is the more common. However, when the position in the word is taken into account, some patterns of probability arise. In word-initial position, there are very few words that start with *ee*; *eel* being the only common one. On the other hand, many words start with *ea*: *each, eager, eagle, east, easy, eat*, etc. Vice versa, in word-final position, there are only a handful of words that end in *ea*: *pea, plea, flea, sea, tea*. In contrast, many words end in *ee*: *agree, bee, fee, free, glee, see, three, tree, wee*. As the V of C(C)VC words, both *ea* and *ee* are common: *beak, bean, beat, beef, bleed, feet, fleece, green, heap, heath, keen, keep, leaf, leash, leave, mean, peace, peach, plead, seek, seem, sleeve, speech, steam*. Indeed, there are a few pairs of homophones, one with *ea*, the other with *ee*: *cheap/cheep; heal/heel; leak/leek; read/reed; steal/steel*. However, although both *ea* and *ee* are common, they should not be introduced together, in case confusion arises. Since *ee* is the more common, introduce that first and make sure the learners have mastered many *ee* words. Then introduce *ea*.

11 **Compound words**. Around age nine, learners can advance to words of more than one syllable. Compound words are usually easy, as the spelling of their two parts does not usually change. Common compound words, with varying degrees of added spelling complexity, include *backbone, backpack, backward, blacksmith, bookcase, football, footprint, homemade, inside, lifetime, limestone, northeast, rainbow, township, upstream*.

12 **Multisyllable words**. Learners can then progress to multisyllable words that are not compounds, but still can be divided into their constituent syllables. Example multisyllable words include *became, carpet, combat, discuss, eaten, rabbit, tennis*.

The above features should be mastered by around age nine.

13 **Affixes**. After age nine, learners can be exposed to more learned vocabulary, including words with prefixes and suffixes, whose spelling rarely changes. Thus, the word *reincarnation* can be broken down into *re* ("again"), *in* ("into"), *carn* ("flesh, body"), and *ation* (noun suffix). Similarly, the various Latin and Greek morphemes outlined in Chapter 22 can be introduced.

While there may be some argument over the precise sequence described here, it is clear that it needs to proceed from one-to-one letter-sound correspondences to more complex ones, from simple syllable structures to ones involving clusters, from single-syllable words to multisyllable ones, from simple vocabulary to more academic vocabulary, etc.

Teaching English Spelling

It is not the intention of this book to provide a number of classroom exercises aimed at teaching and practicing spelling. Many books on the subject already exist, e.g. Lloyd (1998), Nicholson (2005), Shemesh & Waller (2000), Stirling (2011), Stone (2014) using BrE spelling; and *Building spelling skills* (various dates), Fountas & Pinnell (1998), Hoffman (2014, 2017) using AmE spelling. A search for "phonics" on the Amazon online bookstore yields over 70,000 hits, including books, wallcharts, flashcards, etc. There are also many websites devoted to exercises for teaching, practicing, and testing spelling, including many with animations that will appeal to younger learners.

It is also important that teachers select materials that are appropriate for their learners, in three main respects. Firstly, as just mentioned, materials should be selected that use BrE or AmE spelling, whichever is used as the reference by the teacher. Secondly, materials should be selected according to whether the learners are native speakers or foreign learners. Native-speaker learners, i.e. children, may be much younger than foreign learners. While native-speaking children may have reasonably large vocabularies, those vocabularies will comprise more basic words. Thirdly, the age and needs of the learners needs to be taken into account. Non-native learners may range from schoolchildren learning English at secondary level or lower, to tertiary students. Schoolchildren may be learning it because it is a school subject and likely to be of value later in life, with no more specific need, as opposed to university students who may need it in order to read technical journal articles in the language, a very specific need.

Vocabulary Exercises

The learning of English spelling can often go hand-in-hand with the learning of English vocabulary and dictionary use. Writers on vocabulary learning (e.g. Nation, 2013) often recommend the use of word cards. These are small cards, the size of index cards or smaller, on which information about new vocabulary is written. Apart from the meaning of the word, this can include information about the pronunciation (vowel and consonant sounds, transcription, stress placement, etc), grammar (word class, constituent morphemes, collocation, register, frequency, etc), and translation, if a good word-to-word translation exists. Since this is all written on the card, spelling is also involved. Marks can inserted to draw attention to unusual or unexpected aspects of the spelling, e.g. the *b* in *debt*, the double *m* in *accommodation*, the silent *w* in *whose*.

Exercises designed primarily for vocabulary can also be used to teach or check spelling.

Exercise

Write the missing word in the blank. The first and last letters are given.

1   *When the accident took place, news of it s............d like wildfire.*
2   *The witness's story p............d beyond all shadow of doubt that the defendant was lying.*
3   *The holiday park contained various types of a...............n: units, dormitories, and tent and campervan sites.*
4   *I hadn't been in the city for 20 years, and the road system had c............d beyond all recognition.*
5   *The museum contained almost every type of v...............e : cars, buses, trams, and even old carriages and coaches.*
6   *Competitors in the assault course had great physical p...............s.*
7   *C............s animals live by killing other animals and eating them.*
8   *The Burj Al-Arab has every facility. There is even a h...............t for VIPs to reach the airport quickly.*

Features of the spelling of the missing words can be highlighted: the *ea* of *spread*; that *prove* looks like *grove* but is different (it is not magic *e*); the double *m* in *accommodation*; that verbs like *change* that already end in *e* only add *-d* for the participle; that the adjective from *vehicle* (with silent *h*) is *vehicular* (with pronounced *h*); that *prowess*, while being a two-syllable and rare word, nevertheless follows spelling patterns and could not be spelled any other way; that *carnivorous* contains productive morphemes (e.g. it is the same *carn* as in *reincarnation*); similarly *heliport* (cf. *helicopter, airport*).

Word Games

It is usually the case that learners learn better when they are challenged, but at the same time find the class enjoyable. Word games are thus a staple of teachers for engaging the learners while also covering important language points. We start with the two commonest types of word games, crosswords and wordsearches, before looking at variations on them, and other types of word games.

We are all familiar with crosswords. They were first invented in the 18th or 19th century and regularly appear in many newspapers, magazines, etc. Since the answers have to be written into the appropriate squares, they involve spelling the words correctly. There are many websites for teachers with ready-to-use crosswords. There are also many that provide crossword-making programs. Teachers input the words and the clues (often straight definitions or fill-the-gap), and the program creates a crossword using them. The words can thus be chosen to be at the right level for the students, because they have been used in recent reading texts, in order to draw attention to particular spelling patterns that have been recently covered (e.g. using *-gh* words; using magic *e* words).

Crosswords are more passive, individual, perceptual games; the crossword pattern and the words are already determined, the player has to work out what they are, and there is no scoring. Invented in the 1930s, Scrabble, on the other hand, is a more active, interactive, productive version; the crossword pattern and the words are not determined, the players have to create words using the letters they have drawn, attaching these words to words already laid down, and trying to score higher than their opponents.

Similarly, wordsearches are often used by teachers. Again, there are many websites with ready-to-use wordsearches, often on particular themes (e.g. sport, particular countries) as well as websites with programs for creating your own wordsearches.

There are many variants on the basic formats. For instance, The Puzzle Company (n.d.) contains about 20 different types of crossword, varying in terms of size, simple versus cryptic, and themes. An advanced variant is Simon Shuker's Code-Cracker. It contains a regular symmetrical crossword grid. However, there are no clues to the words. Instead, each square has a number representing the same letter each time that number occurs. One or two correspondences are given (e.g. 10 = F; 13 = Y) and, having solved the first word where 10 and 13 occur, the remainder tend to fall into place. Also, each letter of the alphabet is present at least once on the puzzle, so that there is at least one occurrence of rare letters like Q, X, Z. This is thus a good, but advanced, test of vocabulary (and spelling).

W R _ _ _
R I _ _ _ D
M _ _ _ L
S C O _ _ _ R

Figure 27.1 Trio (© The Puzzle Company)

Other types of word game depend on learners' knowledge of vocabulary, but also their understanding of spelling patterns, to be able to arrive at the correct solution.

Trio (Figure 27.1) involves filling in the blank with the same three-letter sequence each time, in order to complete longer words.

The missing three-letter sequence is O T E. There are relatively few five-letter words that start with *wr-*: *wraps, wrath, wreck, wring, wrist, write, wrong,* and *wrote* are the only common ones. Note that the *e* of *rioted* is part of an *-ed* part tense ending, and that in the last word, the *o* is part of a double *oo* digraph.

Word Wheel (Figure 27.2) is a puzzle shaped like a wheel with eight spokes, and thus eight segments. An eight-letter word is inserted either clockwise or anticlockwise, starting in any segment, and one letter is deleted. To solve the puzzle, players have to work out whether the word is clockwise or anticlockwise, what the missing letter is (it is usually a distinctive letter in the word), and thus what the word is.

The word is *reserved*. The *v*, as the most distinctive letter, has been deleted. The *r* at the top is next to an *e*; as a result, this could be *re-* at the beginning of the word, or *-er* at the end. Similarly, the *d* is next to an *e* and could be *de-* at

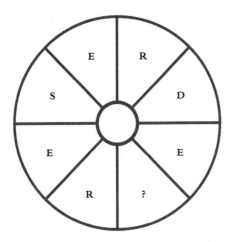

Figure 27.2 Word Wheel (© The Puzzle Company)

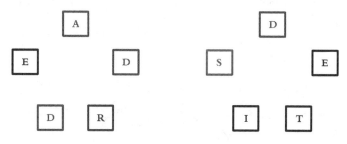

Figure 27.3 Word Builder (© The Puzzle Company)

the beginning or *-ed* at the end. The letters *r* and *d* could be adjacent as in *dress, overdue*, etc. The *reser* sequence is a palindrome, reading the same forwards and backwards, so possibly going in either direction. What is important is not so much how long it takes to arrive at the answer, but the thought processes around English spelling patterns that lead to it.

In Word Builder (Figure 27.3), players are given five letters, and have to find as many words that are three or more letters long as possible. There is always at least one five-letter word.

A, D, R, D, E contains *e* and *d* which form the past tense ending. So, players can look for past tense verbs, in this case, *dared*. Similarly, the five letters contain *e* and *r*, giving the agent ending, in this instance *adder*. The opposite of final *er* is initial *re*, meaning "again"; would you allow *readd* "calculate again"? *Dread*, with the *ea* digraph, is the final five-letter word in this case, and there are many shorter words, e.g. *read, dead, red, Dad*.

D, E, T, I, S similarly contains the *-ed* ending, giving *sited*. The plural ending *s* or *es* gives *diets, edits, tides*. There are other, much less common five-letter words like *deist* "one who believes in God but denies revealed religion" and *stied* "put in a pig sty," as well as many common words with fewer than five letters (*dies, side, tied*, etc.).

Many such puzzles are available in books and on websites. However, all these puzzles can be created by the teacher, adapting them to the learners' level by choosing appropriate words, and by making the puzzle larger or smaller. While puzzles are engaging and fun, they cannot last too long. For this reason, it is a good idea to create a bank of puzzles, to be used as and when they are appropriate, and sometimes as short fillers.

Summary

- It is relatively simple to introduce features of English spelling in a sequence that proceeds from simple to complex.
- There are many materials for teaching spelling, available in book and website form.

- The teaching of spelling can often go hand-in-hand with the teaching of vocabulary.
- Word games that need to be written (i.e. spelled) are an easy way of practicing spelling.

Further Reading

The following websites contain ready-made puzzles, and allow teachers to create their own: Crossword Labs (n.d.), Discovery Education (n.d.), Games Games (n.d.), Instant Online Puzzle-Maker (n.d.), PBS Kids (n.d.), The Teacher's Corner (n.d.). Many of the puzzle formats are reproduced here with the kind permission of The Puzzle Company.

References

Building spelling skills (Grades 1–6) (various dates). Monterey, CA: Evan-Moor Educational Publishers.

Crossword Labs (n.d.). Retrieved from crosswordlabs.com

Discovery Education (n.d.). Retrieved from www.discoveryeducation.com/free-puzzlemaker

Fountas, I., & Pinnell, G. S. (1998). *Word matters: Teaching phonics and spelling in the reading/writing classroom*. Portsmouth, NH: Heinemann.

Games Games (n.d.). Retrieved from www.gamesgames.com/games/spelling

Hoffman, J. (Grades 1–2, 2014; Grades 3–4 2017). *Spelling puzzles*. Grand Haven, MI: School Zone Publishing Company.

Instant Online Puzzle-Maker (n.d.). Retrieved from www.puzzle-maker.com

Lloyd, S. (1998). *The phonics handbook* (3rd edition). Chigwell, UK: Jolly Learning.

Moats, I. C. (2000). *Speech to print: Language essentials for teachers*. Baltimore, MD: Paul H. Brookes.

Nation, I. S. P. (2013). *Learning vocabulary in another language* (2nd edition). Cambridge, UK: Cambridge University Press.

Nicholson, T. (2005). *Phonics handbook*. Chichester, UK: Whurr Publishers.

PBS Kids (n.d.). Retrieved from pbskids.org/games/spelling

Peters, M. (1985). *Spelling, caught or taught?: A new look*. London, UK: Routledge.

Shemesh, R., & Waller, S. (2000). *Teaching English spelling*. Cambridge, UK: Cambridge University Press.

Stirling, J. (2011). *Teaching spelling to English language learners*. Raleigh, NC: Lulu.

Stone, L. (2014). *Spelling for life*. Abingdon, UK: Routledge.

The Puzzle Company (n.d.). Retrieved from www.thepuzzlecompany.co.nz.

The Teacher's Corner (n.d.). Retrieved from www.theteacherscorner.net

Venezky, R. L. (1999). *The American way of spelling: The structure and origins of American English orthography*. New York, NY: The Guildford Press.

28 Testing English Spelling

Learning Objectives

At the end of this chapter, readers will be able to:

- critically evaluate currently used testing methods
- devise assessments that meet testing criteria (validity, reliability, practicality, fairness).

Introduction

ELT institutions, and ELT teachers, use tests widely. They are the obvious way to check entrants' ability, their progress, and the institution's curriculum and teaching methods. Tests of English spelling ability are, in certain respects, easier and more reliable than other ELT tests, but the whole process of testing spelling can be improved. This chapter starts with a general introduction to the purpose of tests and the characteristics of good tests, both with a focus on spelling. Finally, we take a closer look at how learners are prepared, and can prepare themselves, for spelling tests.

The Purpose of Tests

While tests may often be looked on as a necessary evil, they fulfill several different important purposes for institutions and teachers. Commentators generally distinguish four main types of language test:

> *Proficiency* tests measure overall language ability. The two most common worldwide examples of this are IELTS and TOEFL. However, testing agencies are often secretive about exactly what is scored and how. There is no indication on the IELTS website that spelling is taken into account in the writing test format (IELTS, n.d., a) or in the way the writing test is scored (IELTS, n.d., b). Similarly, with TOEFL (n.d.). Nevertheless, it would be naïve to imagine that spelling plays no part in a marker's subjective assessment of a piece of writing. That is, a grammatical, meaningful piece of writing that is spelled accurately is likely to be marked higher than

one with many spelling mistakes. In relation to IELTS, Cole (n.d.) claims that "it's really quite common for candidates to miss as many as 5/6 answers because of poor spelling and that can certainly change your band score." In relation to TOEFL, Miller (2012) advises, "I'm sorry to say that your spelling will impact your TOEFL writing score. OK, one or two misspelled words will not bring about the end of the world, but if you have systemic spelling problems, then the "Language Use" part of your TOEFL writing score will surely decrease!"

Diagnostic language tests, as the name suggests, diagnose the problems in a learner's ability by identifying their strengths and weaknesses in particular areas. Thus, for example, while a learner may have good grammar and pronunciation, their spelling and listening may need improvement.

Placement tests are used by institutions and teachers to place learners in classes at the appropriate levels (beginner, elementary, lower intermediate, etc.). While spelling is part of these tests, the placement more usually depends on more fundamental aspects, such as grammar and vocabulary.

Achievement tests come at the end of a program of study, and test what was taught in that program. It follows from this that an achievement test of spelling must be preceded by instruction in how to learn the spelling of the words. The common practice for a teacher to give a class a list of a dozen words, with the directive that they will be tested on the spelling of the words the following day, falls down in this respect unless the learners are taught how to learn the spellings.

Characteristics of Tests

Language tests are said to have various characteristics. The ones that are relevant to the testing of spelling are as follows.

Validity

A test is valid if it really tests what it is intended to test. This may seem obvious. However, a distinction needs to be maintained between productive tests of spelling, and perceptual tests. If a spelling test aims to test a learner's ability to spell words, as in writing, then the learner needs to write/type the words. Presenting them with three alternative spellings, and requiring them to choose which one is the right spelling, is not a spelling test in this sense. It is a test of their recognition of the correct spelling. Learners may be able to recognize correct spellings if their memories are jolted by being presented with the correct spelling, along with two distractors, but this will not stand them in good stead when they have to write in English, especially if it is in handwriting and bypasses the possibility of a spell-check.

Various formats of productive and perceptual spelling tests can be used. The commonest productive one is for the teacher to read out the words (or for them to be produced as a soundfile on computer), and for the learners to write or type the word. Spelling bees (see Chapter 16), as live performance events, require the participants to say the spelling out loud, one letter at a time, thereby contributing to the memory element of the performance if the word is relatively long. In a multiple-choice spelling test, participants are presented (on paper or on screen) with the correctly spelled word, along with distractors, and they have to identify which one is the correct spelling. While this may be criticized as being only a perceptual test, it does correspond to the common practice in everyday life of writing the word in different ways and, by looking at them, deciding which is the correct, familiar one. A proofreading-style test is for participants to be presented with a sentence or passage with incorrectly spelled words for them to find and correct.

Reliability

The reliability of a test relates to the consistency and accuracy of the measurement. On reliable tests, candidates should receive the same score if they retake the test, or if it is graded by different markers. Spelling tests should have high reliability.

If a learner has truly learned the spelling of a word, they are unlikely to forget it, unless the teacher makes the mistake of not recycling the word in subsequent exercise passages, etc.

The beauty of a spelling test, as opposed to a test of grammar or pronunciation, is that there is usually only one correct answer. There is little room for alternative answers. The only departure from this is where a word has geographical or other variation, e.g. *artefact* (BrE) vs *artifact* (AmE), *disc* vs *disk* (see Chapter 15). If there is only one correct answer, then marking is simple, and can be performed by a computer or a teaching assistant. In short, the marking of a spelling test is objective, as opposed to, say, the marking of the intelligibility of learners' pronunciation, which is a much more subjective assessment.

Practicality

There are various practical issues that need to be taken into account. However, since there is usually only one possible correct answer in spelling tests, practical considerations are easy to accommodate.

Tests should have a reasonable time limit, such that an average learner has time to complete everything comfortably. Tests should be kept easy to administer, and should not be expensive to run. The scores should be easy to interpret.

In fact, because of the nature of spelling testing, in particular that there is only one correct answer, it can easily be carried out on computer, and marked by computer. Indeed, there are many websites offering free English spelling tests.

Fairness

A lot has been written on the fairness dimension of tests, and ethical issues related to this. Three considerations related to spelling testing are the following.

Firstly, it does not seem fair to test something that has not been explicitly taught. Indeed, many of the exercises that are used to teach aspects of language can equally be used to test learners; it is only the purpose of the activity that is different, not the nature. This is precisely the problem with the "Learn the spelling of these 20 words by Monday" approach. If the students have not been taught how to learn the spellings, it implies that spellings are learned by rote. While this is inevitable for a small number of very irregularly spelled, visual words, it is not true of the vast majority. Requiring learners to memorize the spellings of words bypasses the very foundation of the English spelling system, namely the alphabetic principle that letters represent sounds, and that there are certain pervasive spelling patterns in English vocabulary.

Secondly, words used in spelling tests have to be selected carefully. They have to be appropriate to the learners' level of proficiency. They are often selected as the words that occur in the reading the learners are currently doing.

Finally, how far should learners be challenged in spelling tests? Should they only be tested on words that they know, or that have been used in the reading? If, for instance, the test contains the words *big, pig*, and *rig* (which they may know), can they also be tested on *brig* and *prig* (words they probably do not know, but which follow exactly the same spelling rules and patterns)? Consideration should also be given to whether it is acceptable that learners get every item correct (20/20), or whether some "separating the men from the boys" is expected. In other aspects of language, it is rare to award maximum marks for grammar, pronunciation, etc. However, since spellings are usually either right or wrong, there is little basis for not awarding maximum marks, if the learner has got all the spellings right. This is not in itself a problem, especially if the test is one of achievement, testing what has recently been taught.

Preparing for Spelling Tests

Spence (2014) summarizes the main problems with the way spelling tests are typically carried out. Even if a learner scores 100% in a spelling test, that does not necessarily mean that they have mastered the spelling of the words. Observation shows that they may subsequently misspell the word. This emphasizes two points. Firstly, learners need to be taught spelling patterns, not just the spelling of individual words. Secondly, unless the words in a spelling test are recycled by being used in readings, spelling exercises, etc., then they are likely to be forgotten as quickly as they were learned.

The title of Spence's article is "Why I don't give a Friday spelling test (and what I do instead)," emphasizing that learning is more important than testing. She reiterates many of the principles outlined in the previous chapter.

The spelling patterns that underlie groups of words should be studied, rather than the spelling of individual words; this allows learners to cope with unfamiliar words encountered when reading. Importance should be given to sight words, namely those words that are high-frequency, and may contain irregularities in their spelling. The practice of keeping a notebook of new words, or a collection of word cards that can be shuffled, is a technique promoted in vocabulary teaching (e.g. Nation, 2013); one feature of a new word that must be recorded is its spelling, perhaps along with other words that contain the same spelling patterns. It is important to recycle words, by incorporating them in reading or, less obviously, by putting commonly misspelled words on the classroom wall. Finally, observation of incorrectly spelled words tells a teacher as much about a learner's mastery of spelling patterns than correctly spelled words do.

Conclusion

Spelling tests ought to be one of the simpler types of language tests administered to learners. Because there is relatively little variation in spelling, there is usually only one correct answer for the spelling of most words. For example, dictionaries give very few alternative spellings for words. Objective testing can therefore be used, and this can be done by computer.

However, it is unethical to test something that has not been explicitly taught. The common practice of giving learners lists of words whose spellings have to be learned for a test is unfair unless the learners have been taught how to learn the spelling of the words. That is, spelling tests must be preceded by explicit study of the words and their spelling patterns.

Summary

- Spelling tests, like other language tests, are of four main types: proficiency, diagnostic, placement, and achievement.
- Like other language tests, spelling tests should be valid, reliable, practical, and fair.
- The familiar regime of giving learners lists of English words for spelling tests fails on the fairness criterion, unless there has been previous instruction in how to learn the spelling. Otherwise, this is simply a rote learning exercise, ignoring spelling patterns.

Exercises

1 Think of other languages that you know. When you learned them, were you given explicit instruction in spelling? Were you tested on spelling?
2 This book has contained several test-like exercises. Have you scored 100% on them all, or have you discovered that there are some words of

English whose spelling you are unsure of?

Further Reading

General introductions to testing in language learning are Brown, H. D. (2004) and Brown, J. D. (2005), Douglas (2010), Fox, Wesche, Bayliss, Cheng, Turner & Doe (Eds.) (2007), Fulcher (2010), Hughes (2002), McNamara (2000) and McNamara & Roever (2006).

References

Brown, H. D. (2010). *Language assessment: Principles and classroom practices* (2nd edition). White Plains, NY: Pearson Education.

Brown, J. D. (2005). *Testing in language programs: A comprehensive guide to English language assessment.* New York, NY: McGraw-Hill.

Cole, D. (n.d.). *Spelling and IELTS: A test and some tips.* Retrieved from www.dcielts. com/ielts-vocabulary/spelling-test-tips

Douglas, D. (2010). *Understanding language testing.* London, UK: Routledge.

Fox, J., Wesche, M., Bayliss, D., Cheng, L., Turner, C. E., & Doe, C. (Eds.) (2007). *Language testing reconsidered.* Ottawa, Canada: University of Ottawa Press.

Fulcher, G. (2010). *Practical language testing.* London, UK: Hodder Education.

Hughes, A. (2002). *Testing for language teachers* (2nd edition). Cambridge, UK: Cambridge University Press.

IELTS (n.d., a). Retrieved from www.ielts.org/about-the-test/test-format-in-detail

IELTS (n.d., b). Retrieved from www.ielts.org/about-the-test/how-ielts-is-scored

McNamara, T. F. (2000). *Language testing.* Oxford, UK: Oxford University Press.

McNamara, T., & Roever, C. (2006). *Language testing: The social dimension.* Malden, MA: Blackwell.

Miller, J. (2012). *Does spelling matter on TOEFL writing?* Retrieved from english successacademy.com/toefl-writing-spelling

Nation, I. S. P. (2013). *Learning vocabulary in another language* (2nd edition). Cambridge, UK: Cambridge University Press.

Spence, B. (2014). *Why I don't give a Friday spelling test (and what I do instead).* This Reading Mama. Retrieved from thisreadingmama.com/no-friday-spelling-test

TOEFL (n.d.). Retrieved from www.ets.org/toefl

Section 6

The Future

29 Spelling Reform

Learning Objectives

At the end of this chapter, readers will be able to:

- explain why spelling reform would be a solution to many of the problems of English spelling
- list the pros and cons of spelling reform from a language perspective
- describe many of the barriers to spelling reform from a social perspective.

Introduction

As has been made clear in many places in this book, the alphabetic correspondence between sounds and spellings in English is far from 100%. This irregularity is the result of various episodes in the 17-century history of English, and is the cause of much misspelling by both native speakers and non-native learners.

Throughout its history, many people have attempted to bring English spelling more in line with its pronunciation. The first spelling reformer for English may have been a monk by the name of Orm who is believed to have lived around 1200. He wrote a work of biblical exegesis called the Ormulum in an idiosyncratic spelling more closely representing the pronunciation of the time. More widespread attempts at spelling reform took place in the 16th century by Sir John Cheke (1514–1557), Sir Thomas Smith (1513–1577), John Hart (died 1574), and Richard Mulcaster (c.1531–1611). The Royal Society, founded in 1662, had a committee for English language, including spelling reform, with members such as the poet John Dryden (1631–1700). Spelling reform in English thus has a history spanning several centuries.

One possible reason for the failure of spelling reform proposals may relate to the terminology used. While being the most common term used, *spelling reform* has a bad reputation, perhaps because of some of the extreme proposals from some reformers. Alternative terms used include *regularized spelling* (referring to the fact that English spelling is in many respects irregular), *simplified spelling* (designed to create a system that is easier for native children and foreigners to learn), and *improved spelling* (implying that there is room for improvement).

Pros and Cons of Spelling Reform

There are many arguments on both sides of the debate.

Pros

Because of the irregular nature of aspects of English spelling, many foreign learners of English, especially those whose native language does not use the alphabetic principle in its spelling system, adopt a rote learning strategy for English, thereby overlooking the many regularities that do exist. For instance, learners (and many native users) who misspell *occasion* as *occassion* (Chapter 21) do not understand existing rules – in this case that a doubled consonant letter implies a short preceding vowel, as in *passion*. A reformed spelling system would reinforce regularities and the alphabetic principle.

Reformed spellings often correspond to misspellings already made by even otherwise proficient speakers of the language. When speakers play with the standard spellings of words (often called traditional orthography, TO), the result is often spellings that are more regular than the standard version. However, reformed spelling should not be thought of as pandering to the inadequacies of non-proficient spellers, but rather as eliminating features for which there is no justification.

Since reformed spellings usually eliminate redundant letters, passages are usually between 5–15% shorter than TO in terms of the number of letters, although spaces between words will remain the same. This has huge benefits in terms of the amount of time taken by writers and typists, the economic production costs of publishers and printers, the destruction of forests for paper, the storage capacities of libraries, etc. Even in this modern age of e-books, the equivalent saving of time and computer storage is considerable.

For teachers of English, a reformed spelling system would make reading and writing easier for three groups of people. Firstly, illiteracy rates would fall for native speakers with learning difficulties, with resultant implications for individual, national, and international progress.

> Some ten years ago I had a private [dyslexic] pupil called Tony. He was 12 years old, and after one lesson he said, "I do wish we could spell words as we say them – but you'd be out of a job then, wouldn't you?" I replied, "Tony, I wouldn't mind if it were easier for you to read and write."
> (Hutchins, 1989, p. 5)

Secondly, native children without learning difficulties would master reading and writing faster, as there would be fewer irregularities to cope with. Thirdly, many foreigners learn English primarily through the written medium. Spelling pronunciations (see Chapter 18) are often the result of silent letters. Since spelling reform always eliminates silent letters, these spelling pronunciations would disappear.

Perhaps the main advantage of spelling reform in English is that it would be an acknowledgement that a spelling system is a manmade construct that needs to be consciously managed, rather than left on its own to go wild. Otherwise, we have the situation in standard English spelling of a garden that has turned into a jungle. The management of spelling reform is nothing new in many major world languages. Table 29.1 gives some examples of spelling reforms in various languages.

Cons

If a reformed spelling system were adopted, books would need to be reprinted using the new system. However, this already happens. For instance, if you buy a copy of Shakespeare in a bookshop, what you are buying is not what

Table 29.1 Some spelling reforms in languages

1612	Italian	1943	Brazilian Portuguese
1735	French	1945	Portugal Portuguese
1815	Dutch	1946	Japanese
1815	Spanish	1947	Indonesian
1835	French	1948	Danish
1860	Romanian	1950s	Czech
1878	French	1954	Dutch
1901	German	1957	Irish
1904	Romanian	1956	Mainland Chinese
1906	Swedish	1956	Japanese
1907	Norwegian	1959	Spanish
1909	Albanian	1971	Brazilian Portuguese
1909	Norwegian	1972	Malay/Indonesian
1912	Brazilian Portuguese	1972	Japanese
1915	Portugal Portuguese	1973	Portugal Portuguese
1917	Norwegian	1981	Norwegian
1917	Russian	1982	Greek
1920s	Vietnamese	1987	Filipino
1922	Japanese	1990	All Portuguese-speaking countries
1924	Armenian	1990	Dutch
1928	Turkish	1990	French
1934	Dutch	1996	German
1938	Norwegian	2005	Dutch
1941	Norwegian	2005	Norwegian

The glaring absentee is English.

Shakespeare wrote; it is a version with updated spelling. The earliest printed versions of Shakespeare look like the following.

To be, or not to be, that is the Queftion:

Whether 'tis Nobler in the minde to fuffer

The Slings and Arrowes of outragious Fortune

Or to take Armes againft a Sea of troubles,

And by oppofing end them: to dye, to fleepe

No more; and by a fleepe, to fay we end

The Heart-ake, and the thoufand naturall fhockes

That Flefh is heyre too?

It is envisaged that, if a spelling reform is implemented, present-day TO will look as quaint in a century's time as Shakespeare's original spelling does to us today.

Many people claim that by reforming spelling, we would be losing part of our cultural and linguistic heritage, in that TO reflects the historical origins of words and the morphological relations between words. This question has already been addressed in Chapter 22 on the morphological strategy.

There would need to be a transition period, during which both the old and new spelling systems were in use. This might lead to initial confusion but would be overcome eventually as people became used to the new system and recognized its benefits. Similar transition periods have occurred, for instance when Britain converted in 1971 from the £sd monetary system to the decimal £p.

One of the greatest problems is that people would have to learn to respell English the new way. Inertia is the problem, in that people who can already read and write English well enough would be reluctant to have to change.

Further pros and cons of spelling reform are discussed in Chapter 30, where the irregular English spelling system is contrasted with the regular Malay spelling system.

Types of Spelling Reforms

Proposed reforms of English spelling can be categorized into three types according to how much they depart from the current spelling:

1   *Supplanting* reforms replace the current spelling system with a completely new and different alphabet.
2   *Augmenting* reforms use the current alphabet, but supplement the existing alphabet with some new letters.
3   *Standardizing* reforms keep the existing alphabet, but change the way the current letters are used.

Supplanting Reforms

The most famous example of a supplanting reform is the Shavian alphabet, named after the Irish playwright George Bernard Shaw (1856–1950). This is ironic, as Shaw himself did not use the alphabet that is named after him; he used Pitman's shorthand. He was interested in English spelling, having been a member of the BBC's Advisory Committee on Spoken English at a time when spelling reform was a fashionable topic of debate. When Shaw died in 1950, a trust was set up in his will for a competition to devise an alphabet that conformed to three principles. Firstly, like modern phonemic transcription, symbols should represent sounds in a one-to-one fashion, as far as possible. Secondly, since English – regardless of which variety of pronunciation (British, American, etc.) was taken as the reference – has more distinctive sounds (phonemes) than the 26-letter Roman alphabet can handle in this way, the new alphabet would have at least 40 letters. And finally, in order to have a clean sweep and avoid the impression that the new system was simply the old system misspelled, the new alphabet would not be based on the Roman alphabet.

The winning alphabet and spelling system contained some features that might be considered a benefit. The distinction between capital and lowercase letters (see Chapter 11) was not retained, while other features of punctuation and word spacing were retained. Each letter in the Shavian alphabet could be written with one stroke of the pen, without lifting it as is the case with *t* or *i*. Some element of the relationship in pronunciation of letters was represented in their shape. For instance, tall letters (like ascenders; see Chapter 6) represented voiceless consonants, while the same letters rotated 180° or flipped vertically (like descenders) represented their voiced equivalents. This is similar to the current situation with *b* and *p* although, since it is debatable whether Modern English-users recognize this relationship – probably not, as it does not apply to *d* and *q*, and confusion of *b, p, d,* and *q* is a common feature of dyslexia – it is debatable whether it is a worthwhile relationship.

Because of funding problems, only one book was published using the Shavian alphabet: a version of Shaw's play *Androcles and the lion* (1962). Since 2010, other works have been published in Shavian; however, these have all been dilettante projects, rather than a serious attempt to promote its adoption for English. Ultimately, the Shavian alphabet suffers from the same drawbacks as many other supplanting reforms for English. Users would need to learn from scratch a completely new and unfamiliar alphabet. Printers would need to devise new font styles (like present-day Times New Roman, Arial, etc.) for the alphabet in order to avoid all text looking exactly the same. And so on. The consensus among spelling reformers is that supplanting reforms are not the answer.

Augmenting Reforms

As we have seen earlier in this book, the basic problem with English spelling is that it uses the 26-letter Roman alphabet to represent the 40-odd (depending on accent) sounds in English pronunciation, and this problem has existed since missionaries from Rome brought the Roman alphabet to Britain in the 6th century. Even back then, the alphabet had to be augmented by adding four new letters (ash, eth, thorn, and wynn; see Chapter 5) and by using combinations of letters (digraphs) to represent some single sounds.

This section describes a 20th century attempt to augment the Roman alphabet in order to make sound-spelling correspondences more regular. The Initial Teaching Alphabet (ITA) was devised in 1959 in England by Sir James Pitman, the grandson of Sir Isaac Pitman who popularized shorthand. It was based on the reformed system contained in the 1844 book *Phonotypy* written by his grandfather (Kelly, 1981), as well as the Nue Spelling reform system of the Simplified Spelling Society (now the Spelling Society), of which Sir James was a member.

The alphabet originally had 43 symbols, roughly the same number as the phonemes of Standard Southern British English. It was intended as a writing system that could be used to teach native English-speaking children to read and write, more easily than using TO. The theory was that once the ITA had been mastered, and the child could read and write with some confidence, they would then transfer smoothly to TO. Thus, it was not a spelling reform as such, in that it did not intend to do away with TO, but to act as a stepping stone to TO. Nor was it a quasi-phonemic transcription for English, because it had to take into account the various TO spellings of the sounds.

The symbols of the ITA, with their pronunciation equivalent, are shown in Figure 29.1.

Noteworthy features of the system, that show it is not a purely phonemic system, but one that keeps an eye on TO, include the following. There was no ITA symbol for schwa; instead, the symbol corresponded to whatever the vowel letter was in TO. Words like *back* and *fetch*, that use more than one letter in TO to represent single sounds (/k, tʃ/) were written with more than one symbol in ITA, e.g. both *c* and *k* for *back*. Whenever an *s* letter is used in TO to represent a /z/ sound, e.g. *dogs*, it is represented in ITA by the backwards *z* symbol.

As in many reformed spelling systems, there were no capital versions of symbols.

The ITA was adopted by some "progressive" schools in the U.K. and U.S.A. in the 1960s. While the ITA was not intended to presuppose a particular approach to the teaching of spelling, it was often associated with phonics (see Chapter 24). When phonics became unfashionable after the 1960s with the rise of the whole language approach, so the ITA also fell out of use. Pitman established institutions devoted to the ITA in both the U.K. and U.S.A., but they closed because of funding problems. Nevertheless, a group of passionate ITA advocates set up the Initial Teaching Alphabet Federation in 1978 (ITA Foundation, n.d.), and it continues to be used in some institutions in Australia, Canada, Malta, Nigeria, South Africa, Spain, the U.K., and the U.S.A.

Consonants

b c d f g h j k l m n

b k d f g h dʒ k l m n

bib · cake · dad · fife · gag · hat · judge · kick · lull · mime · noon

ŋ p r s ʒ t v w y z ʒ

ŋ p r s z t v w j z ʒ

sing · pipe · roar · sauce · is · tot · valve · will · yes · zoo · vision

Joined consonants

Short vowels

ch ſh th ᴛh wh a e i o u ω

tʃ ʃ θ ð ʍ æ ɛ ɪ ɒ ʌ ʊ

church · shush · thin · then · whale · at · egg · in · odd · up · book

Long vowels / diphthongs

ɑ æ au ee œ ω ue ie oi ou

ɑː eɪ ɔː iː oʊ uː juː aɪ ɔɪ aʊ

father · ape · all · eat · oak · ooze · use · ice · oil · owl

Also, *ſſ* is used following a vowel letter to write the sound in "earn" etc

Figure 29.1 The Initial Teaching Alphabet

Reactions to the ITA are divided. In the 1960s, it was analyzed experimentally by Downing (1964, 1968; Downing, Fyfe, & Lyon, 1967; Downing & Latham, 1967) for both normal and educationally subnormal children, with positive findings. Initial reactions in the 1960s were also enthusiastic; for instance, the title of Mazurkiewicz's (1965) article is "The Initial Teaching Alphabet for reading? Yes!" In a study of the effect of spelling on beginning readers, Thorstad (1991) studied 70 Italian children aged 6–11, 90 English children aged 6–7 learning TO, and 33 English children aged 6–7 learning ITA. She found that the Italian and English ITA children learned to read in one year what would take English TO children three to five years to achieve. The Bullock Report (a 1975 U.K. government publication enti‑ tled *A language for life*; see McArthur, 1998) declared, "It would appear that the best way to learn to read in traditional orthography is to learn to read in the initial teaching alphabet." The beneficial effect of using the ITA with dyslexic children has been documented by Flynn (1994, 2000).

Critics of the ITA argue that, while children may have learned quickly using the ITA, some found it difficult to then transfer to TO, and were con‑ fused by having two alphabets to contend with. Spelling reformers point out that the irregularities of TO are not removed, only postponed. There is thus the economic problem that texts need to be printed in both ITA and TO.

In an article commemorating the 40th anniversary of the ITA, Lane (2001) collected the following readers' memories and reactions, ranging from the enthusiastic to the resentful.

- I love ITA and have a book of famous quotes, speeches and poetry all "translated" into ITA.
- I had a couple of Ladybird books written in ITA . . . I don't recall it doing me any harm.
- We could write notes to each other without our parents or teachers in the grown-up children's classes being able to read them.
- I was in my second year's teaching in Luton in 1968. ITA seemed to be a brilliant way of pushing the children on and they learned to read much earlier than usual. But – and the but is enormous – some could not make the transition.
- I am dyslexic and learned ITA at school. I was already able to read and write simple words when I arrived at school but ITA crippled me. This was because when I wrote the words I knew to be correct I was told they were wrong.
- A big problem with ITA was that phonetic spelling doesn't account for regional accents. Anyone used to hearing words pronounced with a Scots, Welsh or Scouse accent was completely lost.

Standardizing Reforms

Probably the most promising type of spelling reform that could be proposed is one that standardizes the current spelling system. That is, no new alphabet or new letters are proposed. The reform is simply an attempt to make the current letters and their use more regular. Given that the correspondence between sounds and letters in the current state of English spelling is poor, a gradual approach has often been proposed, first making the minor changes that have the largest benefit without facing opposition from users, thus accustoming users to the idea of reforming spelling, before later embarking on more major or less pervasive changes.

A good example of a minor first-stage reform is Lindgren's (1969) Spelling Reform step 1 (known as SR1). This proposed one simple step: make the /e/ vowel, as in *bed*, regularly spelled with just *e*. At present, that is the most common spelling for the sound. As Carney (1994) shows (see Appendix 1), /e/ is spelled *e* 84% of the time in connected speech. The next most common spelling is *ea*, as in *dead* (6%). Then come a number of minor correspondences, each with few examples (in most people's pronunciations): *a* (*any, many*), *ai* (*again, said*), *ei* (*heifer*), *eo* (*jeopardy, leopard*), *u* (*bury*). In some cases, it is not clear whether to consider a pattern as an example of a sound-spelling correspondence for /e/, or as a silent letter. We have treated the *i* in *friend* as silent, rather than part of an *ie* digraph representing /e/. The *u* in *guess* is probably better treated as belonging with the *g* rather than the *e*, because it makes the *g* "hard" /g/ as opposed to "soft" /dʒ/ as in *gesture*. The following poem (Simplified Spelling Society, 1982, p. 2) is constructed to illustrate the spelling resulting from Lindgren's SR1.

> Draw a breth for progress,
>
> Tred abrest ahed.
>
> Fight agenst old spelling,
>
> Better *red* than *read*.
>
> Spred the words at brekfast,
>
> Mesure them in bed,
>
> Dream of welth and tresure,
>
> Better *ded* than *dead*.

(While the new spellings (*breth, tred*, etc) attract the attention, note that *progress, spelling, better, them*, and *bed* remain unchanged.)

This spelling should not cause any problems of intelligibility, and does not look too different from TO. We are already familiar with some of these new spellings from creative examples such as *Def Leppard, Led Zeppelin*. The more traditional form of the name *Geoffrey* is often spelled *Jeffrey*. The new forms *abrest* and *ahed* would still retain their historical link with *breast* and *head* (now *brest* and *hed*). Is the current spelling *breakfast* really connected in most speakers' minds with *break*? It is not pronounced the same (/e/ rather than /eɪ/) and its etymology may not be clear: it is the morning meal when you wake up from sleep, not having eaten during the night. If the connection is considered very tenuous, then *brekfast* could become *breckfast*, following the rule that short vowel sounds followed by /k/ are spelled *ck*, e.g. *tack, speck, brick, clock, truck*. (Spelling reformers often propose that all these *ck*s may be subsequently simplified to *k: tak*, etc.). Similarly, if the doubled consonant rule were retained, *ready* would become *redy* by SR1, but might then become *reddy*.

SR1 was adopted as a minor first-stage reform by the Simplified Spelling Society (now the English Spelling Society), along with four other minor changes:

1   **SR1** (/e/ is spelled *e*)
2   **DUE** (drop useless *e*s). In Chapter 13, we saw that *e* is often silent, in that it does not represent a sound. However, it may or may not have a function. In magic *e*, it works in conjunction with the vowel sound to "make the vowel say its name," as in *game, mete, line, stone, tune*. In contrast, in empty examples of silent *e*, the *e* has no function (is "useless") and could be deleted leaving a plausible spelling for the pronunciation. Thus, in *have, live* (verb), *give, come, some*, the *e* is empty (it is not magic *e*) and DUE thus gives *hav, liv, giv, com, som*, in contrast to *behave, live* (adjective), *five, dome*, where it is magic *e*. Other examples of empty *e* would also be dropped, e.g. *are, freeze, involve, leave, opposite, serve, sleeve, valley, were* would become *ar, freez, involv, leav, opposit, serv, sleev, vally, wer*. Note that many of these examples involve a final /v/ sound, so the current rule whereby words do not end in the *v* letter would have to disappear.
3   *ph* would be spelled with *f* wherever it represents the /f/ sound, e.g. *photo, physical* would become *foto, fysical*. Again, such spellings can be found nowadays in creative spellings such as *Vodafone, Freefone*. This rule would not affect examples where *ph* represents /ph/, e.g. *haphazard*.
4   *ough* spellings would all change, and this anomalous pattern, so beloved by commentators on English spelling, would be done away with once and for all. Where it is pronounced /u:/, it would be changed to *u* (*thru*); where /oʊ/ to *o* (*tho*); where /aʊ/ to *ou* (*drout*); where /ɔ:/ to *au* (*baut, thaut*); where *gh* represents the consonant /f/, to *of* or *uf* depending on the vowel sound (*cof, enuf*).
5   *augh* similarly changes to *au* when it represents /ɔ:/ (*caut, dauter*); where *gh* represents the consonant /f/, to *af* (*laf*).

Cut Spelling

This section describes and illustrates one proposed reformed spelling system for English, called Cut Spelling (CS). It is a standardizing reform, in that it does not propose any new alphabet or letters, but proposes a more regular use of existing letters. It goes much further than Lindgren's SR1, which only proposed one change, and further than the four extra changes just described. However, it does not depart from TO so much that it is likely to encounter strong resistance from speakers/writers of English. As the name Cut Spelling suggests, most of the changes involve omitting letters.

There are three main rules, which address the main features of TO described in previous chapters.

Firstly, letters that are irrelevant to the spelling (i.e. are silent) are omitted. Examples relating to vowel letters include omitting the *a* of *measure* (cf. Lindgren's SR1), *e* in *heart, i* in *friend, o* in *people,* and *u* in *guild.* In this way, *heart* and *guild* would be spelled *hart* and *gild,* which correspond to the spelling of existing words with which they are homophones.

Secondly, letters representing unstressed vowels, usually /ə/, before *l, m, n,* and *r* are omitted. The pronunciation as schwa causes this to be a problem in TO, since it fails to tell writers which vowel letter to use. It is often redundant and can be cut as shown by analogous sets such as *apple, chapel;* (BrE) *centre, enter; prison, prism; fathom, rhythm; resistant, insistent, mightn't.* In CS, these are spelled in a way that reflects this similarity of pronunciation: *apl, chapl; centr, entr; prisn, prism; fathm, rythm; resistnt, insistnt, mytnt.*

A similar cut is that of vowels in certain suffixes. Plural nouns and third person singular present tense verbs are all regularly spelled in CS as just *-s;* past tense/participle *-d;* and progressive *-ng* after stems ending in a consonant (the gain from this will be apparent from the third rule below). Also, the confusing *-able* and *-ible* suffixes are simplified to *-bl.* Thus, *apples, cent(e) red, resisting, eatable,* and *edible* become *apls, centrd, resistng, eatbl,* and *edbl.*

Thirdly, doubled consonant letters are simplified. TO words that are regularly misspelled because of doubled consonant letters become much less of a problem as CS *acomodation, necesry, adress, comitee, embarass, harass, Mediteranean, ocasionly, paralel.* In conjunction with the second rule above, TO pairs related to magic *e,* such as *matting/mating* are distinguished as CS *matng/mating.*

Three further simple substitutions are made with troublesome TO features. The phoneme /f/ is spelled *f,* /dʒ/ as *j,* and /aɪ/ as *y* except in cases of magic *e* (e.g. *dive*). This gives us CS spellings such as *cof, tuf, jeolojy, jinjr, flyt,* and *syn* (TO *sign,* not *sine*). In conjunction with the first main rule above, this gets rid of all the *-ough* and *-igh* chestnuts in one fell swoop.

Other minor CS rules relate to punctuation and simplify the use of capital letters and apostrophes.

So that you can experience how little disruption is caused by these changes, here is a paragraph in Cut Spelling (which in CS is spelled *Cut Spelng*).

> Wen readrs first se Cut Spelng, as in this sentnce, they ofn hesitate slytly, but then quikly becom acustmd to th shortnd words and soon find text in Cut Spelng as esy to read as Traditional Orthografy, but it is th riter ho realy apreciates th advantajs of Cut Spelng, as many of th most trublsm uncertntis hav been elimnated.

You may have hesitated over words like *se* and *ho,* but then it probably dawned on you that *se* now follows the same pattern as *be, he, me,* etc., and that the *w* that is so familiar in TO *who* is empty.

Summary

- Spelling reform has taken place in many major world languages, and led to spelling systems that are regular and easy to learn.
- While spelling reform has been attempted at various stages in the history of English, no reformed system has been adopted widely or led to substantial changes in spelling.
- There are pros and cons to all proposals for spelling reform.
- The three types of reformed spelling proposals are supplanting, augmenting, and standardizing.
- Minor standardizing reforms are the most promising.

Exercise

The following passage (from the English Spelling Society, 1942) illustrates a reformed spelling proposed decades ago, known as Nue Spelling. Firstly, work out what it says. Secondly, decide whether Nue Spelling or Cut Spelling is more likely to be successful as a spelling reform system, and why.

> We spel our wurdz widh leterz and diegraafs dhat survd to reprezent, raadher rufly, dhe pronunsyaeshon dhae had in Elizabeethan tiemz; leterz and diegraafs maenly due to Angloe-French rieterz huu stroev to rekord dhe soundz aafter dhe French maner.

Further Reading

On the pros and cons, and history, of spelling reform for English, see the various articles on the website of the English Spelling Society (n.d.). How variation in English around the world could be accommodated in a reformed spelling is discussed by Gregersen (2000).

References

Carney, E. (1994). *A survey of English spelling*. London, UK: Routledge.

Downing, J. (1964). The I.T.A. (Initial Teaching Alphabet) reading experiment. *The Reading Teacher, 18*(2), 105–110.

Downing, J. (1968). The Initial Teaching Alphabet and educationally sub-normal children. *Developmental Medicine and Child Neurology, 10*(2), 200–205. doi: 10.1111/j.1469-8749.1968.tb02868.x

Downing, J., & Latham, W. (1967). *Evaluating the Initial Teaching Alphabet: A study of the influence of English orthography on learning to read and write*. London, UK: Cassell.

Downing, J., Fyfe, T., & Lyon, M. (1967). The effects of the Initial Teaching Alphabet (i.t.a.) on young children's written composition. *Educational Research, 9*(2), 137–144.

English Spelling Society (1942). *A breef history ov inglish speling*, Simplified Spelling Society Pamphlet 5. Retrieved from spellingsociety.org/uploaded_pamphlets/p5breefhistory-pamphlet.pdf

English Spelling Society (n.d.). Retrieved from spellingsociety.org

Flynn, J. M. (1994). *The use of the Initial Teaching Alphabet for remediation of dyslexia.* New York, NY: Initial Teaching Alphabet Foundation.

Flynn, J. M. (2000). *Synthesis of research on the use of the Initial Teaching Alphabet for remediation of dyslexia.* Initial Teaching Alphabet Foundation occasional paper 4. Retrieved from s320709369.onlinehome.us/wp-content/uploads/2014/12/SynthesisResearchITA.pdf

Gregersen, E. A. (2000). Compromise spellings and World English. *Journal of the Simplified Spelling Society, 27,* 16–18. Retrieved from spellingsociety.org/uploaded_journals/j27-journal.pdf

Hutchins, J. (1989). Dyslexia and simplified spelling. *Journal of the Simplified Spelling Society, 1989*(3), 5–9.

ITA Foundation (n.d.). Retrieved from itafoundation.org

Kelly, J. (1981). The 1847 alphabet: An episode of phonotypy. In R. E. Asher & E. J. A. Henderson (Eds.), *Towards a history of phonetics* (pp. 248–264). Edinburgh, UK: Edinburgh University Press.

Lane, M. (2001). Educashunal lunacie or wizdom? Retrieved from news.bbc.co.uk/2/hi/uk_news/1523708.stm

Lindgren, H. (1969). *Spelling reform: A new approach.* Sydney, Australia: Alpha Books.

Mazurkiewicz, A. J. (1965). The Initial Teaching Alphabet for reading? Yes! *Educational Leadership, 22*(6), 390–393 & 437–438. Retrieved from www.ascd.org/ASCD/pdf/journals/ed_lead/el_196503_mazurkiewicz.pdf

McArthur, T. (1998). The Bullock Report. In *Concise Oxford Companion to the English Language.* Oxford, UK: Oxford University Press.

Shaw, G. B. (1962). *Androcles and the lion* (Shavian alphabet and TO edition). London, UK: Penguin Books.

Simplified Spelling Society (1982). *Newsletter Winter 1982.* Retrieved from spellingsociety.org/uploaded_newsletters/news1-newsletter.pdf

Thorstad, G. (1991). The effect of orthography on the acquisition of literacy skills. *British Journal of Psychology, 82,* 527–537.

30 English Spelling and Malay Spelling

Learning Objectives

At the end of this chapter, readers will be able to:

- contrast the regularity of Malay spelling with the irregularity of English spelling
- list reasons why Malay spelling has been managed, while English spelling faces many obstacles in this respect
- contrast the problems that English spelling causes with the lack of problems in Malay
- better understand the English spelling problems and attitudes of their learners, who may come from a country with a language that has a regular spelling system.

Introduction

The purpose of this chapter is to compare and contrast the spelling system of English with that of another language. Malay has been selected because it is at the other end of the spectrum from English. The spelling system is very regular, and most of the spelling problems that beset English learners simply do not exist in Malay.

Malay / Indonesian is the major language of the Austronesian language family. The family consists of related languages in Southeast Asia, Oceania, Madagascar, and Taiwan. Malay is spoken by about 77 million people in Malaysia, Singapore, Brunei, southern Thailand, and the southern Philippines. It is closely related to Indonesian; however, since the Indonesian spelling system differs from that of Malay, because of the historical influence of Dutch on Indonesia, the following discussion only relates to Malay as spoken in the former regions. The Indonesian spelling system is nevertheless similarly regular to that of Malay.

Around the 1st century BC, maritime trading links were established by Malaysia / Indonesia with China and India. The Indian influence led to what is known as the Hindu-Buddhist era, which lasted until the 13th century. Documents were written using the Indian Pallava alphabet, followed by the Kawi alphabet (8th to 16th centuries), which is derived from Pallava, and the

Rencong alphabet native to Malaysia / Indonesia (13th to 16th centuries). The kingdom of Pasai in Indonesia is thought to have been founded in 1267 by Merah Silu, who converted to Islam. Thus began Muslim influence in the region. Indonesia is nowadays the largest Muslim country in the world, and Malaysia is also Muslim-majority. In terms of spelling, previous alphabets began to be replaced by the Arabic alphabet, this form of Malay orthography being known as Jawi. It is still commonly found in Malaysia. From the 16th century, under Portuguese, Dutch, and British influence, Jawi was gradually replaced by the Roman alphabet as the main way of writing Malay.

Malay Spelling in a Nutshell

It is simple to describe all the main elements of the Malay spelling system in one page. Rondthaler (1993) contemplates one benefit of the similar regularity of Spanish spelling:

> If you are flying to Mexico, you can hold in your hand a little card that shows the spelling of every Spanish sound. Then, when the plane lands, you can pronounce, in Spanish, virtually every word on every sign you see. You won't know the meaning of many of the words, but you can pronounce them, and that's a good start toward learning the language.
>
> (Rondthaler, 1993, pp. 31–32)

A similar card can easily be produced for Malay:

Vowels		
a /a/ (/ə/ word-finally)	*e* /e/ or /ə/	*oi* /oi/
ai /ai/	*i* /i/	*u* /u/
au /au/	*o* /o/	
Consonants		
b /b/	*k* /k/ ([ʔ] syllable-finally)	*r* /r/
c /tʃ/	*l* /l/	*s* /s/
d /d/	*m* /m/	*sy* /ʃ/
f /f/	*n* /n/	*t* /t/
g /g/	*ng* /ŋ/	*w* /w/
h /h/	*ny* /ɲ/	*y* /j/
j /dʒ/	*p* /p/	

Figure 30.1 Spelling-to-sound correspondences in Malay

A little explanation would be needed for those not familiar with phonetic symbols (e.g. "/ai/ as in English *sigh*"). Likewise, there is one sound that would need to be explained because it does not occur in English: /ɲ/. However, apart from that, Figure 30.1 is a simple card that could be produced for Malay (like Spanish) giving spelling-sound correspondences. Tourists could then pronounce Malay well enough, although they would not of course know the meaning of the words they were pronouncing. As Rondthaler says, it's a good start.

Rondthaler then points out the difficulty for English:

> The reverse is not true. No immigrant coming to the US can hold in his hand a card that shows the spelling of English sounds. Such a card would be the size of a refrigerator door, since we spell our 42 sounds in a potpourri of over 400 different ways. Scores of rules and exceptions add to the confusion.
>
> (Rondthaler, 1993, pp. 31–32)

To illustrate the problem, here is a card for the spelling-sound correspondences for one English letter: *c*:

In English, *c*:
- is sometimes pronounced /k/, e.g. *academy, balcony, romantic*
- is sometimes pronounced /s/, e.g. *cent, acid, excise, fancy*
- is sometimes part of the representation of /ʃ/, e.g. *vicious, ocean, social*
- When part of *ck*, is sometimes redundant, being followed by the identical sounding *k*, e.g. *rock*, or is only required to avoid implications of a long preceding vowel, e.g. *hockey* (cf. *hokey* /hoʊki/)
- when part of *ck*, is occasionally completely redundant, e.g. *blackguard, Cockburn*
- is sometimes redundant, being preceded by the identical sounding *s*, e.g. *science, muscle, luscious*
- is sometimes redundantly doubled, e.g. *account, accommodation* (cf. *acoustic*)
- is sometimes not redundantly doubled, e.g. in *accident, vaccine* the first *c* represents /k/ and the second /s/
- is /tʃ/ in Italian loanwords, e.g. *cello, concerto*
- as *cc* is /tʃ/ in Italian words, e.g. *cappuccino*
- when part of *ch* is usually /tʃ/, e.g. *chancellor, coach*
- when part of *ch* is /k/ in Greek loanwords, e.g. *Christmas, cholesterol, orchid*
- when part of *ch* is /ʃ/ in French loanwords, e.g. *charade, machine, panache*
- when part of *ch* is sometimes /dʒ/, e.g. *Norwich, spinach, sandwich*
- when part of *ch* is the velar fricative /x/ in some loanwords (if pronounced this way), e.g. *loch, Bach*
- is occasionally redundant, e.g. *acquit* (cf. *aquatic*), *victuals, indict, yacht, Connecticut, blancmange, Tucson, czar*
- is sometimes in free variation, e.g. *defence ~ defense, disc ~ disk*

Figure 30.2 Spelling-to-sound correspondences for *c* in English

The card for the whole Malay spelling system is smaller than that for one letter of English. Admittedly, the letter c was chosen because it is probably the one with the most spelling-sound correspondences. Nevertheless, the point is clear: Malay spelling is simple compared with English. There are simple correspondences; for instance, c = /tʃ/, and /tʃ/ = c, and it is never silent. There is only one letter of the alphabet where we can say the same for English: v = /v/, and /v/ = v, and it is never silent. All other letters have one-to-many and many-to-one correspondences, and may be silent.

An interesting question is how long it would take you to learn the spelling of Malay. You may indeed feel that it is so simple that you have already learned it by reading the last couple of pages, barring one or two unfamiliar sounds (e.g. /ɲ/) and correspondences that are not so self-evident (e.g. *sy*). In contrast, teachers of English spend a lot of time teaching and correcting the spelling of English.

Comparing Malay Spelling with English Spelling

History

In comparing the status of Malay spelling with that of English, it is necessary to bear in mind similarities and differences in the histories of the two languages.

As was detailed in Chapter 4, the English language is usually considered to date back to the Anglo-Saxon tribes in the 5th century. Similarly, the earliest passage in Old Malay is the Kedukan Bukit inscription (Haryono, 1995) discovered in South Sumatra (modern Indonesia), and dating to the 7th century. Naturally, documents and inscriptions in Old English and Old Malay from that time differ significantly from Modern English and Malay, because of language change over the centuries.

There is, however, a large difference in the length of time for which the Roman (Latin) alphabet has been used to write these languages. The alphabet was introduced for English by Irish Christian missionaries in the 6th century. In contrast, it was introduced for Malay by the Portuguese in the 16th century; the earliest attempt to write Malay using the Roman alphabet was in 1518 by Duarte Barbosa, a Portuguese writer and traveler, seven years after the Portuguese conquered Melaka. Four years later, Italian Antonio Pigafetta, a companion of Ferdinand Magellan, compiled a Malay-European dictionary using the Roman alphabet. English has thus used the Roman alphabet for 1,000 years longer than Malay.

Language Management

As was mentioned in Chapter 29, "English spelling has never been officially managed. There is no recognised academy or educational agency in Britain appointed to monitor the use and development of the language, as there often is for the languages of other countries" (Carney, 1994, p. 468). Some bodies, and some works such as dictionaries, may have a normalizing effect, but there is no one, universally accepted, worldwide governing body for English.

In contrast, there is such a body for Malay: the Dewan Bahasa dan Pustaka ("Institute of Language and Literature"), established in 1956 and headquartered in Kuala Lumpur, the Malaysian capital. Its website (Dewan Bahasa dan Pustaka, n.d.) states its objectives as:

- To develop and enrich the national language in all fields, including science and technology;
- To develop literary talent, particularly in the national language;
- To print or publish or assist in the printing or publication of books, magazines, pamphlets and other forms of literature in the national language and in other languages;
- To standardize spelling and pronunciation, and devise appropriate terminologies in the national language;
- To encourage the proper usage of the national language; and
- To encourage the usage of the national language so that it will be extensively used for all purposes in accordance with the law for the time being in force.

Note that its mission is to standardize the spelling and pronunciation of Malay (point 4), as well as its grammar, morphology, etc. (point 5). In this respect, it is similar to the Académie Française for French (see Wikipedia, n.d. a).

Asmah Haji Omar (1989, §14) explains the achievement of this management: "The Malay spelling reform was a success in three ways. Firstly, it resulted in giving a standard norm in spelling the language in place of a situation where many norms existed. Secondly, with its practicality and flexibility it has paved the way for a tremendous growth and development of the language. Finally, it brought together the Malay speaking countries in a close cultural and linguistic network."

Countries Where the Language Is Spoken

The areas of the world where English and Malay are spoken differ greatly.

English is spoken in virtually every country of the world. Often-quoted statistics from Crystal (1997) are that there are 320–380 million native speakers of English, 150–300 million second-language speakers, and 100–1,000 million foreign-language speakers.

Malay, on the other hand, is spoken in a limited geographical area in southeast Asia: Malaysia, Singapore, Brunei, southern Thailand, and the southern Philippines. The total number of speakers in these areas is about 77 million. It is therefore much easier to gain consensus about management and possible reform of the spelling system.

Spelling Reform

English has never undergone any wholesale, global spelling reform. As explained in Chapter 29, small-scale reforms have occurred at various times, but nothing extensive.

On the other hand, Malay has undergone several rounds of spelling reform. In the 20th century, reforms with varying degrees of change and pervasiveness occurred in 1904, 1924, 1956, and 1972 (Asmah Haji Omar, 1989).

Phonology

In fairness, it has to be pointed out that Malay phonology is simpler than English.

In terms of vowels, as is shown in Figure 30.1, Malay has six monophthong (single-state) vowels (phonemes), and two diphthongs (vowels with tongue and/or lip movement: /ai, au/). This compares with 20 vowels (12 monophthongs and eight diphthongs) in (standard British) English.

In terms of consonants, Malay has 20, excluding those only found in loanwords. English, on the other hand, has 24, again excluding any sounds found in loanwords, such as the /x/ in (some people's pronunciation of) *loch, Bach.*

Given that Malay has a total of 28 vowel and consonant phonemes, while (standard British) English has 44, it is not surprising that sound-spelling and spelling-sound correspondences in English are much more complex than in Malay, and that regularizing the correspondences in Malay is thus much simpler.

The syllable structure of Malay is simpler than of English. English syllables may have up to three consonants in the pronunciation at the beginning, e.g. *spring*, and up to four at the end, e.g. *sculpts.* Malay, on the other hand, is a CVC language, only allowing a maximum of one consonant in both initial and final position. There are thus no consonant clusters.

The difference in stress between syllables is far less in Malay than it is in English. In English, unstressed syllables are typically weakened, often reducing to the schwa vowel /ə/, as in *arena* /əriːnə/. This in turn leads to problems in knowing which letter represents that schwa vowel, e.g. *purer, juror*, as discussed in Chapter 14.

In contrast, schwa in Malay is less to do with stress. Indeed, it is possible to find Malay words where each vowel is schwa, e.g. /səgərə/ "fresh." The spelling of these vowels is predictable too: word-finally, it is *a*, elsewhere it is *e*, thus *segera*.

Loanwords

As we saw in Chapter 16, English has borrowed words from a large number of languages over the course of its history. More to the point, English has generally not regularized loanwords so that they conform to the pronunciation and spelling of English.

Table 30.1 Loanwords in Malay

Lending language	Word in Malay	Meaning
Arabic	*Ahad*	Sunday (literally "one")
	kamus	dictionary
	maaf	sorry
Dutch	*rokok*	smoke
	sepanduk	banner
Persian	*dewan*	hall
	gandum	wheat
	piala	cup, trophy
Portuguese	*almari*	cupboard
	bomba	fire brigade
	keju	cheese
Sanskrit	*anugerah*	award
	bahasa	language
	kuda	horse
Tamil	*kedai*	foodstall
	kolam	pool
	peta	map

In contrast, Malay regularly adapts loanwords in terms of pronunciation and spelling. However, the two main sources of loanwords nowadays are English (especially for science and technology) and Arabic (especially concepts related to Islam). Table 30.1 gives a few examples. Some of these were borrowed into the language so long ago that modern Malay speakers may not realize that they were originally loanwords.

Malay has borrowed words from a few languages: Arabic, Dutch, Persian, Portuguese, Sanskrit, Tamil, and various Chinese dialects, usually as a result of speakers of those languages traveling to Malaysia. In contrast, the number of languages that English has borrowed words from is much larger (see Chapter 16), often as a result of English speakers traveling to those countries during colonial times.

Exercise

As for the huge number of words borrowed from English, can you identify the following English loanwords from their Malay spelling? (All their English equivalents contain the letter *c*. They have been regularized in Malay because the letter *c* unambiguously represents /tʃ/, not /k/ or /s/.)

akademi

akaun

asid

balkoni

canselor

eksaiz

hoki

kalsium

koc

kolesterol

krismas

orkid

pakej

rok

romantik

sains

sen

sivik

vaksin

(English equivalents are given at the end of this chapter, if you really cannot work them out.)

26-letter Roman Alphabet

Does Malay use all the 26 letters of the Roman alphabet? From Figure 30.1, we can see that *q*, *v*, *x*, and *z* are missing. In fact these letters are used, but rarely and specifically for loanwords. The same is true of the digraphs *gh* and *kh*. See Table 30.2.

Table 30.2 Rare Roman alphabet letters in Malay

Letter(s)	Origin of loanword	Malay example	Meaning
q	Arabic	*Quran*	Muslim holy book
v	English	*video*	video
x	English	*X-ray*	X-ray
z	Arabic, English	*zarafah*	giraffe
		zon	zone
gh	Arabic	*Maghribi*	Morocco
kh	Arabic	*khas*	special
		tarikh	date

No Doubled Consonant Letters

There are no doubled consonant letters in Malay. Occasionally it happens that two instances of the same letters occur one after the other, but they belong to the representations of different sounds. For example, *gg* sometimes occurs; however, the first *g* is part of the *ng* digraph (for /ŋ/) while the second represents /g/, e.g. *inggeris* "English," *guna* "use" > *pengguna* "user."

No Silent Letters

There are no silent letters in Malay. Historical change has not caused letters to become silent, and the management of the Malay spelling system has ensured that this remains true. The lack of consonant clusters in Malay, and the smaller difference between stressed and unstressed syllables means that sounds are seldom omitted (elided). In loanwords, this may happen, however. For example, English *process* is borrowed into Malay as *peroses*. Note that the two-syllable English word has become a three-syllable Malay word because the initial cluster /pr-/ is not allowed in Malay phonology. However, Malay speakers, most of whom speak some English, often elide the first schwa sound, making it the same as in English, with the /pr-/ cluster, and thus a silent *e*.

No Phonemic Transcription in Malay Dictionaries

Because the pronunciation is virtually 100% predictable from the spelling, and vice versa, there is no need for phonemic transcriptions (or any other kind of pronunciation guide) in Malay dictionaries, of the type found in all English dictionaries.

No Spelling Bees in Malay

Similarly, spelling bees do not occur in Malay. Since the spelling is predictable from the pronunciation and unambiguous, contestants would never get any items wrong, unless they were not fully competent in the language.

Ability to Pronounce Malay Without Understanding

As the pronunciation is predictable from the spelling, anyone who has internalized the Malay correspondences can pronounce any word from its spelling. This is regardless of whether they know the language well or are just beginners. This situation is similar to that of the Hungarian professor's grandchild quoted in Chapter 3. It also means that people can sing Malay karaoke even though they may not know the meaning of what they are singing.

No Homophones or Homographs in Malay

The ambiguity caused by English homophones and homographs (Chapter 20) is absent from Malay. There are no homophones (words that are spelled differently but pronounced the same) and very few homographs. The only scope for homographs is cases like *e* representing /e/ or /ə/. The spelling *perang* can therefore be either /peraŋ/ "brown hair colour" or /pəraŋ/ "war."

No Variant Spellings in Malay

Malay has no equivalent to the English words *disc* and *disk*, which are used somewhat interchangeably. In English /k/ can be spelled with either *c* or *k*, whereas in Malay it can only be *k*.

Phonological Strategy

The phonological strategy of relating sounds to spelling, and spelling to sounds, is all that is required to learn to read and speak Malay. The other strategies (morphological, analogical, etymological, visual) described in Chapters 22, 23, 25, and 26 relate to English, and are not needed in Malay. Malay has no spelling pronunciations. As a result, it is easy to learn Malay pronunciation and spelling. This is true for all learners, whether foreigners learning the language, or children learning it as their native language. Difficulties experienced by learners relate to phenomena such as dyslexia (Wan Mohammad, Vijayaletchumy, Abd Aziz, & Abdul Rahim, 2012), rather than being caused by inherent difficulties in the spelling system. In school, little time is spent teaching and correcting the spelling of Malay.

Literacy

The bottom line for any spelling system is whether it enables the speakers of the language to read and write, and thus achieve literacy and advance their education. Literacy rates in Malaysia are high: 98% for those in the 15–24 age range, although lower for older speakers (UNESCO, 2016).

Literacy rates for English-speaking countries are often absent in global literacy lists (e.g. UNESCO, n.d.). However, literacy is lower than one would expect, given that English-speaking countries are generally wealthier countries.

> According to a study conducted in late April [2013] by the U.S. Department of Education and the National Institute of Literacy, 32 million adults in the U.S. can't read. That's 14 percent of the population. 21 percent of adults in the U.S. read below a 5th grade level, and 19 percent of high school graduates can't read.
>
> (Huffington Post, 2013)

Similarly, in a 2013 study by the Organisation for Economic Co-operation and Development (OECD), England came 22nd for literacy out of 24 OECD countries (BBC News, 2013). The top places were taken by non-English-speaking countries. There are many other factors involved; however, the difficulty of the English spelling system must contribute to this shortfall.

Conclusion

Linguists are always wary of labeling languages as simple or complex. A language consists of many subsystems, including grammar, morphology, and phonology, and while one language may have, say, a simple grammar, it may have a complex phonology. However, spelling is one area where one can talk about simplicity and complexity, because it is essentially man-made and conscious. Malay has a simple spelling system, and the many benefits outlined in this chapter follow from this. However, English has a complex spelling system, meaning that many problems arise.

Summary

- Malay has a much more regular spelling system than English. This is partly due to the management of the spelling system that has taken place at various times.
- There are many benefits to a regular spelling system. One major result that the regular spelling system contributes to is high rates of literacy.

English Equivalents

Academy, account, acid, balcony, chancellor, excise, hockey, calcium, coach, cholesterol, Christmas, orchid, package, rock, romantic, science, cent, civic, vaccine.

Exercise

Here is a passage in Malay. In fact, it is the words of the Malaysian national anthem (Wikipedia, n.d. b). You probably do not know Malay, so this is totally unfamiliar to you. However, this chapter has introduced you to the basics of Malay phonology and spelling. Try applying this new knowledge and read the passage out loud.

	Translation
Negaraku	My homeland
Tanah tumpahnya darahku,	Where I have spilt my blood
Rakyat hidup	The people living
bersatu dan maju,	United and progressive

Rahmat bahagia	May God bestow
tuhan kurniakan,	Blessings and happiness
Raja kita	May our king
selamat bertakhta.	Have a successful reign.

Further Reading

The details of Malay spelling are covered in Omniglot (2017).

References

Asmah Haji Omar (1989). The Malay spelling reform. *Journal of the Simplified Spelling Society, 1989*(2), 9–13. Retrieved from web.archive.org/web/20100706054017/ http://www.spellingsociety.org/journals/j11/malay.php

BBC News (9 October 2013). *England's young adults trail world in literacy and maths.* Retrieved from www.bbc.com/news/education-24433320

Carney, E. (1994). *A survey of English spelling.* London, UK: Routledge.

Crystal, D. (1997). *English as a global language.* Cambridge UK: Cambridge University Press.

Dewan Bahasa dan Pustaka (n.d.). Retrieved from laman.dbp.gov.my and prpm. dbp.gov.my

Haryono, T. (1995). Traces of Buddhism in Sumatra: An archaeological perspective. Paper presented at the International colloquium on "Buddhism in the Himalaya, its expansion and present-day aspect," Kathmandu (Nepal), 22–30 September. Retrieved from en.unesco.org/silkroad/sites/silkroad/files/knowledge-bank-article/traces_of_buddhism_in_sumatra_an_archaeological_perspective.pdf

Huffington Post (6 September 2013). *The U.S. illiteracy rate hasn't changed in 10 years.* Retrieved from www.huffingtonpost.com/2013/09/06/illiteracy-rate_n_3880355.html

Omniglot (2017). *Malay.* Retrieved from www.omniglot.com/writing/malay.htm

Rondthaler, E. (1993). "Informal" spelling as a way to literacy. *Journal of the Simplified Spelling Society, 1993*(2), 31–32.

UNESCO (2016). *Malaysia.* Retrieved from uis.unesco.org/en/country/MY

UNESCO (n.d.). *UNESCO eAtlas of literacy.* Retrieved from uis.unesco.org/en/ topic/literacy

Wan Mohammad, W. M. R., Vijayaletchumy, S., Abd Aziz, A. Y., & Abdul Rahim, N. (2012). Dyslexia in the aspect of Malay language spelling. *International Journal of Academic Research in Business and Social Sciences, 2*(1), 308–314. Retrieved from www.hrmars.com/admin/pics/524.pdf

Wikipedia (n.d. a). *List of language regulators.* Retrieved from en.wikipedia.org/wiki/ List_of_language_regulators

Wikipedia (n.d. b). *Negaraku.* Retrieved from en.wikipedia.org/wiki/Negaraku

31 The Future of English Spelling

Learning Objectives

At the end of this chapter, readers will be able to:

- list some changes and trends in English spelling and punctuation that are ongoing
- speculate on the state of English spelling in, say, 50 years' time.

Introduction

This chapter is necessarily speculative. While we can observe some changes that are taking place now, and extrapolate from them how things are likely to look in the near future, much of what follows is crystal ball-gazing, with little guarantee that the things will happen. The reason for this is that nobody can say for sure what technological changes will take place in terms of word-processing, and digital communication in general. It is also important to note that changes will only take place if the users of the language are happy for the changes to take place. The promotion of any managed changes is therefore important.

Three categories of possible change are discussed in this chapter: changes that can be observed at present in respect of writers' punctuation habits; changes caused by changes in technology; and consensual changes to the spelling system, and perhaps the grammatical system, by some kind of reform.

Punctuation

In Chapter 9, we already alluded to various types of variation in punctuation habits including changes through time that are likely to continue into the future.

British punctuation has always been lighter, using fewer punctuation marks, than American punctuation. This may continue as a trend although, for communication's sake and for the disambiguation of text, it cannot completely disappear, leaving no punctuation.

The semicolon, retained by many, discarded by many others, may or may not be on its way out.

The use of the apostrophe to represent possession (and not to represent simple plurals) is barely understood, and it is often misused (according to traditional rules) by many, including native and non-native writers alike. Its use for possession may lapse, although its other use, to show that letters have been omitted as in *haven't*, is less likely to disappear completely, because of examples like *we'll / well, we'd / wed*.

As another manifestation of lighter punctuation, hyphens seem to be used less. Carter and McCarthy (2006, p. 482) state that "The use of hyphens in compounds and complex words involves a number of different rules, and practice is changing, with fewer hyphens present in contemporary English." Thus, for instance, *nonnative* seems to be preferred to *non-native*.

There seems to be decreasing understanding of what constitutes a grammatically and semantically complete sentence, and therefore what takes a sentence-completing punctuation mark (such as a full stop / period, exclamation mark, or question mark) at the end. In particular, by traditional punctuation rules, commas cannot join sentences. Sentences joined by commas, known as run-on sentences or comma splices, have been commented on for decades, but seem to be increasingly frequent. Paradoxically, the use of commas to mark off introductory adverbial phrases, and in the middle of sentences, seems to be decreasing.

Dashes, traditionally viewed as informal punctuation, seem to be more frequently used, even in relatively formal texts.

Technology

The invention of word-processing with spell-checking meant that writers could rely less on their memory and dictionaries for the correct spelling of words. Similarly, the invention of smartphones, and social media channels such as Facebook and Twitter, has meant that brief communications of the moment are now common.

Spell-checking programs have become more and more sophisticated. In early versions, the program's internal dictionary did not contain many words, and thus relatively few suggestions for correct versions were given. However, they now provide much more in the way of names of people and places, and rarer, perhaps technical, words. Spell-checkers are nowadays generally combined with grammar-checkers, and can for example detect the probable misplacement of spaces, e.g. suggesting that *take sin* (while both perfectly valid English words) may well be a typo for *takes in* (two English words that occur more probably together). More recently, checkers seem to have diverted into the stylistic province of plain English, suggesting that *a large number of* should be replaced by *many*. Further refinement of spell- and grammar-checking programs can be expected. Whether it genuinely helps writers become better spellers remains to be seen.

Speed is of the essence with much written communication via social media. Brevity is also important; for instance, Twitter has a 140-character limit for tweets. As a result, short, fast messages are often conveyed, often with scant editing for spelling and punctuation. Messages can also be transmitted efficiently by using emoticons. These features are probably here to stay for the near future.

As Crystal (2008) argues, this does not necessarily mean the end of proper spelling and punctuation, as we know it. It is impossible to play with the spelling of language (by using abbreviations, for example) if you do not know the spelling of language. Texting is an informal means of communication, but formal means, such as is required for writing a job application, still exist and are important. Spell-checkers can suggest alternative corrections, but a writer cannot choose the correct alternative if they do not know the correct spelling for the word they intend.

To conclude, it is difficult to predict how technological changes will impact spelling, because it is difficult to predict what the technological changes might be. As the quotation attributed to the 6th century B.C. Greek philosopher Heraclitus states, "The only thing that is constant is change." There is no reason for us to suppose that, because of technological change, spelling and punctuation will not be subject to this constant change, even if spelling is a man-made construct.

Reform

Chapter 29 has already outlined the main pros and cons of spelling reform. While spelling reform would theoretically be successful in increasing English literacy and eliminating spelling mistakes, because the purpose of reform is to eliminate irregularities, it faces obstacles. It is not, however, an impossible task. For instance, the word *through* is spelled that way because it was originally pronounced with a final /x/ sound, which was lost. It is Old English in origin, and is related to the modern German *durch*. The *Online Etymological Dictionary* (n.d.) states that it was "not clearly differentiated from *thorough* until early Modern English." From the 15th to the 18th centuries, a common spelling of *through* was *thro*. The spelling *thru* was also possible then, and indeed predates the modern spelling *through* by over 100 years. So, the spelling *thru*, thought of by many as a modern reformed spelling, has a history. It was popularized in the U.S.A. in the 19th century, and is still thought of as informal. Merriam-Webster (n.d.) recalls that

> near the end of 2010, the Associated Press announced that its stylebook, used by many newspaper editors and writers, would now allow for the use of *drive-thru* instead of *drive-through*. At an editor's conference in 2014, there was an audible gasp in the room when this was mentioned.

As the French say, "Plus ça change, plus c'est la même chose" (The more things change, the more they stay the same). Present-day people are concerned about what they perceive as an innovation that in fact corresponds to an older form of the spelling. It would really be an innovation if it became a *dryv-thru*.

Yule (n.d.) outlines some changes that could take place.

As was explained in Chapter 29, one problem faced by English but not by other languages is that it is spoken in many countries of the world, with no governing body. A worldwide association for the English language, with representatives from all major English-speaking countries, would be a good first step.

Hangul Day, 9 October, was established by 16th century King Sejong as a celebration of the Korean writing system he devised. A similar International English Spelling Day could prompt discussions of the nature of English spelling. It is important to note that this is not intended as a day for worldwide spelling bees, but as a forum for better understanding the problems caused by the current system.

Schools could be encouraged to hold "Design your own English spelling system" competitions. Yule suggests that opponents of spelling system should be encouraged to participate.

The most far-reaching of Yule's suggestions is that English grammar could change (with concomitant changes in spelling) in order to make it more regular and decrease the burden on children to learn its irregularities. She suggests that, instead of the current *bring, brought, teach, taught*, these could be made into regular verbs, adding *-ed* to make the past tense. Such a situation already exists between BrE *learnt, spelt* and AmE *learned, spelled*, and AmE *dove, snuck* and BrE *dived, sneaked*. Since most spelling reformers propose reducing part tense endings to simply *-d*, this would result in *bring, bringd; teach, teachd*.

These are spelling changes that many readers may find fanciful. However, they would almost undeniably achieve the objective of reducing irregularities and thereby increasing literacy for native and non-native users.

Summary

- Three types of spelling change may be foreseen: in punctuation habits; those caused by changes in technology; and possible spellings regularized by reform.

Exercise

Do you foresee any other possible changes in English spelling and punctuation? How pervasive are they? What opposition might they face?

References

Carter, R., & McCarthy, M. (2006). *Cambridge grammar of English: A comprehensive guide*. Cambridge, UK: Cambridge University Press.

Crystal, D. (2008). *Txting: The gr8 db8*. Oxford, UK: Oxford University Press.

Merriam-Webster (n.d.). *How "thru" turned into "through" and then to "thru" again*. Retrieved from www.merriam-webster.com/words-at-play/how-thru-turned-into-through

Online Etymological Dictionary (n.d.). Retrieved from www.etymonline.com/word/through

Yule, V. (n.d.). *The future for English spelling*. Oz Ideas. Retrieved from valerieyule.com.au/sfutspe.htm

32 Conclusion

Learning Objectives

At the end of this chapter, readers will be able to:

- reflect on the main problematical features of English spelling
- reflect on possible solutions.

Introduction

This is the final chapter of this book, and it is usual for final chapters to be a recap of the main points of the preceding chapters. However, given that the preceding chapters – all 31 of them – have covered a very wide spectrum of disparate topics (theory, history, technology, strategy, world languages, reform, etc.), it would be difficult to draw threads connecting them.

One thread that can be easily seen from reading the preceding chapters, because it has been emphasized so often, is the peculiar nature of English spelling. Its basis is alphabetic, because it uses the Roman alphabet (not a logographic or syllabary system), which it has used for over a millennium and a half. However, as was pointed out in Chapter 2, it is perhaps the worst (most irregular) example of an alphabetic system in languages of the world.

This is the result of two main factors. Firstly, English has had a Roman alphabet written form since the 6th century, longer than many other languages. Secondly, the English spelling system has never been systematically managed. Lexicographers like Dr. Samuel Johnson and Noah Webster had some effect on standardizing spelling, but it was minor, unsystematic, and a couple of centuries ago.

The fact that English spelling is irregular may not be obvious to native speakers. This is especially the case with monolingual speakers in western societies. Crystal (1987, p. 360) explains.

> People brought up within a western society often think that the mono-lingualism that forms a routine part of their existence is the normal way of life for all but a few 'special' people. They are wrong. Multilingualism is the natural way of life for hundreds of millions all over the world.

Visually (n.d.) shows that in 2009 there were very few countries with only one indigenous language: Bermuda, the British Indian Ocean Territory, the Cayman Islands, the Falkland Islands, the Maldives, North Korea, Saint Helena, the Vatican State. At the other end of the spectrum, Papua New Guinea has 830 indigenous languages.

These statistics relate to countries that are mono-, bi-, or multilingual. The concept can also be applied to individuals: how many people within a country can speak more than one language? Visually (n.d.) shows that only 18% of Americans can speak a language other than English. This bilingualism compares with 53% of Europeans, including 95% of Luxembourgers, and 99% of Latvians.

The upshot of these statistics is that many native English speakers are monolingual and, as a result of that, they may not appreciate the difficulty of English spelling in contrast to the spelling of other languages. Native English-speaking teachers may not realize the contrast between the simplicity of some learners' native languages' spelling systems, and the complexity of English spelling.

A Strategic Approach

Because English spelling is a poor example of an alphabetic system, other strategies for coping with learning spelling have been proposed. In particular, consideration of the constituent morphemes of longer words may help but, as was pointed out in Chapter 22, there are many counterexamples.

While there have been many exercises in the chapters of this book, and many of these can easily be used or adapted for use in the classroom, readers may be a little disappointed that there is no section in this book with exercises on spelling. The conscious decision not to include such exercises was taken because there is a large number of such books, worksheets, etc. available either in print or online, many of them freely downloadable.

A personal favorite is Stirling (2011). It is one of very few books that contain background information so that the reader understands English spelling, as well as classroom exercises to teach and practice its patterns. Also, it does not contain mistakes or unorthodox views on the nature of English spelling.

While both this book and her book cover the various elements of the English spelling system (phonological, morphological, etc.), she labels them "systems" rather than "strategies." To my mind, these elements are not systematic enough to be able to call them systems. Even the most basic element of an alphabetic spelling system, namely that letters represent sounds, is so poorly manifested in English. Instead, I have treated them as strategies for coping with uncertainty. For certain words, a phonological strategy, looking only at letters and sounds, may work. For other words, a morphological strategy, considering the morphemes that make up words, may work. The visual strategy, namely memorizing the spelling of some words because their spelling is so irregular phonologically, morphologically, etc., is essentially a last resort strategy and certainly cannot be called a system.

This visual strategy is the basis of the dilemma found in some words in English. The spelling of the Lea & Perrins product is often explained by saying, "It's written 'Wor-cester-shire Sauce', but it's pronounced 'Wooster'." An American example is the state spelled "Ar-Kansas" but pronounced "Arkan-saw." Simpler examples include, "It's written /debt/ with a *b*, but it's pronounced /det/." Note how such explanation is unnecessary and impossible in other languages.

Also note how brand names, stage names, etc. may be made more memorable by using unconventional, but still possible, spelling. For instance, British musician Dominic Harrison took the stage name *Yungblud* (Vevo, 2018: Wikipedia, n.d.). In pronunciation, this is not a problem; it is only when the name has to be spelled that the departure from the conventional but irregular spelling of *young* and *blood* becomes apparent. Again, this is a situation that does not exist in other languages.

Another situation that does not exist in other languages is the common English question, "How do you spell that?" In languages with a regular alphabetic spelling system, if a word or name is pronounced X, then it can only be spelled Y. In English, there may be more than one possibility. However, English is not totally irregular, so teachers can legitimately ask, "How do you think it is spelled?"

Getting Personal

While it is often considered bad style to use the first person in academic writing, I would like to end this conclusion by recounting a couple of personal episodes, and by taking a personal stance.

I am a native British speaker of English, born and raised near London, U.K., and I went to university in Edinburgh. I still find it fascinating that I did not realize that *idiosyncracy* and *abbrieviation* were misspellings until I was doing my PhD research. *Idiosyncrasy* in fact ends in *-sy*; it comes ultimately from the Greek elements *idios* "one's own" and *synkrasis* "personal characteristics," itself from *syn* "together" and *krasis* "mixture." That is, it is not like *democracy*, from Greek *demos* "people" and *kratos* "rule." Similarly, both *abbreviation* and *brief* come from Latin *brevis* "short." It was borrowed into English in the early 14th century as *bref*. The spelling of the vowel in the adjective *brief* changed to *ie*, but not in the noun *abbreviation*.

There can be few languages where an educated speaker reaches postgraduate level without being able to spell not particularly uncommon or technical words.

I am British and therefore use British spellings. However, this is a book published by Routledge. While Routledge is a British company, it is worldwide, and this book is published by its New York office. Thus, I write in British English (grammar, vocabulary, etc.) but have been asked to use American spelling throughout. As was shown in Chapter 15, the spelling differences between British and American spelling are not great and, as computer spell-checkers can be set to either British or American (or some other varieties of) English, changing to American spelling is not difficult. However, the resultant text may be considered somewhat of a hybrid linguistically.

This is a situation that does not apply in other languages.

Solving the Problem

The situation of English spelling is like that of many things. The current situation is not ideal; the system is so complex that, for native speakers, it takes children much longer than other languages to master, some people never master it, there are low literacy rates, resulting illiteracy is a barrier to getting a job, etc. For non-native learners, English spelling is difficult to learn, is probably much more irregular than learners' native languages, and English teachers have to spend much longer on spelling than teachers do in other languages.

However, there are so many different opinions about how to fix the problem that nothing can be agreed, and as a result nothing is done.

In my opinion, without some form of spelling reform, little can be improved. The fundamental problem lies not in the way teachers teach spelling, but in the features of the spelling system itself. A movement to regularize English spelling by removing some of the most obvious irregularities would be a good start. Most proposals for reformed spelling do away with silent letters, especially those that are empty; that is, have no function (other than to make spelling difficult!).

As spelling reform would affect all English users, a worldwide body would be needed, with representation from all major English-using countries, to propose changes. These changes would have to be acceptable to all, or at least the vast majority of, users.

As this would represent an upheaval in the spelling of the world's foremost language, it would have to be implemented gradually, rather than as a "big bang" all-at-once change. Lindgren's SR1 (Chapter 29), whereby all instances of the /e/ vowel are spelled with *e*, is just such a scheme. It is not a shock to the system, but shows that a minor change can make a big difference in regularizing spelling, eliminating irregular sellings like *leopard, treasure, heifer,* etc.

It is tempting to think that now is a good time to action this, in light of the fact that modern technology has produced media such as email, Facebook, Twitter, where nonce respellings are common and people, especially younger people, are probably more open to the fact that variation in spelling away from irregular TO is possible.

Summary

- Most people in the world are at least bilingual, and can probably see how irregular English spelling is.
- Various strategies are required to cope with the irregularities of English spelling.
- Even well-educated native speakers of English make spelling mistakes.
- Some kind of reform of English spelling seems inevitable, if accurate and correct spelling is to be aimed for.

Exercises

1   Which of the following statements do you agree with?

- "Nothing need be done. English spelling is fine as it is."
- "Nothing can be done. English spelling contains too many problem features."
- "The way I personally spell English is best. Other variations (British, American, other) are worse."
- "A worldwide body for English would be a good idea."
- "A small, first-step change like Lundgren's SR1 would be a good idea."
- "Creative respellings used in Facebook and other social media are fine."
- "English spelling is no worse than that of other languages I know."
- "Words borrowed from other languages should retain their original foreign spelling."
- "I am confident I spell English correctly 100% of the time."
- "As an English teacher, spelling is not a problem in my classes."

2   Play God. If you had ultimate power, how would you suggest the following English words should best be spelled?

accommodation

beggar

choir

choux

friend

genre

have

lawyer

liar

once

plausible

salmon

snorkel

steal

steel

xylophone

References

Crystal, D. (1987). *The Cambridge encyclopedia of language.* Cambridge, UK: Cambridge University Press.
Stirling, J. (2011). *Teaching spelling to English language learners.* Raleigh, NC: Lulu.
Vevo (2018). *Yungblud.* Retrieved from www.vevo.com/artist/yungblud
Visually (n.d.). *Monolingual vs bilingual.* Retrieved from visual.ly/community/infographic/lifestyle/monolingual-vs-bilingual
Wikipedia (n.d). *Yungblud.* Retrieved from en.wikipedia.org/wiki/Yungblud

Appendix 1
Sound-to-spelling Correspondences
for British English

This appendix presupposes a basic knowledge of the sound system and phonemic symbols of English.

Consonants

Consonant sounds are quite uniform in accents of English worldwide. The following table gives the main sound-to-spelling correspondences for the 24 consonant sounds (phonemes) of (British) English (from Carney, 1994).

Phoneme	Spelling	% of the time in connected speech	Example words
/p/	p	95	pan
	pp	5	copper
/b/	b	98	bit
	others	2	
/t/	t	96	ten
	tt	3	pattern
	others	1	
/d/	d	98	dame
	dd	2	sudden
/k/	c	59	car
	k	21	king
	ck	6	back
	others	14	
/g/	g	92	go
	gu	3	guess
	gg	2	ragged
	others	3	
/tʃ/	ch	65	chest
	tch	10	match
	others	25	Palatalization, e.g. *question, ritual*

(continued)

Phoneme	Spelling	% of the time in connected speech	Example words
/dʒ/	g, ge, dge	71	gem, page, badge
	j	29	jug
/f/	f	84	fat
	ph	11	phone
	ff	4	offer
	others	1	
/v/	v	100	very
/θ/	th	100	thigh
/ð/	th	100	then
/s/	s, ss	79	sit, dress
	c	15	cent
	others	6	
/z/	s	93	rise
	z, zz	5	zero, jazz
	others	2	
/ʃ/	sh	37	ship
	ch	1	chef
	others	55	Palatalization, e.g. dictation, repulsion, logician
	others	7	
/ʒ/	s	91	Palatalization, e.g. occasion
	g	4	beige
	others	5	
/h/	h	99*	home
	wh	1*	whole
/m/	m	96	money
	mm	3	summer
	others	1	
/n/	n	97	need
	nn	1	tunnel
	others	2	
/ŋ/	ng	75 *	sing
	n	25 *	sink
/l/	l	75	lamp
	ll	18	follow
	le	8	castle
/r/	r	94	real
	rr	4	carry
	others	2	

/w/	*w*	64	*well*
	qu (= /kw/)	27	*quick*
	wh	5	*wheel*
	u	4	*language*
	others	<1	
/j/	*y*	19	*yet*
	as part of /juː/		*use*
	reduction of an		*behavior*
	underlying		
	/iː, ɪ/		

Vowels

Accents of English differ more in terms of vowel sounds than consonant sounds. As a result, the following table of sound-to-spelling correspondences applies to the 19 vowel sounds of standard (British) English (excluding /ə/), but may need adapting for other accents.

Phoneme	Spelling	% of the time in connected speech	Example words
/ɪ/	*i*	61	*bit*
	y	20	*rhythm*
	e	16	*become*
	a, aCe	2	*spinach, image*
	others	2	
/e/	*e*	84	*ten*
	ea	6	*dead*
	others	9	
/æ/	*a*	100	*bad*
/ʌ/	*u*	63	*mud*
	o	27	*ton*
	ou	8	*touch*
	others	2	
/ɒ/	*o*	92	*not*
	a	6	*wash*
	others	2	
/ʊ/	*oo*	64	*good*
	u	32	*put*
	others	4	

(continued)

(continued)

Phoneme	Spelling	% of the time in connected speech	Example words
/iː/	e, eCe, final ee	38	be, theme, agree
	non-final ee	26	deep
	ea	25	leaf
	non-final ie	5	chief
	i, iCe, final ie	2	motif, police, laddie
	others	4	
/ɑː/	ar	60	park
	a	34	father
	others	6	
/ɔː/	a (+ l)	29	halt
	or, ore, ar	25	cord, core, war
	au	9	author
	aw	9	jaw
	our	8	court
	ough	6	ought
	al ('empty' l)	5	talk
	others	9	
/uː/	oo	39	moon
	u, uCe, ue	27	flu, rule, blue
	o, oCe, oe	15	who, move, shoe
	ew	9	new
	ou	7	group
	others	3	
/ɜː/	er(r)	39	herb
	ir(r)	18	bird
	ur(r)	15	turn
	or(r)	17	word
	ear	8	heard
	others	3	
/eɪ/	a, aCe	65	labor, lake
	final ay	18	day
	ai	12	rail
	others	5	
/aɪ/	i, iCe, final ie, final y	80	bicycle, like, lie, try
	igh	13	high
	non-final y	2	rhyme
	others	5	
/ɔɪ/	oi	61	boil
	oy	39	boy
/oʊ/	o, oCe, oe	75	go, hope, toe
	ow	18	grow
	oa	4	coat
	others	4	

/aʊ/	ou, final ow	93	cloud, cow
	pre-consonantal ow	6	crowd
	others	1	
/ɪə/	ear	28	dear
	ea	12	idea
	er, ere	12	hero, mere
	ia	10	media
	eer	4	deer
	others	34 *	
/eə/	ar, are	59	librarian, care
	air	28	hair
	ear	10	wear
	others	3	
/ʊə/	u + /ə/ in suffix	†	actual, fluent
	u + /ə/ in stem	†	cruel
	oor	†	poor
	our	†	tour
	ure	†	sure

* As Carney (1994, p. 190) says, "/ɪə/ is very divergent" in terms of sound-to-spelling correspondences.

† As Carney (1994, p. 194) notes, many of these words are pronounced with /ɔ:/ by many speakers. For this reason, he does not give percentages for /ʊə/.

Further Reading

For more on the sounds of English, and the symbols used to represent them in transcription, see Brown (2005, 2014).

References

Brown, A. (2005). *Sounds, symbols and spellings* Singapore: McGraw-Hill.

Brown, A. (2014). *Pronunciation and phonetics: A practical guide for English language teachers*. New York, NY: Routledge.

Carney, E. (1994). *A survey of English spelling*. London, UK: Routledge.

Appendix 2
Surnames Exemplifying
Spelling Rules

Introduction

English spelling had been variable for centuries, until about the 18th century. As a result, alternative spellings of words, especially surnames, have been widespread. The surnames listed that follow, including their variant spellings, have existed in the history of English; their prevalence in Modern English societies varies.

Since English is fundamentally a Germanic language (see Chapter 4), it is not always easy to trace which surnames are of German origin (from Anglo-Saxon times), and which are more modern additions through migration from Germany. Some can reliably be called recent German introductions, such as *Trapp* (as in the von Trapp family of *The sound of music* fame) or *Depp* (as in Johnny Depp, the American actor) which only entered U.S. English in the 18th century. Note that doubled final consonant letters are common in the spelling system of German.

Various other caveats have to be expressed:

- Many surnames have to be labeled "uncertain origin"; that is, language historians (etymologists) have been unable to trace the source reliably. While some Anglo-Saxon surnames have been in the language for centuries, others have been introduced from other European languages (French, Dutch, etc.), and from the Gaelic languages of Ireland, Scotland, Wales, and Cornwall.
- English has been spoken with widely differing accents throughout England. As a result, scribes centuries ago in different parts of the country used different spellings to represent their (different) pronunciations. For most of the centuries of the history of English, there has been a low level of literacy among the general public. Some alternative spellings seem to have been the result of simple misspellings by clerks on birth certificates, etc.
- Many surnames are variants of other, perhaps more common, surnames, e.g. *Stedd* is a variant spelling of *Stead; Degg* of *Dagg; Gregg* of *Grieg*.
- The letters *i* and *y* have been interchangeable throughout much of the history of English.

- As has been evident from many of the examples given in Chapter 8, a final *s* and a final silent *e* are common in surnames. The final *s* is thought to have originated in the 13th century for peasant laborers who had no surname of their own; they were therefore given the surname of their master, with a final *s*, a possessive *s* without an apostrophe, to show that they were bonded to him. Thus, *Gibbs* was a worker belonging to master Gibb. As for silent final *e*, this had previously been pronounced (as a schwa) but, when the final schwa disappeared from the pronunciation, the final *e* letter remained in the spelling. Some silent final *e*s were added for a formal prestige effect.

- Some surnames were originally what is known as nickname surnames. For instance, *Short* was originally the nickname of someone who was short (cf. Modern English *shorty*); his ancestors then retained the surname Short. The surname *Baines* is similarly thought to be an original nickname from the Old English word *ban* "bones," for a thin person.

A Fuller List of Surnames with Doubled Final Consonant Letters

Babb, Badd, Batt, Begg, Benn, Bett, Bigg(e)(s), Binn(s), Blogg(s), Bodd, Bogg(s), Bonn(e), Bott, Brett, Brigg(e)(s), Budd, Bugg(e), Bunn(e), Butt, Capp, Chubb, Chugg, Clapp, Clegg(e)(s), Cobb, Copp(s), Cott, Crabb(e), Cragg(e), Cramm, Crapp, Cromm, Cropp(s), Crumm, Cumm(e), Cupp, Dabb, Dagg, Dann(e)(s), Degg, Digg(es), Dinn(e), Dobbs, Dodd(s), Dogg, Domm(e), Donn(e), Drumm, Dudd, Dumm, Dunn(e), Dynne, Fagg, Fann, Fatt, Fenn, Figg(e)(s), Finn, Fitt(s), Flegg, Flett, Flinn, Flynn, Fogg(e), Fripp, Fudd, Gadd, Gann, Gatt, Gedd, Gemm, Gibb(s), Gigg(s), Ginn, Gladd, Glynn(e), Gomm(e), Gregg, Gritt, Gumm, Gunn, Gwynne, Hagg, Hamm, Hann, Hatt, Hedd, Higg(e)(s), Hobb(e)s, Hodd, Hogg(e), Hott, Hudd, Hugg, Humm, Hutt, Jett, Jigg(s), Judd, Jugg, Kegg, Kidd, Knagg(s), Knott, Ladd, Lagg, Lamm, Latt, Legg(e), Lett, Limm, Linn, Lipp, Logg, Lott, Lugg, Lumm, Lunn, Lutt, Lymm(e), Lynn, Matt, McCann, McNutt, Meggs, Miggs, Mimm(s), Minn(e)(s), Mitts, Mobbs, Mogg(s), Mudd, Mugg, Munn(e)(s), Mynn(e)(s), (K)Natt, Nedd, Nobbs, Nunn, (K)Nutt, Pegg(e), Penn, Pett, Pigg(e), Pimm(e), Pinn, Pitt, Platt, Plumm(e), Pogg, Pott(s), Pratt, Pymm(e), Ragg(e), Ratt, Redd, Repp, Rhett, Rigg(e)(s), Robb, Rodd, Rudd, Rutt, Scott, Scragg, Scripp(s), Scrogg(e)s, Scruggs, Simm(s), Spratt, Stagg, Stedd, Stepp(e), Stodd, Stott, Stubb(e)s, Studd, Symm, Tabb, Tadd, Tapp, Tatt, Tedd, Tett, Tibbs, Timm(s), Tinn, Tipps, Todd, Topp(s), Tott, Trogg, Tubbs, Tunn, Tupp, Tutt, Twigg(e), Tymms, Venn, Watt(s), Webb, Wigg, Wragg(e), Wynn.

A Fuller List of Surnames with Doubled Final *r* Letters

Barr, Burr(e), Carr, Corr, Dorr, Farr(e), Firr, Garr, Kerr, Orr, Parr, Starr, Storr, Tarr, Torr

Further Reading

The following sources are useful in tracing the origins of surnames: Davis (2010), *Find my past* (n.d.), *Forebears* (n.d.), *My heritage* (n.d.), *The internet surname database* (n.d.). *House of names* (n.d.) also gives names of settlers to the U.S.A., Australia, and New Zealand.

References

Davis, G. (2010). *Research your surname and your family tree.* Begbroke, UK: How To Books.

Find my past (n.d.). Retrieved from www.findmypast.co.uk

Forebears (n.d.). Retrieved from forebears.io

House of names (n.d.). Retrieved from www.houseofnames.com

My heritage (n.d.). Retrieved from lastnames.myheritage.com

The internet surname database (n.d.). Retrieved from www.surnamedb.com

Appendix 3
The Main Uses of Punctuation
in English

As quoted in Chapter 9, punctuation is governed "two-thirds by rule and one-third by personal taste." The following are therefore rules that most proficient writers of English follow, although there is variation and the rules may be adjusted on occasion for effect.

In typing, do not leave a space before a punctuation mark, but leave one space after. See Chapter 10 for one or two counterexamples.

Apostrophes are used:

- in contractions, e.g. *we'll, they'd*
- in unusual plurals, e.g. *Mind your p's and q's. This research was carried out in the 1970's. If you're sending mail to Europe, it's advisable to use European 1's and 7's in the address.*
- in possessives; put the apostrophe after the noun that possesses, e.g. *the boy's books* (the books of the boy), *the boys' books* (the books of the boys).

Brackets are of two main types: (round) brackets ( ) called *parentheses* in American English, and square brackets [ ] simply called *brackets* in American English. Both always occur in pairs.

Round brackets are used:

- for supplementary information, or asides, e.g. *Margaret (or Maggie for short).* In this usage, they are similar to pairs of commas or dashes
- around *s* or *es*, to signal singulars and plurals, e.g. *any payment(s).*

Square brackets are used:

- to add explanatory material in quotations, e.g. *"I came, I saw, I conquered [Britain]."*
- for brackets inside brackets, e.g. *(as hyperbole [see definition])*
- to correct or point out the error in a quotation, e.g. *"my parent[s],"* *"irregardless [sic]."*

Capital Letters

See the discussion and list of uses in Chapter 11.

Colons are used:

- to indicate that what follows the colon is an explanation or elaboration of what precedes it, e.g. *There was only one problem: Richard. There was only one problem: Richard had forgotten the food.*

Do not follow a colon with any other punctuation, such as a hyphen/dash.

Commas are used:

- in lists, e.g. *We went to France, Germany, Switzerland, and Italy.* (In British English, there is no comma after *Switzerland.*)
- to separate adjectives unless they belong together, e.g. *He wore a double-breasted, blue suit. He wore a dark blue suit.*
- to separate parts of a long sentence where the second part starts with a connecting word, e.g. *The speaker has challenged us with a really important question, and a solution must be found soon.*
- to enclose asides or apposition (which could also be put in brackets), e.g. *I was not, needless to say, impressed by the result. His sister, Jane West, was by his side.*
- to finish quoted speech, when the main sentence continues, e.g. *"You're late," he said.*
- to separate an introductory expression of time, place, or reason from the rest of the sentence, e.g. *The very next day, she had changed her mind. At the back of the class, the children were playing loudly. Because of this, I have to deny your request.*
- to prevent the reader from connecting words that do not belong together, e.g. *While I cooked, the baby played nearby.*

Dashes are used:

- to indicate a strong interruption, e.g. *My advice – if you want it – is to pay it in full.*
- in pairs, unless the interruption finishes the sentence, e.g. *He told you to pay in full – and that's my advice too.*

Ellipsis is used:

- when words have been omitted in a quotation, e.g. *"John . . . is my brother."*

- when a sentence is unfinished, e.g. *I know it's wrong but . . .*

Exclamation marks are used:

- at the end of exclamations, e.g. *What a load of nonsense!*

Full stops are used:

- at the end of a sentence, e.g. *My train arrived late.*

Americans often put full stops (periods) in abbreviations, e.g. *Dr. Jones, C.I.A.*

Hyphens are used:

- in compound premodifiers, e.g. a *five-dollar note*
- in compound premodifiers, to show what belongs together, e.g. *twenty five-dollar notes, twenty-five dollar notes, twenty-five-dollar notes*
- often in compound words, but you should check a dictionary, e.g. *eye-shadow*
- often after prefixes, especially to avoid ambiguity or awkwardness, and where they are followed by capital letters or numbers, e.g. *post-war, re-use, non-ASEAN countries, pre-1900.*

Question marks are used:

- at the end of direct questions, e.g. *What is the problem?*
- at the end of quoted questions, e.g. *"When did you arrive?" she asked.*

Quotation marks are used:

- to show direct quotations, e.g. *"How nice to see you again!" she gushed.*
- to show that a word is being used in a strange, non-literal sense, e.g. *Nonverbal features are the "glue" that hold conversation together.*

Semicolons are used:

- to join two complete sentences into a single written sentence when (i) the two sentences are felt to be too closely related to be separated by a full stop, (ii) there is no connecting word which would require a comma, such as *and* or *but*, and (iii) the special conditions requiring a colon are absent. E.g. *It was the best of times; it was the worst of times.*

Further Reading

For more detailed discussion of punctuation marks and their uses, there are many standard reference books on punctuation, including the following.

Allen, R. (2002). *Punctuation*. Oxford, UK: Oxford University Press.

Casagrande, J. (2014). *The best punctuation book, period: A comprehensive guide for every writer, editor, student, and businessperson*. Berkeley, CA: Ten Speed Press.

Trask, R. L. (2004). *The Penguin guide to punctuation*. London, UK: Penguin Books.

Appendix 4
Answers

Chapter 2 Types of Spelling System

Some further logograms in English:

+ *plus*	£ *pound* (and other currencies)
- *minus*	# *number*
± *plus or minus*	° *degree* (temperature)
× *times*	@ *at*
÷ *divided by*	" "if pronounced *quote, unquote*
= *equals*	/ if pronounced *slash* in a URL
% *percent* (and other mathematical symbols)	¶ *paragraph*
$ *dollar*	§ *section*

Chapter 5 History of English Spelling

chaste	*chastity*	*austere*	*austerity*
humane	*humanity*	*serene*	*serenity*
shade	*shadow*	*female*	*feminine*
grateful	*gratitude*	*credence*	*credulous*
mania	*manic*	*hero*	*heroine*
tenacious	*tenacity*	*obscene*	*obscenity*
hilarious	*hilarity*	*severe*	*severity*
opaque	*opacity*	*legal*	*legislate*
vale	*valley*	*supreme*	*supremacy*

Bible	*biblical*	*atrocious*	*atrocity*
five	*fifth/fifteen/fifty*	*floral*	*florist/florid*
mime	*mimic*	*provoke*	*provocative*
crime	*criminal*	*close*	*closet*
line	*linear*	*holy*	*holiday*
mine	*mineral*	*sole*	*solitude*
define	*definitive*	*phone*	*phonics*
satire	*satirical*	*omen*	*ominous*
type	*typical*	*tone*	*tonic*

Chapter 7 Technology

Exercise 1

The following dates are indicative of roughly when the terms were first used.

& ("ampersand"): 1st century (in Latin)

luv ("love"): 1825

NIMBY ("not in my back yard"): 1980s

SWAK (sealed with a kiss"): c 1925

thanx ("thanks"): early 20th century

thru ("through"): 1839

TTFN ("tata for now"): c 1940

wot ("what"): 1945

Exercise 2

Here is an explanation, if you need it, from Bänziger (2007, p. 1).

Text language	Expanded text language	Standard modern form
dad@hvn	dad at heaven	our Father who art in heaven
urspshl	you're special	hallowed be thy name
we want wot u want	we want what you want	thy kingdom come, thy will be done
&urth2b like hvn	and earth to be like heaven	on earth, as it is in heaven

giv us food	give us food	give us this day our daily bread
&4giv r sins	and forgive our sins	and forgive us our trespasses
lyk we 4giv uvaz	like we forgive others	as we forgive those who trespass against us
don't test us!	don't test us!	and lead us not into temptation
save us!	save us!	but deliver us from evil
bcos we kno ur boss	because we know you're boss	for thine is the kingdom
ur tuf	you're tough	and the power
&ur cool 4 eva!	and you're cool forever!	and the glory, for ever and ever
ok?	OK?	Amen

Chapter 8 Rules of English Spelling

Strict

1 *Anyone who violates this rule will be severely punished.*
4 *I understand the basic rules of chess.*
6 *Under the rules, the company must publish its annual accounts.*
9 *There are no hard and fast rules about what to wear to classes.*

Not-so-strict

2 *As a general rule, burglars are wary about gaining entry from the front or side of a building.*
3 *There's an unwritten rule that you never call an actor before 10 a.m.*
5 *Hanson's golden rule is to add value to whatever business he buys.*
7 *Early marriage used to be the rule in that part of the world.*
8 *As a rule of thumb, a cup of filter coffee contains about 80mg of caffeine.*
10 *It is a rule of English that adjectives generally precede the noun they modify.*

Chapter 9 Punctuation

The Importance of Punctuation

1 *I told the girl that the boy kissed, a story.*
  The ambiguity here relates to the word *that*, which can be either (i) a subordinator introducing what I told the girl (cf. *I told the girl that Mary had gone home*), and this is the more likely first reading, or (ii) a relative pronoun, which is what it actually is here. A comma disambiguates this.

2   *These two dogs are my parents'.*
   That is, they are my parents' dogs; they belong to my parents. The word *dog* would not normally be repeated, as understood.

3   *Let's eat, Grandpa!*
   We are not going to resort to cannibalism and eat Grandpa. As several cartoons on the internet summarize, "Commas save lives."

4   *The boy and the girl in jeans were late.*
   The boy, and the girl in jeans, were late.
   The question here is how many of them were wearing jeans. If they were both wearing jeans, then first one is appropriate; if only the girl was wearing jeans, the second.

5   *If you understand the instructions clearly, there's no problem.*
   If you understand the instructions, clearly there's no problem.
   The ambiguity here is what the word *clearly* relates to. If you have a clear understanding, the comma comes after *clearly*; if it is clear that there is no problem, then before.

6   *The secretary remembered that, in addition to the printer she had been asked to order, a number of other items needed replacing.*
   Most people misread this on first reading as *The secretary remembered that in addition to the printer, she had been asked to order a number of other items.* and then *needed replacing* shows that this reading is wrong.

7   *The children the doorman admitted were a nuisance.*
   The children, the doorman admitted, were a nuisance.
   The ambiguity relates to the word *admitted*, which has two possible meanings: (i) allowed to enter (first version), or (ii) acknowledged (second version). notice that in the second version, that phrase can be moved to other places in the sentence: *The doorman admitted (that) the children were a nuisance. The children were a nuisance, the doorman admitted.* If the doorman's words are quoted verbatim, then quotation marks would be appropriate: "The children," the doorman admitted, "were a nuisance."

8   *John said, "The teacher is stupid."* The teacher is stupid and we are quoting John's words verbatim.
   John said the teacher is stupid. The teacher is stupid but John's words are paraphrased.
   "John," said the teacher, "is stupid." John is stupid and we are quoting the teacher's words verbatim. This is possible because phrases like *said the teacher* can be moved to different parts of the sentence: *"John is stupid," said the teacher.*

9   You've left too much space between *fish* and *and*; and *and* and *chips*.
   Imagine someone commenting to the designer of a sign for a fish and chip shop. Italics show that some words are being quoted as words.

10 This clever example (from Trask, 1997, p. 3) has five possible versions:
   We had one problem: only Janet knew we faced bankruptcy.

We had one problem only: Janet knew we faced bankruptcy.

We had one problem only, Janet knew: we faced bankruptcy.

We had one problem only Janet knew: we faced bankruptcy.

We had one problem only Janet knew we faced: bankruptcy.

Dear John Letter

This clever example from About Education (n.d.) illustrates how punctuation can completely change the meaning of a passage. If Jane loves John, it will be:

Dear John

I want a man who knows what love is all about. You are generous, kind, thoughtful. People who are not like you admit to being useless and inferior. You have ruined me for other men. I yearn for you. I have no feelings whatsoever when we're apart. I can be forever happy. Will you let me be yours?

Jane

On the other hand, if she loathes John, it will be:

Dear John

I want a man who knows what love is. All about you are generous, kind, thoughtful people, who are not like you. Admit to being useless and inferior. You have ruined me. For other men, I yearn. For you, I have no feelings whatsoever. When we're apart, I can be forever happy. Will you let me be?

Yours,

Jane

Harry Potter Passage

Here is the original passage with punctuation.

"Want a hand?" It was one of the red-haired twins he'd followed through the barrier.

"Yes, please," Harry panted.

"Oy, Fred! C'mere and help!"

With the twins' help, Harry's trunk was at last tucked away in a corner of the compartment.

"Thanks," said Harry, pushing his sweaty hair out of his eyes.

"What's that?" said one of the twins suddenly, pointing at Harry's lightning scar.

"Blimey," said the other twin. "Are you – ?"

"He is," said the first twin. "Aren't you?" he added to Harry.

"What?" said Harry.

"Harry Potter." chorused the twins.

"Oh, him," said Harry. "I mean, yes, I am."

The two boys gawked at him, and Harry felt himself turning red. Then, to his relief, a voice came floating in through the train's open door.

"Fred? George? Are you there?"

"Coming, Mom."

With a last look at Harry, the twins hopped off the train.

Harry sat down next to the window where, half hidden, he could watch the red-haired family on the platform and hear what they were saying. Their mother had just taken out her handkerchief.

"Ron, you've got something on your nose."

The youngest boy tried to jerk out of the way, but she grabbed him and began rubbing the end of his nose.

"Mom – geroff" He wriggled free.

"Aaah, has ickle Ronnie got somefink on his nosie?" said one of the twins.

"Shut up," said Ron.

"Where's Percy?" said their mother.

"He's coming now."

Chapter 10 Spaces and Hyphens

Solid, Hyphenated or Spaced?

The spellings given in dictionaries are as follows.

Cobuild	Oxford	Longman	Merriam-Webster	Random House	American Heritage
car park, carpark	car park	car park	car park	car park	car park
dry-cleaning, dry cleaning	dry-cleaning	dry-cleaning	dry-cleaning	dry-cleaning	dry cleaning
firefly, fire fly	firefly	firefly	firefly	firefly	firefly
onlooker	onlooker	onlooker	onlooker	onlooker, on-looker	onlooker
orangutan	orang-utan	orangutang	orangutan	orangutan, orang-utan	orangutan
riff-raff, riffraff	riff-raff	riff-raff	riffraff	riffraff	riffraff
saddlebag, saddle-bag	saddlebag	saddle bag	saddlebag	saddlebag	saddlebag
sledgehammer, sledge-hammer	sledgehammer	sledgehammer	sledgehammer	sledgehammer	sledgehammer
tape recorder, tape-recorder	tape recorder	tape recorder	tape recorder	tape recorder	tape recorder
trainspotting, train spotting, train-spotting	trainspotting	trainspotting	train spotting	trainspotting, train-spotting	
troubleshooter, trouble-shoot	troubleshooter	troubleshooter	troubleshooter	troubleshooter, trouble-shooter	troubleshooter, trouble-shoot
wellbeing	well-being	well-being	well-being	well-being	well-being

Compounds with "Window"

The spellings given in dictionaries are as follows.

Cobuild	Oxford	Longman	Merriam-Webster	Random House	American Heritage
window box	*window box*	*window box*	*window box*	*window box*	*window box*
windowpane , window pane	*windowpane*	*windowpane*	*windowpane*	*windowpane*	*windowpane*
window seat	*window seat*	*window seat*	*window seat*	*window seat*	*window seat*
window shopping, window-shopping	*window-shopping*	*window-shopping, window shopping*	*window-shopping*	*window-shopping*	*window-shopping*
windowsill, window sill	*windowsill*	*windowsill*	*windowsill*	*windowsill, window sill*	*windowsill*

1 Types of "Word"

Orthographic word

- Write an essay of about 1,000 words.
- A picture is worth a thousand words.
- A good typist can reach over 100 words a minute.

Word-form

- The five commonest words in written are *the, of, to, and*, and *a*.
- *Forewent* is a rare word in English.
- I can't read the doctor's handwriting – what is this word?

Lexeme

- The *Longman Dictionary of Contemporary English* contains entries for over 80,000 words.
- At age 4, native speaker children know an average of 700 words.
- There are two words *bank*: one meaning a place where you deposit money, the other the side of a river.

Chapter 11 Capital Letters

Here is the passage with capital letters.

Bertram 'Bert' Albert Patenaude passed to the great dressing room in the sky certain that a place in FIFA World Cup history had been unfairly denied him, for he always claimed that on 17 July 1930 he had scored a hat-trick – two days before Argentinian Guillermo Stabile bagged a famous 'first' with three goals against Mexico. In his own version of events the historic feat was achieved when the United States beat Paraguay 3-0 in the inaugural World Cup. Bert opened the scoring in the 10th minute and also notched the final goal in the 50th minute. Yet for some reason, Bert had not been officially credited with a second goal in the 15th minute. One source gave it to the US player Tom Florie and another tagged it an own goal by Paraguay's Aurelio Gonzalez. Nothing would have changed but for a group of dogged statisticians unearthing the original sources. First they checked the 1930 World Cup report submitted to the United States Football Association by manager Alfred Cummings – it credited Patenaude with all three goals. Then they found three survivors of the game who backed Bert to the hilt. Some 1930 newspaper reports were equally convincing – the Argentinian daily *La Prensa* not only gave Bert the hat-trick, but issued diagrams of how the goals were scored. So that is how Bert Patenaude finally secured World

Cup immortality and found his way into the *Guinness World Records Book* to boot. He will remain forever the scorer of the World Cup's first hat-trick.

Chapter 12 Silent Letters

An Alphabet of Silent Letters

Here are some examples of silent letters. There are many more examples. The only letter that never seems to be silent is *v*.

A: *bread*

B: *debt, limb*

C: *science*

D: *handsome*

E: *have, give, bye*

F: *halfpenny*

G: *gnaw*

H: *whales, vehicle, orchestra*

I: *friend*

J: *marijuana*

K: *knew*

L: *should, would, could, salmon, almond*

M: *mnemonic*

N: *autumn*

O: *young, southern, leopard, people*

P: *psychology, pneumonia, receipt*

Q: *racquet*

R: *Worcester, laisser-faire, iron*

S: *island, chassis*

T: *ballet, fasten, Christmas, mortgage*

U: *Gloucester, build*

V: [None]

W: *wring*

X: *grand prix*

Y: *key*

Z: *rendezvous*

Empty, Auxiliary and Inert Letters

Empty	Inert	
column	Word	Related words
lamb	*bomb*	*bombard, bombardier*
have	*debt*	*debit*
Auxiliary	*hasten*	*haste*
huge	*receipt*	*reception*
	two	*twin, twelve, twenty, between*

Chapter 13 Doubled Consonant Letters

Which Letters Can Be Doubled?

Consonants

The following letters can double: *b* (*robber*), *d* (*redden*), *f* (*puffing*), *g* (*digger*), *l* (*fall*), *m* (*summer*), *n* (*sinner*), *p* (*copper*), *r* (*furry*), *s* (*fuss*), *t* (*matting*), *z* (*fizzy*).

The following letters cannot double: *ch, h, j, k, q, sh, th, w, x, y.*

While *v* can double, it only does so in very few words, all of which are somewhat informal, especially British:

- *bevvy, civvy, divvy, navvy, revving.* Historically (and perhaps in present-day English), these are abbreviations from *beverage, civilian, divide, navigator,* and *revolution.*
- *bovver* (an informal respelling of *bother*), *chivvy, flivver, luvvie* (a respelling of *lovey*), *savvy, skivvy, spivvy.*

The case of *c* is discussed in the chapter.

Brandnames are sometimes created to flout these rules, for marketing effect, e.g. *Exxon.*

Vowels

The vowel letters *e* (*sleep*), and *o* (*room*) can double. The vowel letter *i* can double, but in very few examples, e.g. *taxiing, skiing* (see Chapter 16, where *taxi* and *ski* are shown to be irregular loanwords). The vowel letters *a* and *u* (and *y*, when it represents a vowel sound) cannot double, except in loanwords, e.g. *aardvark.*

Non-existent Words

Because of the presence vs absence of doubled consonant letters, they would be pronounced as follows.

Doubled consonant letter, thus short vowel

blunnish, fammy, pladded, quiggen, sheggle, snoppy, spedder, thritted,

Single consonant letter, thus long vowel

buny, fruded, rotish, swable, swibes, tropers, wabing

Chapter 14 Spelling of Unstressed Vowels

Note that most of these, being newly created adjectives, take *-able.*

1 *hackable*
2 *paintable*
3 *burnable*
4 *fliable* (the *y* of *fly* must change to *i* before adding the ending, cf. *certifiable*)
5 *debuggable* (the final *g* must double, cf. *huggable*)
6 *googlable* (the *e* of google is dropped, cf. *whistlable*)
7 *enticeable* (the *e* of *entice* must remain, in order to represent /s/, cf. *inexplicable*)
8 *garageable* (the *g* of *garage* must remain, in order to represent /dʒ/)
9 *movable* or *moveable* (*moveable* is an older spelling, nowadays only found in *moveable feast*, a Christian event such as Easter that occurs on different days in different years)
10 *convinceable* or *convincible* (the former is regular, the latter is based on *invincible*)

Chapter 16 Loanwords

Scripps Spelling Bee Words

Word	Meaning	Language of origin
koinonia	dress fabric	French
marocain	Christian fellowship	Greek
gesellschaft	an association of individuals for common goals, as for entertainment, intellectual, or cultural purposes or for business reasons.	German
nunatak	an isolated mountain peak projecting through the surface of surrounding glacial ice	Inuit
scherenschnitte	the art of paper cutting design	German
stichomythia	a form of dialogue originating in Greek drama in which single lines are uttered by alternate speakers	Greek
feuilleton	the part of a European newspaper carrying review, serialized fiction, etc.	French
knaidel	a dumpling	Yiddish
guetapens	a trap	French
cymotrichous	with wavy hair	Greek
stromuhr	An instrument for measuring the quantity of blood that flows per unit of time through a blood vessel.	German
appoggiatura	a musical note of embellishment preceding another note and taking a portion of its time.	Italian
autochthonous	aboriginal	Greek
succedaneum	a substitute, esp any medical drug or agent that may be taken or prescribed in place of another	Latin

Do you think these are all words that 14-year-olds need to know?

Words Starting with ka-

kabob	Arabic *kabab*
kaffeeklatch	German, from *Kaffee* "coffee" + *Klatsch* "gossip"
kaffir	Arabic
kaftan	Turkish, from Persian
kagoul	French "balaklava"
Kalashnikov	Russian, from the name of the inventor, Mikhail Kalashnikov
kale	Old English, from German *Kohl*. Persists as the first part of *cauliflower* and, indirectly via Dutch, *coleslaw*.
kaleidoscope	Greek *kalos* "beautiful" + *eidos* "form" + *scopos* "aim"
kamikaze	Japanese *kami* "divinity" + *kaze* "wind"
kanga	Kiswahili (east Africa)
kangaroo	Probably Guugu Yimidhirr, an extinct Aboriginal language of North Queensland, Australia
kaolin	Chinese *gao ling*, literally "high hill"
kapok	Malay *kapuk*
kaput	German *kaputt*
karaoke	Japanese, *kara* "empty" *oke*, an abbreviation of *okesutora* "orchestra"
karat	Arabic *qirat*
karate	Japanese *kara* "empty" + *te* "hand"
karma	Sanskrit
katydid	Onomatopoeia, ie the sound of the word mimics the sound of the object
kayak	Inuit *qayaq*
kazoo	Origin uncertain, perhaps onomatopoeia

The history (etymology) of some of these words can be traced further back by using an etymological dictionary.

Words Ending in -i

Word	Language
alibi	Latin "elsewhere"
basmati	Hindi "fragrant"
bikini	Name of atoll
borzoi	Russian "fast"
broccoli	Italian
chai	Chinese
chilli	Nahuatl (Mexico)
deli	Shortening of German *Delikatesse* "dainty"
envoi	Old French "send"
hajji	Arabic
jacuzzi	U.S. brand name (Jacuzzi Bros, Italian immigrants)
khaki	Persian "dusty"

(continued)

(continued)

Word	Language
kiwi	Māori
koi	Japanese
lei	Hawaiian
mini	Shortening of minimum or miniature, both from Latin
muesli	German
Nazi	Shortening of German *Nationalsozialist*
okapi	Bambuba (Congo)
pi	Greek letter, Hebrew "little mouth."
rabbi	Hebrew "my master"
roti	Hindi
salami	Italian
taxi	Shortening of taxicab, ultimately from Latin *taxa* "charge."
wadi	Arabic "it flowed"
wasabi	Japanese
yeti	Tibetan

Chapter 17 Names of Letters

apresheat (appreciate): the name of *a* is /eɪ/

hape (happy): the name of *e* is /iː/

indd (indeed): the name of *d* is /diː/

lbo (elbow): the names of *l* and *o* are /el/ and /oʊ/

nd (end): the name of *n* is /en/

pa (pay): the name of *a* is /eɪ/

pn (pen): the name of *n* is /en/

qt (cute): the name of *q* is /kjuː/

ski (sky): the name of *i* is /aɪ/

tm (team): the name of *t* is /tiː/

Chapter 18 Spelling Pronunciation

Beaulieu	/bjuːli/	*Leominster*	/lemstə(r)/
Belvoir	/biːvə(r)/	*Lewes*	/luːɪs/
Brough	/brʌf/	*Mousehole*	/maʊzəl/
Burpham	/bɜː(r)fəm/	*Ruislip*	/raɪslɪp/

Frome	/fru:m/	Slough	/slaʊ/
Gotham	/goʊtəm/	Welwyn	/welɪn/
Birmingham, England	/bɜ:(r)mɪŋəm/	Birmingham, Alabama	/bɜ:rmɪŋhæm /
Cairo, Egypt	/kaɪroʊ/	Cairo, Indiana/ Georgia	/keɪroʊ/
Milan, Italy	/mɪlæn/	Milan, Indiana/ Ohio	/maɪlæn/
Peru, South America	/pəru:/	Peru, Indiana	/pi:ru:/
Versailles, France	/veəsaɪ, versaɪ/	Versailles, Indiana	/vərseɪlz/

Chapter 20 Homophones and Homographs

Exercise 1

Alter, altar; ascent, assent; baron, barren; brood, brewed; ceiling, sealing; choose, chews; cygnet, signet; hole, whole; lesson, lessen; minor, miner; moose, mousse; naval, navel; piece, peace; plane, plain; profit, prophet; roll, role; serial, cereal; shoot, chute; steel, steal; straight, strait; sword, soared; tighten, titan; waste, waist; wrecks, Rex

    Beetle, betel, Beatle; cord, chord, cored; heel, heal, he'll; knows, nose, nos; main, mane, Maine; meat, meet, mete; praise, prays, preys; rain, rein, reign; road, rode, rowed; vain, vein, vane; wise, whys, Ys; your, you're, yore

    Cue, queue, Q, Kew; mark, Mark, Mach, marque; peas, pees, pease, Ps; seize, sees, seas, Cs; tease, teas, tees, Ts; you, ewe, yew, U

Exercise 2

Rather than provide a long list of homographs with explanations, we suggest you look up any you cannot solve in a dictionary.

Exercise 3

arm of a chair	foot of a mountain
back of a chair	hand of a clock
brow of a hill	heart of the forest
chest: treasure chest	limb = "branch"
finger: fish fingers	mouth of a river

neck of a guitar, bottle

nose of an airplane

rib of an umbrella

shoulder of the road

spine of a book

teeth of a comb

tongue of a shoe

Exercise 4

There is no right or wrong answer for your intuitions. Here are the answers from the historical point of view; that is, examples of polysemy have the same historical origin, while homonyms do not.

Homonymy

Pupil, ear, corn, meal, steer,

Polysemy

Earth, eye, sole, fork, bank

Chapter 22 Morphological Strategy

Exercise 1

cent: centenary, centennial, Centigrade, centimeter, centipede, centisecond, centurion, century

corp: corporal, corporate, corporation, corporeal, corps, corpse, corpulent, corpus, corpuscle, incorporate

loc: locus, locum, local, locale, locality, localize, locate, location, allocate, collocate, dislocate, relocate, locomotion, locomotive

mari: marina, marine, submarine, aquamarine, mariner, maritime, marinate, calamari

nav: naval, navigate, navigable, navigator, nave (of church)

port: portable, portly, portfolio, apport (arch.), deport, export, import, purport, report, support, transport, comportment, deportment, important, portmanteau, portage

sanct: sanctum, sanction, sanctify, sanctuary, sanctimonious, sacrosanct

scrib/scrip: scribe, scribble, script, scrivener, ascribe, circumscribe, conscript, describe, inscribe, prescribe, proscribe, subscribe, manuscript, nondescript, postscript

uni: unanimous, unicorn, uniform, unison, universe, university, unicycle, unisex, unidimensional, unidirectional, unite, unify, unification, unilateral, union, uniped, unique, unit, Unitarian

Exercise 2

Your *just deserts* are what you *deserve* (with one *s*).

The adjective from *grammar* is *grammatical* (with an *a*), not *grammetical*.

The word *health* is related to the verb *heal* (both with *ea*).

The word *integrate* is related to the noun *integrity* which, because of the /e/ vowel in the second syllable, could not be spelled with *er*.

A *memento* is something that helps you *remember* in your *memory* (all three with *e*).

The noun from *necessary* is *necessity*, which must have a double *s* letter because of the preceding short /e/ vowel (cf. *obesity*).

The noun that the adjective *sacrilegious* comes from is *sacrilege*, not *sacrelige*.

The verb that *writing* comes from, with no change of vowel sound, is *write* (with one *t*).

Chapter 23 Etymological Strategy

bicompartmental: "composed of two compartments"

autothermic: "such that generated heat sustains a chemical reaction"

quadrupedal: "having four feet"

carditis: "inflammation of the heart"

illimitability: "the state of being incapable of being limited, boundless"

ichthyoid: "characteristic of fish"

demigoddesshood: "the state of being a female half-god"

glossectomy: "the surgical removal of all or part of the tongue"

agrometeorology: "the study of weather in order to increase crop production"

hydrogeomorphology: "the study of landforms created or modified by water"

Chapter 24 Phonological Strategy

Exercise 1

- *The building had gone to rack and ruin.* (/r/)
- *My brother and I are like chalk and cheese.* (/tʃ/)
- *Marking is part and parcel of being a teacher.* (/p/)
- *She chooses her clothes so that she can mix and match.* (/m/)
- *My kids were so excited they jumped for joy.* (/dʒ/)
- *A new haircut works wonders for your confidence.* (/w/)
- *She keeps her house spick and span.* (/sp/)
- *His face was black and blue.* (/bl/)

Exercise 2

Answers can be found in any rhyming dictionary (e.g. Rhyme Zone, n.d.). Rhyme Zone also distinguishes common words from uncommon ones.

Exercise 3

A rocket inventor named Wright
Once traveled much faster than light.
He departed one day
In a relative way
And returned on the previous night.

There was a young lady of Kent
Whose nose was remarkably bent
One day, they suppose,
She followed her nose,
For no one knows which way she went.

There once was a fly on the wall
I wondered, "Why doesn't it fall?
Are its feet stuck?
Or is it just luck?
Or does gravity miss things so small?"

There once was a young boy named Sid
Who thought he knew more than he did.
He thought that a shark
Would turn tail if you bark,
So he swam out to try it.
Poor kid!

A crossword compiler
named Moss,
Who found himself quite
at a loss,
When asked, "Why so blue?"
Said, "I haven't a clue.
I'm 2 Down to put 1 Across."

Chapter 25 Analogical Strategy

Exercise 1

brougham	/bruːəm/
clough	/klʌf/

doughty	/daʊti/
hough	/hɒk/ (BrE), /hɑːk/ (AmE)
slough	(noun) /slaʊ/
	(verb) /slʌf/
sough	/saʊ/

Exercise 2

Bough	/bɒf/ (BrE), /bɔːf/ (AmE)
Broughton	/brɔːtən/
Coughton	/koʊtən/
Gough	/gɒf/ (BrE), /gɑːf/ (AmE)
Loughborough	/lʌfbərə/
Poughill	/pɒfil/(BrE), /pɑːfil/ (AmE)
Stoughton	/stoʊtən/
Troughton	/traʊtən/

Chapter 26 Visual Strategy

The 20 Most Frequent Words

Many of the top 20 words are grammatical function words that are unstressed in connected speech, often with the /ə/ vowel (see Chapter 14). Nevertheless, they may be pronounced as strong forms with full vowels, and those pronunciations are taken as the basis for stating whether they are regular or not.

Totally regular: *and, a, in, it, for, not, on, at.* These words all have simple and regular letter-sound correspondences.

Regular with complexities.

- *Be* and *he* both involve word-final *e* = /iː/, found in very few other words (*me, she, we*), all of them also grammatical function words.
- *The* is another example of this, and *the* and *that* both contain the complexity that the digraph *th* = /ð/.
- *You* contains the rare correspondence *ou* = /uː/, found in *youth* and French loanwords like *bivouac, caribou, silhouette, Louise.*

Irregular

- *To* and *do* are the only words where *o* = /uː/, apart from *who* and (especially BrE) *lasso*.
- *Of* is the only word where final *f* = /v/.
- *Have* is not an example of magic *e* (as in *behave*). The *e* is empty (see Chapter 12).
- *I* (i) is always spelled with a capital letter, and (ii) is the only native English word where final *i* = /aɪ/ (excluding foreign words like *alibi, pi, rabbi*, Latin plurals like *cacti*, and the interjection *hi*).
- *With* is the only word where final *th* = /ð/. All other words, being lexical content words, have /θ/, e.g. *kith, smith, zenith*.
- *As* is the only word that is not a plural noun where final *s* = /z/.

In short, many of the most common words in English have complexities or irregularities in their spelling.

Chapter 30 English Spelling and Malay Spelling

Here is the Malay spelling (left) with a phonemic transcription (right)

	Transcription
Negaraku	/nəgaraku/
Tanah tumpahnya darahku,	/tanah tumpahɲə darahku/
Rakyat hidup	/raʔjat hidup/
bersatu dan maju,	/bərsatu dan madʒu/
Rahmat bahagia	/rahmat bahagiə/
tuhan kurniakan,	/tuhan kurniakan/
Raja kita	/radʒə kitə/
selamat bertakhta.	/səlamat bertaxtə/

Notice how the Malay spelling is very close to being a phonemic transcription. Various videos of the Malay national anthem being sung can be found on YouTube.

References

About Education (n.d.). *A brief history of punctuation*. Retrieved from grammar. about.com/od/punctuationandmechanics/a/PunctuationHistory.htm

Bänziger, S. (2007). *Still praying strong: An empirical study of the praying practices in a secular society*. Retrieved from repository.ubn.ru.nl/bitstream/ handle/2066/56672/56672.pdf

Rhyme Zone (n.d.). Retrieved from www.rhymezone.com

Trask, R. L. (1997). *Penguin guide to punctuation*. London, UK: Penguin.

Glossary

Alliteration   Words alliterate if they start with the same consonant sounds.

Alphabetic writing system   The commonest type of writing system, where letters represent sounds (phonemes).

Ash   An Old English letter (æ) pronounced /æ/ and eventually replaced by *a*.

Augmenting spelling reform   A system that uses the current alphabet but augments it with some extra, new letters and symbols.

Auxiliary letter   A letter that has no sound of its own (is silent) but does have a function, and so cannot be omitted. Magic *e* is an example.

Bulking up   Increasing the number of letters in a word, for instance, making function words at least three letters long.

Camel case   A pattern of capital and lowercase letters (e.g. *PowerPoint*) where one or more letters in the middle of the word are given capitals.

Capital   Large versions of letters (*A, B, C,* etc.), as opposed to lowercase. Capitals are also called uppercase, because in traditional movable type printing they were stored in the upper of two cases, with lowercase in the lower.

Content word   A noun, main verb, adjective, or adverb.

Cupertino effect   Unintended words entered by auto-correct. It is named after the word *Cupertino* being inserted for mistypings of *cooperation*.

Dash   A horizontal line between words. There are three lengths of horizontal line: hyphen (shortest), en-dash (middle), and em-dash (longest).

Desktop publishing   Using a computer, often without using specialist publishing software, to produce a high-quality document from the typography point of view.

Digraph   Two letters representing one sound (phoneme), e.g. *th* = /θ/.

Dual-route hypothesis   The theory that familiar, common words are recognized as a whole by visual strategy, while less common, unfamiliar, and new words are processed by a phonological strategy of relating letters to sounds.

Early Modern English   The period from the late 15th century to the late 17th century.

Empty letter   A letter that both has no sound (i.e. is silent) and has no function. It could therefore be omitted, leaving a plausible spelling for the pronunciation, e.g. the *a* of *bread*.

Eth   An Old English letter (ð) pronounced /ð/ and eventually replaced by *th*.

Etymology   The historical origin of a word.

Font   Letter shapes such as Arial, Century. See *serif*.

Function word   A word other than a noun, main verb, adjective, or adverb. For instance, an article, auxiliary verb, conjunction, preposition, or pronoun.

Golfball typewriter   A typewriter such as the IBM Selectric, where the letters were placed around a sphere resembling a golfball. Fonts could be changed by changing the golfball.

Hanging indent   An indent where the first line of each paragraph is not indented but all subsequent lines are. This is common in reference lists.

Homograph   Two words are homographs if they are spelled the same, but pronounced differently, e.g. *wind*.

Homonym   Two words are homonyms if they are both spelled and pronounced the same, but are different words (in terms of meaning and etymology), e.g. *bark*.

Homophone   Two words are homophones if they are pronounced the same, but spelled differently, e.g. *beach, beech*.

Inert letter   A letter that has no sound in the word under consideration (e.g. the *g* of *sign*), but does have a sound in morphologically-related words, e.g. *signature*.

Loanword   A word that came into the language from another language.

Logographic writing system   A writing system, where the individual symbols (characters) represent words, phrases, or morphemes, rather than sounds.

Lowercase   Small versions of letters (*a, b, c*, etc.), as opposed to capitals. In traditional movable type printing, they were stored in the lower of two cases, with capitals in the upper.

Magic e   An auxiliary *e* that is silent, in that it represents no sound, but has the function of "making the vowel say its name," e.g. the *e* of *tube* vs *tub*.

Middle English   The period from the Norman Conquest (1066) until the late 15th century.

Minim   A short, vertical stroke used by scribes for the letters *i* (one minim), *n* and *u* (two), and *m* (three).

Mnemonic   A device to help someone remember the spelling of irregular words, e.g. *Rhythm has your two hips moving* (*rhythm*).

Morpheme   A unit of meaning used to create longer, multimorphemic words, e.g. *dehumidifiers* is composed of the morphemes *de, humid, ify, er* and *s*.

Myelinization   A process occurring in later childhood where myelin, a white fatty substance, forms an insulating sheath around the auditory nerve, improving hearing in the higher-frequency range, as is needed for fricative sounds.

Non-proportional font   A font where the width of a letter is the same, regardless of the letter. This was typical of typewriter fonts.

Old English   The period from the mid-5th century (invasion of Anglo-Saxon tribes) to the Norman Conquest of 1066.

Orthographic depth (opacity, irregularity)   The amount of irregularity in an alphabetic writing system usually, as for English, because the language has a long history, and has never been systematically managed. As a result, the spelling may reflect the historical forms of words, may represent the units of meaning (morphemes) in a word as much as its component sounds, and must be processed by a more visual strategy. Languages with good letter-sound correspondence are said to be shallow or transparent.

Oxford comma   A comma used before the second-to-last item in a list. Also called a serial comma in AmE.

Phonological awareness   The ability to divide words into their syllables, and those syllables into their onset and rhyme, and those components into their constituent sounds.

Polysemy   The process whereby one word (e.g. *head*) has a basic, literal meaning ("topmost part of the body"), which is extended to a more metaphorical sense ("topmost member of a department").

Pronunciation spelling   A nonstandard spelling that reflects the (often quite common) pronunciation of a word, e.g. *yep*.

Proportional font   A font where the width of a letter is not standard, but depends on the particular letter. This is typical of computer fonts.

QWERTY   The keyboard arrangement most commonly used in computers and typewriters. It is named after the first six characters on the top row of letters. Other arrangements have been proposed.

Rhotic   An accent of English in which the /r/ sound is pronounced syllable-finally in words such as *departure*.

Rhyme   The vowel of a syllable, plus any following consonants. Two words are said to rhyme if all sounds from the vowel of the stressed syllable onwards are the same, e.g. *made* and *displayed*.

Runes   The original alphabet used for Old English, eventually replaced by the Roman alphabet.

Sans serif   See *serif*.

Schwa   The vowel /ə/, as in the first and last syllables of *arena*.

Serif   The little extensions at the ends of the strokes of a letter. Century is a serif font, while Arial is sans serif.

Sight word   Very common words that, it is proposed, should be learned by rote with little reference to the regular letter-sound correspondences. Two famous lists of sight words are by Dolch and Fry.

Silent letter   See *empty letter, auxiliary letter,* and *inert letter*.

Smart quotation marks   Quotation marks which have different shapes according to whether they open or close the quotation. This can be automatically assigned by the computer.

Spelling pronunciation   A pronunciation that differs from the standard pronunciation under the influence of irregular spelling, e.g. pronouncing an /l/ in *salmon*.

Standardizing spelling reform   A reform that uses the existing alphabet, but changes the way the current letters are used, in order to be more regular.

Supplanting spelling reform   A reform that replaces the current spelling system with a completely new and different alphabet.

Syllabic writing system   A system in which symbols represent whole syllables, e.g. the hiragana and katakana systems of Japanese.

Thorn   An Old English letter (þ) pronounced /θ, ð/ and eventually replaced by *th*.

Traditional orthography   The standard modern spelling of words, including major variation (BrE versus AmE). Often used in contrast to reformed spelling.

Wynn   An Old English letter (ƿ) pronounced /w/ and eventually replaced by *w*.

Index